Badwater and Beyond

A Thousand Races, Places & Faces

Michael Brooks

To Fran
Run well and stay healthy.
Thanks for your support and kind words.

Mike Brooks

Badwater and Beyond

A Thousand Races, Places, and Faces

ISBN-13: 978-1984195982
ISBN-10: 1984195980

Give feedback on the book at: mjbruns2@hotmail.com

First Edition
Printed in the U.S.A

DEDICATION

I would like to dedicate this book to my brother Paul, who passed away in his sleep on July 30, 2015. Born October 5, 1949, he was the youngest of the three Brooks brothers and we thought the healthiest. Paul was fun loving and a practical joker who enjoyed taking care of his grandchildren with his wife Barb. Paul loved his family dearly and is missed by all who knew him. Rest in peace my friend and dear brother.

Also to my parents Walter and Mary Brooks who did the best they could with what they had to work with. I miss them dearly.

After Glow

I'd like the memory of me to be a happy one, I'd like to leave an afterglow of smiles when my life is done. I'd like to leave an echo whispering softly down the ways, of happy times and laughing times and bright sunny days. I'd like the tears of those who grieve to dry before the sun, of happy memories that leave when life is done.

Contents

1   Chapter 1: Introduction

3   Chapter 2: The Cast of Characters

41   Chapter 3: Denise Brooks

45   Chapter 4: The Early Years

53   Chapter 5: I Start Training and Running

63   Chapter 6: Some Lessons Learned

71   Chapter 7: The Badwater Years Begin

77   Chapter 8: The Badwater Years Continue: 2003

87   Chapter 9: Mike Brooks Smith and Camp Sunshine

93   Chapter 10: My Turn for Badwater: 2004

113   Chapter 11: 2005 Western States and More

119   Chapter 12: Lots of Races in 2006

133   Chapter 13: Pacing, Races, and More in 2007

141   Chapter 14: Plenty of Races in 2008; Coronary Artery Disease

145   Chapter 15: My Toughest Race

153   Chapter 16: Another Cross Country Trip

161   Chapter 17: More Ultras and My 300th Marathon

171   Chapter 18: Ironhorse and Other Races: 2012-2013

173   Chapter 19: I Make it to Ironhorse 100k

185   Chapter 20: Clint Burleson and Mainly Marathons

193   Chapter 21: My Favorite Marathons (More Bad News)

213   The Future

215   The Future: An Update

221   Running Clubs I belong to

225   Acknowledgements

227   Mike's Marathons

CHAPTER 1: INTRODUCTION

I think the title of this book pretty much explains what the book is about. I have done Badwater and gone beyond that in doing 491 miles in a 10-day race. I found the 10-day race harder than Badwater. I started doing races 20 years ago and have done over a thousand since then. About 100 were ultras and 400 were marathons. I now average about 70 races a year, with half of these marathons and ultras plus a number of shorter races (what I refer to as training runs). Having done a marathon or ultra in every state 5 times I have probably been to a thousand places. When I do a race, especially outside my native New England, I visit state capitols, national parks, museums, zoos, and many other attractions. A thousand faces is just an estimate of the many people I have met in my travels. Most of these are fellow runners and quite a few are now friends. I talk an awful lot while running long races and meet many runners this way. It seems like my closest running friends are the ones I have run ultras with. Several of these runners have contributed their thoughts and reminiscences for this book. Reading about them you will soon learn there are some really nutty runners out there. Since I wrote this book mostly by memory there may be some mistakes here and there with dates, times, or the order I have races listed. However, it is as honest and accurate as I could make it.

It would be impossible and pretty boring if I wrote about every single one of my marathons and ultras so I have tried to write only about the ones that I thought would interest the reader. There will be a list of all ultras and marathons in the appendix. Looking at this list with my finish times, you will quickly realize I started running about mid-pack and have now gone to the very back of the pack. About the only talent I have ever had is being able to put one foot in front of the other. I have been told by two cardiologists not to run, one even telling me I could drop dead like Jim Fixx. I'm taking several medications that affect my running, plus I do not train. My races are my training. These help explain the reasons for my slow times. Another excuse is my weight; if I lost some pounds, I possibly could run faster. If I didn't like beer and peanuts so much, losing weight would be a lot easier.

I have been asked many times why I run and travel so much. The answer is pretty simple. I love to run, meet people, and travel to different places. Another reason for my running is that it has enabled me to raise money for non-profit organizations like the National Multiple Sclerosis Society, the Dempsey Cancer Center Healing Tree for Children, and Camp Sunshine.

What I find funny or fun, others might not. At times puking, diarrhea, and some other gross things are funny to me. You might have to be a long distance runner to find certain things humorous. I'm sometimes called crazy or abnormal for doing some of the races I have done. My doctor thinks I have obsessive compulsive disorder. Well if I have to have OCD, let it be about running.

Hope you enjoy the book, and please remember to not do what I have done. If I suggest some running tip, don't listen to me.

CHAPTER 2: THE CAST OF CHARACTERS

This is a listing, by no means exhaustive, of some of my running friends who played an instrumental role in my adventures. You will meet these people several times in my book but I thought it might be useful to have an alphabetical listing with some biographical information, often in their own words, plus a memory or two of how we met (prefaced by MB, or according to Mike Brooks).

Allen, Gary:

- From Cranberry Isles, Maine, and founder and race director for the Mount Desert Island Marathon.
- Gary's been a runner for 45 years and has logged over 100,000 lifetime miles.
- He's also completed 95 marathons and 8 ultras with 68 sub 3 hour marathons in consecutive decades 70s, 80s, 90s, 00s, 10s.
- He ran 700 miles from Maine to DC for charity and 500 miles from Maine to Super bowl XLVIII for charity.
- He raised over $36,000 from charity runs to help others.
- Gary currently ranks 10th in the world for greatest span below 3 hours.
- He bettered Ted Corbitt's American record for 20 miles on track.

Mike's comments: I first met Gary when I did his 24 hour race in Bar Harbor. I also have done the Great Cranberry Island 50k and MDI Marathon both many times; Gary is race director of both.

Bartocci, Frank:

Frank describes Mike Brooks as a lover of kids, dogs, beer, friends, inner peace, kicking butt and taking no prisoners, and life.

Frank's statistics:
- 642 marathons, 70 ultras
- 50 States Marathon finisher 9 times
- Pikes Peak Marathon 6 times
- 1 100 mile race (Leanhorse at age 61), MN Voyageur 50 mile finisher
- Edmund Fitzgerald 100km twice
- Savage 7 series 4 times (finished 3 of these and at least 100 marathons with Mike)
- TinMan Triathlons 2 times
- American Birkebeiner 53k Cross Country Ski races 20 times

Mike Brooks (aka. Mikey) and I have run at least 100 marathons together. Mikey is my buddy, but mostly my running buddy. And not just an ordinary soul... As we used to say on the streets of Chicago, Mikey is 'one tough sumbitch' running buddy. In fact, I think they invented that phrase after watching Mikey do his thing on the various courses that he has traversed over his running career. But I've observed a few other characteristics over the span of almost 2 decades that I've known and run races with him. He just loves to stop and say something nice to kids on the side of the road during a race or pet a dog. And we've shared ideas on politics, beer, friends, inner peace, kicking butt (always our own), and life.

I've had the honor of laughing 'at' the jokes of runners traveling with us on the course and basically just enjoying the present moment. But the struggle out there is also notable and tends to bring us closer, we are like brothers out there trying to achieve a common goal. Physical toughness is a given but so is mental toughness, and not everyone has these to the degree required to finish what is started. Mike's 'track' record speaks for itself. Of those races that he has entered he's finished all and a great many, as I've said, we've run together at some point in the race. You heard that right...he starts it; he'll finish it...at least those short distances like the marathon! Nobody wants to quit...right? To say that we don't quit is to say that today the sun is expected to rise in the East. It's just a fact of life!

The short essay that follows is about a particularly special race that I might not have finished were it not for the help of this guy. This one shared experience stands out for me among all the others. In some way, it represents one of those 'by the skin of your teeth finishes' where you have to struggle a bit to get 'er done, and where the strength of those around you is revealed.

It was a warm spring day in Kentucky. We were at the starting line of the Land Between the Lakes 60k Ultra. I was asked to lead Mikey and another runner (let's just call her Lois for the sake of this story) through the multi-loop course. It was Lois's 1st ultra, and since I had done this race several times, I was asked to lead the group: I was the 'expert'. I am the 'expert'? This should have been code to mean 'we are all doomed!' Yes, as we were soon to discover: this was to be one of those times where I, for one, would be sorely tested.

We all started off strong enough. My idea was to do the ultra thing: 'walk the hills, run the flats and downs.' Well, we were all doing great until midway on the last lap where I got so dehydrated that I was panting up the hills and was struggling to maintain any kind of pace. I was obviously so excited about leading us to victory, I forgot to drink enough water myself! I resigned to walk it in the last 5 miles or so to salvage the race so that I'd finish. I felt cramping in my legs and knew that the heat had taken its toll on me.

I insisted that Lois and Mikey take off - so I could deal with the rest of the course, internalize my shameful performance thus far, and reach down for the strength needed to finish those last miles. Lois decided to go ahead and she finished strong. In fact, she did quite well and drank enough when the weather got too hot. Mikey though refused to leave my side. He said that I looked like crap and he'd never seen me look that bad, he knew I was in trouble, and just wanted to stay with me to the finish. I knew I'd finish although I also knew it wouldn't be pretty, but Mikey just ignored me when I told him to 'take off' - I had to stop and stretch a few times along the way. I felt cramps coming and wanted to delay the problems as best I could - those last miles seemed to go on forever – Mikey was so supportive. Finally, we were a block away from the finish and Mikey suggested we run it in. I looked at him like he was crazy! I was barely hobbling in, and Mikey still wouldn't move out and finish. What a tremendous display of sportsmanship. I thank him for this to this day. (I like to say that his Irish stock went up that day---I will never forget it).

Now we were finished (in more ways than one) and I'm sitting (collapsed) in a chair 'cause I couldn't function very well and all of a sudden my leg cramps. Sharp spike in pain -- those of you who have experienced a dehydration cramp know that it is truly a joy to behold. I knew what it was but was yelping just the same. There was one guy that had come over and was doing what I asked - pushing on the forefoot to work against the cramp and work it out - wow, it worked. It took about an hour before I wanted to drink anything, then after that I started to come alive again...slowly...but I was definitely on the mend...

I guess if you run these races long enough, you will probably experience this. Especially if you decide to finish no matter what! These are the races that, upon reflection, are most meaningful... and they have the most value. For this particular day in Kentucky, it was about the struggle, it was about the value of the finish, and it was about the greatness of runners around us that help us to the finish...the greatness of one runner in particular.

Berkowitz, Lois:

- Riverview, MI
- Running since 10/16/1978, marathoning since 4/1990
- 399 marathons/ultras as of 2/25/15
- Longest race completed: Catalina Island 50 Miler
- 1st 50 States finish: Birmingham, AL 1997
- 2nd 50 States finish: Hartford, CT 2002
- 3rd 50 States finish: Bellingham Bay, WA 2009
- 4th 50 States finish: Providence, Rhode Island 2012
- Completed all provinces/territories of Canada 2002
- Edits newsletters for the 50 States Marathon Club and for Toledo (OH) roadrunners and has published articles in Marathon & Beyond magazine

Lois remembers four specific runs with Mike, two of which probably wouldn't have been completed without his help. Here she writes about the Presque Isle/Erie Marathon in Erie, PA, the Land Between the Lakes 60k, the Bear Lake Double, and the Rio marathon.

I had known Mike for a number of years as a friend and member of the 50 States Marathon Club. The first time I can remember running with him was at Erie, Pennsylvania. I have done Erie multiple times – it's an easy if boring four-hour drive for me. I met up with Mike at the beginning of the race and we had some conversation. I had no plan for the day other than to complete, get a shower, and go home. I started talking with Mike, and he explained the heart issues he was dealing with, and that he was monitoring his heart rate. Whenever his heart rate went over a certain point, Mike would stop and walk until it went down. I said, "Ok, I can follow that." I had a good, easy run around Presque Isle, thanks to Mike.

Land Between the Lakes was one of those races you don't think too much about if you do it; my philosophy is, if you're going to do something hard, don't overthink it! The other maxim is, always try to do some hard stuff! I had completed one 50 miler and was hornswoggled into signing up for the LBL 60k, which was to be my third longest race completed. LBL is almost all trail, and not a walk in the park, if you get my drift.

I was more confident when I found that Mike Brooks was going to do it. Mike is calm, makes good conversation, does not yell. I informed Mike that he was pacing me, since I knew that I could keep the same pace as he did, and he had a calm sort of confidence that could keep me going – I can handle 26.2 easily enough, but longer than that and my mind goes. We were reinforced by the appearance of Frank Bartocci, who will do anything everywhere.

I didn't realize until race morning that Mike doesn't really like trails all that well! I assumed that if you could do 100 milers and other multi-day races, you could do anything! Frank was his backup. It was a fun team effort. For most of the race, Frank led, I brought up the middle, and Mike was the caboose. Luckily they were usually within sight, but far enough off that they could not hear me swearing.

We were in what I would judge the last quarter of the race, on the trail, when I looked down and saw quite a bit of red stuff on the trail. I thought, "I hope that is red Gatorade, but I don't think so...." Then I trotted a bit further to catch up with Frank, and overheard his conversation with a youngish woman running alongside him...the gist was that she had fallen, broken her nose, and the red stuff was...blood! She was happy, though, because this race was in the 40's for her marathon/state-wise.

Mike was not exactly the star of the second exciting incident of the day, but demonstrated his character in it. At some point Frank slowed up rather dramatically and Mike was with him. I passed them, but tried to stay with them. Frank kept urging us to go ahead – he did not look particularly healthy. I listened to a couple of urgings from Frank, then went ahead, after all, he was the most experienced of any of us – and we were pretty close to the end. I ran off the trail onto the road at the end, and through the finish line.

I greeted Nancy Broadbridge who had finished ahead of me, and we waited for Frank and Mike. They came, not too long after, Frank slugged over the finish line and immediately doubled over and screamed as I have never heard him scream before, overcome with extreme leg cramps. He had, of course, just finished another tough 60k. Nancy and I made him sit down and massaged his legs for a while, helped him to the building where the food was, got him food, and waited while he threw it up once or twice. Mike had recognized what trouble Frank was in, and stuck with him throughout. This is Mike!

Not so exciting but another good display of Mike's character came with the Bear Lake Double in Idaho/Utah in 2010. This was a great double and Dave Bell had offered a time share condo to me if I could fill it, which I did, to capacity.... One day we started in Idaho and ran 26.2 miles around the lake until we got into Utah, then we stopped. The next day we started in Utah, and ran 26.2 miles around the lake until we stopped in Idaho. This race was very challenging for me for another reason – though it was very beautiful, it could be incredibly boring, as it was all road. The older I get, the less I like running on roads all the time in the same direction, even if they have great scenery around them. Mentally, I simply need stimulation – rocks, obstructions, anything interesting!

I designated Mike again as my pacer. One of the great things about Mike is that we are close to the same pace. Once it is fixed in my head that he is pacing me, I simply go into neutral, the ozone, whatever you want to call it, and follow. If he walks, I walk. If he runs, I run. There was conversation, we discussed spouses, we talked about the scenery, and Mike remained calm. I admire that quality, to remain calm in all situations, in a person. The races were completed successfully, in no small part to my pacer.

I should also mention one of my few international trips, the 50 States Marathon Club world tour to Rio de Janeiro. I ran the race with Mike and it was exciting in its own way. Around mile 20, a protest group of roughly 30 people were standing ON the course. We assessed the situation and decided it was safer to circumvent the group. Toward the end of the course, markings were rather unclear, and so we had a mini-adventure finding our way to the finish line. Thank you, Mike, for sharing another adventure!

Mike's comments: Lois donates a lot of her time to the Toledo Road Runners and 50 States Club. I think she must be hiding from me lately. I have not seen her in a race since the Bay of Fundy marathon 2 years ago. That is too bad because I like running with her and enjoy her company. Maybe if she does the Maine Marathon she will stay over at my home again.

Boone, Paula
Boone, Steve

- Steve – born 1949
- Paula – born 1966 (lucky Steve)
- Sock Monkey – "born" 2011

Steve and Paula Boone reside in Humble, Texas. He has completed 603 marathons and each of the US states five times. She has completed 314 marathons and each of the US states three times. They are founding members of the 50 States Marathon Club which was established in 2001 and now has a membership of over 3,700 members.

They started and fund the Marathon Challenge Program which awards t-shirts to local elementary school children who complete the marathon distance during the academic school year. Over the last 22 years, the program has grown from 14 finishers the first year to 9,300 finishers in 2014. In 2014, Steve and Paula traveled to Kochi, India to start a similar program in their local elementary schools.

Paula recalls: As far as I can remember, we met at Brent's race in May 2001. Mike was running the double and I ran the marathon. We ended up running many miles together. We have since run lots of races together. My last fast marathon was when I ran with Mike in Maine 2008. He helped me through the race until we caught up to Steve.

Mike's comments: I have known Steve and Paula since 2001 or so. Steve runs a lot faster than me so it is Paula whom I have run with so many times.

Bowe, Kathy:

I volunteer at many races; I started running 12 years ago. I was a late bloomer; my first race was the Beach 2 Beacon 10k. Since then I have run too many races to count, but I run Beach 2 Beacon every year. One year I had a goal of running a 10k every month. I started in May and ended in October. I couldn't find any other 10k's in Maine.

My first marathon was the Maine Marathon in 2007. Mike approached me at the Trail to Ale 10k with a beer in his hand and asked if I would like a pacer for this marathon and he offered to pace me. I warned him I was slow but he didn't care. He paced me the entire 26.2 talking to me and other runners during every step. After 19 miles he started introducing me as his daughter and that this was my first marathon. His encouragement and motivation made an impact on my run that day and beyond. He is such an inspiration. Since then, I have run 3 more marathons; Manchester City, Disney, and Marine Corps.

Five years ago I started helping out with a local group run and began mentoring beginning runners. Eventually I received my RRCA coach certification. I'm now the registration coordinator and director for the Maine Marathon.

Mike's comments: Kathy, along with Janice Gagnier, are my running daughters. Both are young enough to be. Kathy did a great job in the Maine Marathon and running with her made my day. I still see Kathy at a lot of races and she still refers to me as dad and claims she is my daughter. If she is not running she is volunteering.

Brainerd, Bob

- Licensed Athletic Trainer, Health/ Exercise Science Educator
- Nationally Certified Strength and Conditioning coach
- Elite Marathon Runner- 37 marathons - 9 Bostons
- Life Time Achievement Award by MaineTrack club
- Coach/ Friend to Many for 30 years - Greatest Joy has been coaching others to accomplish their goals
- 10 ultramarathoners
- Over 30 Boston qualifiers
- Over 15 Ironman Finishers
- Individuals who competed in Nationals in swimming, triathloning, and running

Mike's comments: I first met Bob in 1995. One of the many things I like most about Bob is that as a coach he pays the same amount of attention to all athletes no matter their ability.

Bob coaches for the Maine Track Club in Auburn, Maine. Most MTC members live in the Greater Portland area where they also have a training program. Bob does such a good job and is so well liked he draws runners to his training sessions from all over including greater Portland.

I was the first ultra runner Bob trained and considering what he had to work with he did an excellent job. Bob paced and crewed for me at Badwater and the Vermont 100 miler. He also climbed Mt. Whitney with me.

Bob has also helped me when I have had an injury. His favorite line is, "you should not run BUT if you are going to..." Bob has helped countless athletes recover from injuries and lose weight. He is known simply as Coach Bob to hundreds of runners. Thanks, Bob, for all the help and good times you have given me.

Brooks, Mike

- First Race -1995
- All races are totals to January 1, 2015
- Number of Races -1057
- Ultra Marathons - 94
- Marathons - 349
- Total Marathons and ultra Marathons - 443
- Races won - One (I also finished last, only runner in 24 hour race)
- D.N.F. (Did Not Finish Race) 3 Ultra Marathons.
- D.F.L (Dead Freakin' Last) – 4

- Best Accomplishment - Raising over $60,000 for the National Multiple Sclerosis Society, Healing Tree for Children and Camp Sunshine.
- Toughest Race for me - 2009-Self Transcendence Ten Day - 491 miles - age 63
- Toughest race runners THINK -2004- Badwater 135 miles plus 22 up Mt. Whitney and back- age 58

Brooks, Walter (Mike's brother):

Walter worked in retail for over 45 years and had every job imaginable from stock boy-shipper-receiver-salesperson-store manager-buyer to merchandise manager. He hated the inside work and loved being outdoors! Freedom at last -after 30 years of marriage he separated in 2001-both kids married in 2000-retired from CVS after 20 years.

He always wanted to travel and see the country. Mike asked if I would be interested in a marathon trip. I said yes and in June 2006 I made my first trip with him to the Teton Dam marathon in Rexburg, Idaho. I enjoyed the trip and got the travel bug!

Since then I've traveled to more than 125 marathons and visited every state at least once. I've also been to South Africa, Canada, and Mexico. I've driven cross-country twice, each trip about 10,000 miles and over 1 month. Mike did the easy part (running); I was the designated driver in total about 50,000 miles. I was also responsible for keeping the after-race beer cold and to keep him out of trouble.

Due to my skilled driving we had no accidents and only a few tickets in Alaska and Minnesota (plus a few warnings). While Mike was running slowly I had plenty of time on my hands. I became a tourist and visited the attractions...almost every National Park and hundreds of other local venues including casinos. While he was busting his ass, I was racking in the big bucks.

Traveling with Mike has afforded me the opportunity to see just about everything in this beautiful country. I've also met many of Mike's running pals, a unique cast of characters! They are all dedicated fanatics and love running. Some are in the Guinness Book of World Records. Others have through-hiked the Appalachian Trail and ascended Mt. Kilimanjaro. I also got to bond with my Bro and to appreciate his gutsy determination and his appreciation for good brew.

Bruckert, Gene:

Born in 1935 and has been running since high school. His first marathon was the 2000 Green Bay Marathon. Since then he has completed 472 marathons including 220 ultras, twelve 50 milers and one 100 miler.

Gene states that he can't meet the time limit for most marathons anymore, so he does timed runs and races where the race director doesn't care about finishing time - these are mostly runs coupled with a much longer race.

He's won a few races, but all were part of multiple events, and he states he was the RD in each and the only entrant in the particular event he ran in.

Gene admits he is probably the champion of the DFL category.

There are three tough races that stand out: Leadville (altitude sickness), little su (-20 degrees and much sinking in the snow, and Pike's Peak 30 mile (actually 33 miles with last 13 (surprise!) without aid).

Although he really enjoys trails he can no longer do runs with 1.5 mile rises as his knees can't take coming down the hills. The health benefits of running long are becoming well known but it is the nice people you meet that make an ultra special.

Gagnier, Janice

Janice has the following to say about her "running Dad" Mike Brooks:

I met Mike while watching my daughter Melissa Gagnier-Albani run races put on by the Maine Track Club. He and my daughter encouraged me to join them in running a race. I decided to run the 2003 Portland Sea Dogs Mother's Day race.

I knew immediately that I was bitten by the running bug. I would continue to see Mike at other local races and MTC events. I ran my 1st half marathon in 2005 in the Sportshoe Center Maine Marathon. Mike would run up to me and run a few miles to be sure that I was doing okay, then he would proceed forward to the next runner and encourage them and then move on to the next runner. Mike would tell me about his interesting running adventures and the miles would fly by. Hearing his stories made me want to run marathons.

In 2007, I entered into a MTC lottery for the Boston Marathon and was chosen! Mike, always so generous, gave me his 1996 100th Boston Marathon shirt! He also loaned me his book, "Boston: A Century of Running," to help motivate me. I remember seeing people wearing Marathon Maniacs and 50 States Marathon Club shirts, and I asked Mike about them. I told him that I'd like to become a Marathon Maniac, but didn't know if I could do it. He assured me that I could and he'd run a back to back race with me so I would qualify! We ran the Space Coast Marathon and Palm Beaches Marathon in 2009 so I would qualify to become a Marathon Maniac, #2312. Mike and I ran in the 2009 Gasparilla Ultra Challenge and the Goofy Challenge.

When we run races, he tells people that he's my dad. It's so funny when people start cheering, "Come on Dad"..."Go Dad!!!" I'm proud to have him as my running Dad! I have learned so much about running and staying motivated from him! I've learned it's okay not to be the fastest, instead it's about getting out and having fun and enjoying the adventure! He is the only person I know that can outtalk me when running a race. On one of our runs he told me about the "The Savage Seven" series of races, 7 marathons in 7 days!!! Mike assured me that I could do it and he agreed to run it with me.

Mike's Comments: Janice is very outgoing and does not mind me referring to her as my daughter. She is much younger than me. At the Space Coast marathon, she did not win the race but did win best costume. She was also sick with the flu when she ran Boston, that is determination. Glad to have a daughter like this.

Hunt, Carl and Fay

Here is how Carl remembers meeting and running with Mike:

Back a dozen or so years ago, I decided to participate in the Delaware Triple Crown Races and run the marathon. It was a reasonably short drive to Newark from my CT home and a trail marathon sounded like fun. At this point in my running life, I felt like a seasoned veteran since I had been running marathons for a whopping two years and must have done at least a phenomenal number of a dozen or so. Wow! That's more than two a year! Little did I know how much a simple thing like a pre-race pasta dinner could change the flow of one's life forever. After dinner, I somehow felt different about running. Like what's next? How soon can I go beyond the marathon, go faster, do more of them, doubles, triples, drive farther, update your airline accounts and start to fly a lot, expand your list of hotels to stay at, find good ways do the 50 states and maybe think about the "U" word – ultramarathon. My life was irrevocably changed. Maybe for the better. Then again....... I had met Mike Brooks.

The Delaware marathon was a mud fest of fun where the best part was traversing the wide freezing cold river to cool off your feet and clean up your shoes. Falling in was a bonus which allowed you to clean the mud from parts other than your shoes. All in all, it was a great race and a lot of fun. I exchanged emails with Mike after the race and we chatted. Soon he had me convinced that I could do an ultra. Since the Maine Track Club, of which Mike just happened to be a member, just happened to be putting on such an event soon, I signed up. Why not? The thought of 50 miles was a bit much for me. Luckily, I think, Mike and a good friend, Ron Paquette, were doing the 50k. We stayed together for the race and had a blast.

We talked about many things during that run, but my favorite was the life lesson that was imparted upon me somewhere about mile 27. Mike informed me that we are all born with a finite number of brain cells. When you run marathons, you deplete the supply. When you get down to zero, you start running ultras.

Since you can only go farther into the rabbit hole by continuing to run, you have to replenish the brain cell supply. The only way to replenish the supply is to drink beer. Good lesson, but, it requires practice.

Mike and Ron tolerated my whining and abysmally slow pace and we approached the finish line in about 5:53. We decided that it would be really cool to just stand there for a couple of minutes about 50 yards from the finish and go through at 5:55:55. We did that and it is still a very pleasant memory of my first time. Ultrarunning that is.

In order to complete the circle to insanity, Mike convinced me that I needed to do a double. Finding one was easy. I had been looking for a marathon to do Sunday as the 50k was on Saturday. It just so happened that there was a marathon in MA which happened to be on the way up to the Maine race. We stopped in Lowell and signed up.

I was full of fear and doubt as to whether I was capable of actually completing it the day after the 50k. Mike and Ron convinced me I could do it. They were right. The thing they forgot to mention was how much it would hurt a day or two later. It didn't matter, I was hooked. It was a no brainer that 100 miles would soon be on the agenda. That 100 miler turned out to be Umstead. I ran with Mike Smith and Andy Velazco again. This was my first 100 miler and it was a fantastic day. I ran a sub-24 with both Mike and Andy doing the same. Great day.

I once made the mistake of watching a movie called Running on the Sun, about a bunch of lunatics who go to Death Valley, the hottest place on earth, and run 135 miles in a race called Badwater. In July. In temps reaching in the 120's and 130's. Traversing two mountain ranges and finishing on the third. Blisters like you've never seen, vomiting, hallucinations, near death experiences, heat exhaustion, black toenails and absolutely brutal training techniques. Crazy. Absolutely insane. Best movie I ever saw!

Mike decided he was going to do Badwater. He had already been telling me tales about his being there and crewing for both Mike "the younger" Smith and Andy Velazco. I had been trying to find a way to get into that race and Mike "the elder" offered me the opportunity to increase the odds of my being accepted by having me crew for him.

His plan was to do the full course which includes a trip up to the top of Mt. Whitney after the race, an additional 22 miles for the round trip on Mt. Whitney. Mike, Andy, Walt Prescott, and another friend, Bob Brainerd, were going to crew the race and he needed me to help get him up Mt. Whitney.

I had met Mike, Andy, and Walter on other races, but I really got to know them at Badwater. That environment will do that.

Somewhere along the line, the guys let me pace Mike a bit during the race. When they wanted a break, I'd go out again. This worked out very well and gave me an experience that I will never forget.

One night while we were parked near Lone Pine, Walter was telling me about hallucinations and strange sounds that he had experienced in that area of the run. I kept waiting to see demons coming from the shadows, but they never materialized. Guess that it wasn't my turn. Strange things happen, though, after you've been awake for 30 plus hours.

Mike, my friend, gentle Mike, became a real bitch. He would cuss, yell, and do all manner of "un-Mikey" things. We finished the race without killing each other and went to the awards dinner. When Mike received his buckle, he had a huge smile on his face. Then it was time for round two, a round trip up Mt. Whitney. That meant climbing 14,505' after 135 miles.

It was a trip to remember.

We nearly didn't get there. We started in the middle of the night on a course that we had never seen before. Not too smart. Walking up from the portals in the dark requires that one knows where the start of the hiking trail is and that you follow it. We didn't. Walked quite a bit past the entryway and it took us a while to figure out that we had missed it. Lesson learned.

During our time walking on parts of the trail, it was so dark that we couldn't see a thing. We knew there was a canyon waiting to kill us off to our left but were never sure where it was. We could hear water rushing by us down below, not very far away, just down. Doing this in the dark was not a bright idea. We had several close escapes: nearly falling off the side of the mountain from lack of sleep, walking through snow drifts 4 feet high, trying to get some sleep under the stars part way up; these were all part of the journey.

The best part was being able to get to know your friends better and see-ing some of the most beautiful views in the world. Coming down was another epic adventure. By now, Mike was in really tough shape. We all were, but he had done the race. Tired was an understatement. Ask Mike about his experi-ences on the switchbacks coming down.

Getting to know your friends better took on new dimensions on that day. Wouldn't have traded that trip for anything.

Having done the crew part of Badwater, it was my turn to apply the next year. First I had to do some running. Mike recommended Across the Years as a good training run. Do the 48 hour and teach yourself to run tired. Excellent idea. Run until you feel like dying would be a better option and then go on. Cool. Did it. Ran in the rain, the wind, and the cold. In Phoenix. Met some of the best and nicest people at Nardini Manor that I will ever know. That was a wonderful race with champagne and fireworks on New Year's Eve. Mike and I ran an awful lot of miles together in that race. Talking about who knows what. Doesn't matter. That race was fun.

Then it was Umstead again. This was my last long training race before the Badwater application needed to be sent in. That concept had worked for Mike and I was hopeful that it would work for me, too.

It did. I got in. Now what?

The logistics and planning for the Badwater race are actually worse than running it. Or so Mike told me. You can drive yourself to distraction trying to prepare. Without help from your friends, you won't make it. When the race begins, without an outstanding crew, you won't make it.

Fortunately for me, I had the best crew that was on the course that day. My friends Mike the elder Brooks, Mike the younger Smith, Andy Velazco, Ron Paquette, and Kyle Gancher willingly gave up a week of their personal lives to get me through the race. I will never forget what they did out there for me. Your crew has to think for you. They did. It worked and I made it.

Mike somehow almost missed the finish. It was his turn to police up the gear and to get some rest. His calculations had us getting into Lone Pine and finishing the last half marathon in 6 hours. He wasn't counting on Andy and his walking stick. Andy had taken a fall and twisted his ankle pretty badly coming down the hill into Panamint Springs. He was pretty much unable to walk for the rest of the day.

Going into the last uphill segment, Andy met me with his walking stick. His ankle was still quite stiff, but he had a good rest. We saw a pair of runners on the switchbacks a half mile up the road who had passed us a bit earlier. Next thing I know, I heard Andy tapping the road in a metronomic manner telling me "target ahead, one half mile". Nothing else. As we moved on, Mr. Metronome quickens the pace again and again.

On the way up, we pass a turnout where Mike Smith and Kyle were parked. My six pairs of shoes were all over the place. Mike was telling me that my shoes were missing. Didn't make sense to me since I thought I saw them all over the place. For some reason, Mike woke up in the hotel and decided that he and Ron needed to get up and to the portals of Mt. Whitney, the finish, early. I am thankful that he did. He was off by two hours thanks to Andy's pushing the pace. One of my best memories ever was having all of my crew up there with me and all of us running in the last half mile and crossing the finish line together. One parting gift from the crew was the announcement that I had to go back and do it again because mine wasn't an official finish.

Say what?

Seems that the temperature for the event when Mike the younger did it was 126. For Andy it was 132 and for Mike the elder it was 124. They claimed that the temperature in Furnace Creek when I ran was only 118 and that wasn't an official finish.

Nice, guys.

I'm near dead and they want to play.

Mike decided that it would be a good idea if a bunch of us went out to Leadville, CO, to run the marathon. Not much oxygen up there, but, why not? Once again, the mountains provided the majesty and spectacular views that folks cannot begin to appreciate unless they make the journey. We met up with a few other friends while there and had a really good time. Couldn't really breathe, but that's way overrated anyway when compared to the camaraderie of these races.

While trying to do the 50 States, Mike suggested I do the Sugarloaf marathon so as to get my marathon for Maine completed. I thought that it would be a good place to run as well as bring the family.

The grandsons saw their first moose and that was exciting. They were 5 and 7 at the time and they still remember that. They also saw a beautiful river near the hotel and of course decided that they would go swimming.

"Boys, it's Maine," says Mike. The water is a little cold. No problem. They found out differently after they tried. Uncle Mike was right.

In addition to all of that excitement for the boys, Mike took them down to visit his former fire station. The boys got a tour of the firehouse, sat in the cab of a fire truck, rang bells, and flashed the lights. They will never forget that. Mike drew the line at letting them sound the siren as several firemen were upstairs sleeping. Mike and I ran Sugarloaf together and had a ball.

Pineland Farms is another wonderful race with great organization, volunteers, and runners. It runs through open fields and covered forests. While your legs get a thorough trashing, you get an opportunity to discover that the state bird of Maine is, in fact, the dive bomber mosquito.

My grandsons spent the time while we were running with my wife and Denise, Mike's wonderful wife. During the course of the day, they were able to witness the birth of a fawn. What an awesome experience for them.

One year, I got "lucky" and hit the Western States 100 lottery. Mike the elder, Andy, and I had crewed for Mike the younger and Walt Prescott the year before so we had a good idea of what we needed to do for my shot at it. Mike and his brother, Walt, agreed to crew me for the race.

On race day, everything was going well. We had breakfast and at Squaw Valley, Starbucks was open prior to the shotgun start. Good way to begin a race. Temps were rising by early morning and by the time I hit the area between Red Star Ridge and Duncan Canyon, I was walking around light headed and faint.

It was 100 plus in the sun and I found a nearby tree to sit down under for a while. I made it to Duncan Canyon 4 minutes beyond the cut-off. When I was told that I would not be allowed to continue, I didn't even think to argue.

Again, my only concern was Mike and Walt. They were waiting for me at Robinson Flat and I had no way to get there. The aid station folks radioed ahead and hoped to get the message to Mike to meet me at Foresthill where the volunteers would bring me. Luckily, the volunteers at Robinson found Mike and told him what had happened. I really felt bad letting them down again but they both took it well and we were on our way.

I tried the lottery again for Western States the following year. Woohoo! Got in again. Two years in a row. Time to buy a Powerball ticket!

Mike and Walt agreed to try it again. Mike told me he had just finished a major race and he would only be able to pace me the last 22 miles from Rucky Chucky. Andy was there to give it a try for himself, with his wife and daughter to crew for him. Breakfast, Starbucks, and shotgun.

Off we go again. Mike and Walt wave and we agree to meet in Robinson Flat. Hopefully. I make it past Duncan Canyon this time. That's a good sign. Mike and Walt are glad to see me at Robinson Flat. Andy had taken a serious fall just out of Duncan Canyon and told me to keep going.

I felt really bad for him as he was doing great up to that point. I hoped we'd meet up later in the day. Mike and Walt tell me what I need to do next. Nice. No thinking necessary. Just move. Off I go. I cruise through the next few miles but the heat and the valleys are taking their toll. By the time I get to the climb up Devil's thumb and El Dorado Creek, I had some good blisters and ankle pain. Over the top and into Michigan Bluff. Andy, Kathy, and their daughter were there to cheer me on. Andy had to bail on the race because of the earlier fall that he had taken. My trusty crew met me and urged me onward as I had no time to spare. Seems that I had taken quite a bit of time to get up the hills. I was whining pretty well on the way out as Mike was urging me on. He basically told me to quit whining and get on with it. I didn't have a choice, so, on we go.

A little bit down the road was Mike. He had taken in my condition and decided that he was going to get me through it. We walked a bit, he gave me some Advil, and off we went. Slow, but, steady. Mike kept pulling me on. And on. We made it past No Hands Bridge and I was hit with an unpleasant trip up another pair of hills. Again, Mike pushed the no whining policy and just urged me on. We topped Robie Point and Mike was finally able to convince me that we were going to make it. We crossed the finish line with about 15 minutes to spare. Unreal. Mike took me about 45 miles instead of the "I can only do about 20 miles with you." If he hadn't, I would not have made it. Thank you, Mike. Andy and family were at the finish to meet me. Thanks for hanging out, Andy.

I managed to make it through the Vermont 100 race three times. Mike was there crewing and pacing me for all three. Mike played a major role on my getting through each of them. There are far too many stories to tell about these runs, but suffice it to say there was at least one of them that I would not have made it were it not for Mike.

As I mentioned before, one of the best things about doing all of this travelling and running is getting together with the guys and the camaraderie. Never fails for me, so, when Mike suggests that we all deplete the bank account and register for the Disney Goofy races, what could I do? I had run Disney a couple of times previously and swore never to do it again. At the time, you went through the sewer treatment plant, very little of the parks, and it just seemed that you were paying a lot of money for little return. But, here we go again with Mike hooking you with the beautiful medal story.

On the course this time, I ran with Mike and he let me know that there is an aid station at some point that he remembered from several years back and the guys had beer there. Who else but Mike would know that? Soon enough, we were there and the guy gave him a beer. Now Mike seemed to be getting smarter. Maybe he has replenished his brain cells. The post-race dinner found a bunch of us with our families at a Texas Roadhouse. My 7 and 9-year-old grandsons were getting a bit anxious to get back to the hotel pool. That is, until they got hit with a peanut. Looked around and they couldn't figure where it came from. Mike the younger and wife Sandra were being bad and the peanut wars had begun. It continued out into the parking lot with all of the "adults" involved.

In 2005, I was somehow roped into taking over the RD slot for the Jack Bristol Lake Waramaug Ultramarathon. The previous RD had had enough and the race was about to die along with its storied history. I had some help that year from quite a few of my friends and we were able to pull it off. It was a lot of work and a lot of stress, but, once it went off, it was worth it. We had 27 finishers that year in the three races.

Over the ten years that I pulled the RD duties, we were able to build it up and improve it each year. My last year, 2014, we had 124 finishers. Mike and Ron were there almost every one of those years. They would come down the day before and help with setup, packet stuffing, food and aid station prep, loading of the trucks and trailer and whatever else needed to be done. Mike the elder, the retired firefighter, made the chicken parm and pasta dinner at my house for the bunch of us that were working.

Next day, we'd get up at 3:30 am, eat, load the food and what-not, and be on the road by 4:30 am. One thing that I should have mentioned earlier is that Mike and Ron can't hear worth a hoot. As a result, their communications with others are a bit loud. Individually, it's not bad, but, together, oh well. If ever you've run with them, no explanation is required.

One year, we dropped our first aid station gear off at 5:00 am. Sounds carry quite a bit on a quiet lake that early in the morning. We got out of the trucks and in a normal-for-Mike-and-Ron audio level, we began to unload. A shhhh from me and the boys tried to quiet it down.

Too late. One of the neighbors from across the street came out of his house and began to read us the riot act, threatening to turn us in to the police and have us hung up by a yardarm. He was doing this from about 75 yards away so it was likely that he was louder than us, but, he lived there, we didn't. I did what I could to keep the peace and it seemed like it worked.

Later on in the day, however, I was making my rounds on the lake and visiting the aid stations. As soon as I got out of my truck, the aid station guys at the beach were asking what in the world we had done to get the guy across the street so riled up. Apparently, he was still irate and had been there yelling at them.

The fact that Mike and Ron are a bit loud is something that I like to tease them about. They always take it good naturedly. In the last few years, my wife has complained to me that I have the TV up too loud and I find myself saying what did you say more than I did before. Might be I'm as bad as them, but, please don't tell them that I said that.

After the beach aid station was set up, we'd head down to the other stations and set up the start line. Mike and Ron would handle the packet pickup and race day registration. That was huge for me as it freed me up to pay attention to runner questions, get the early start together, do the safety briefing, and all of that. When things slowed down a bit, they'd get ready and run the race. It was a busy day for the boys, with the long drive back to Maine afterwards.

On the way down to CT from Maine, Mike had a favorite package store in NH where he could find beer at a good price with no sales tax and no bottle deposit. Always looking for a bargain. He always made sure to bring some for me and for the runners who asked for it too. That's Mike. Always looking out for the rest of us. Brain cell restoration.

Mike really likes to run the long distance timed events. We had a blast at the Across the Years races so the Sri Chimnoy 6 and 10 day races looked like a perfect fit for him. His plan was to drive down to Flushing Meadow and do the race. Fay and I would come down near the end of the race and I would drive him in his car back to my house to get cleaned up and rest.

We had a really fun time down there meeting all of the world class ultrarunners as well as the truly nice people associated with the race. It was a wonderful experience for us. We made it back to the house okay and the next day Mike drove home. He whined a bit for about two weeks about being sore and achy and all of that, but, otherwise, he had a good experience.

So much so, that he decided that 6 days wasn't enough and that the 10-day race would be next. We followed the same basic plan and everything went smoothly. With one exception. On the way home, about ¼ mile from my house, Mike said something to me, don't remember what, and my eyes were diverted from the road for a second.

Next thing I hear from Mike is a very loud shout of caution. I swerved the wheel to miss a car that had stopped right in front of us to make a turn. Too late. I hit the rear of the car ahead and made a mess out of the fender and hood on Mike's beloved 100-year-old Honda. Nobody was hurt so all was good. That showed me that there was nothing that Mike wouldn't do for me. He even let me wreck his car. Thank you, Mike.

Mike's comments: As you can tell by reading what Carl wrote, we have done a lot of races together, crewed and paced each other. We have stayed at each other's homes, our spouses are now friends and I know his sons and grandchildren. I cannot think of anything we have done together that I now regret, even those really tough races.

Kurth, Sabra

- 53 marathons
- Lots of halfs
- No ultras
- Sabra has been running for over 30 years--last 20 were in pursuit of that elusive bird, the marathon

She remembers: I met Mike Brooks at Dust Bowl 2013. My first memory of him was running with Frank Bartocci in Oklahoma and Mike was behind us on a stretch in a residential area. Every time we would come through, the dogs would bark at Mike. I decided to finish the run with Mike that day. We did New Mexico together and later met up at Center of the Nation 2013. Mike is great fun to run with, he has a story for every occasion. When I would be helping out at the food tables with Hanne and the others, he would always advise them not to lend me any money (always sound advice).

Another memory of running with Mike was Riverboat 2014 in Arkansas. It was lightning and thunder and pouring rain. Clint stopped his bike in front of us and said, "Sabra, you can wait in your car, Mike, you need to keep running." I am looking forward to more adventures this year. Thanks for many laughs, Mike.

Mike's comments: Sabra always has a smile on her face and helps out at many of Clint's races. I always enjoy running with her.

Macon, Larry

- Born December 31, 1944
- Has completed over 1600 marathons and ultras
- Guinness World Record for Most Marathons in a year (239)
- Won Bear Lake 2008 (Don't ask how many participants)
- Completed 19 circuits of the 50 States
- Mike's younger and better looking brother

Larry relates his memories of Mike:

When I first met Mike Brooks, it was not love at first sight; it was not even "like" at first sight. The rugged, gruff, plain spoken, retired fireman who grew up in the rough and tough part of Boston was sitting outside a tent at 5 a.m. We were running some long forgotten all night race, and here was Mike drinking a beer. I was certain he didn't have a thing in common with me. Fast forward a few hundred marathons, and now I'm changing my marathon schedule just to share some time with Mike – at least until at some point during our races when he gets tired of walking and takes off, leaving me humiliated and miles behind. That's Mike – charging ahead no matter what.

From that chance meeting in the wee hours of the morn, my appreciation and respect for Mike has grown - a tough, persevering, generous, one of a kind guy who knows no bounds. There is no challenge too treacherous or pain too great to keep Mike away from a goal. Whether it is seven days of races or a trail too steep for a mountain goat, Mike will go for it . . . AND finish with bells on. I have seen him hobbling from his car up to a marathon's starting line and get his medal at the end. I have watched him continue on in spite of flu that had him throwing up for half the race (and for the other half, well, he was dashing into the porta potties!). I have spotted him taking what I thought might surely be his last breath to somehow beat a young dude crossing the mat. Why even on one of those blazing, sun-scorching days when all aid stations are out of water and he's about to succumb to dehydration, Mike always thanks the volunteers.

Be it in Montana or Florida or Maine or Texas, Mike goes and goes and goes, and where there's Mike, there's generosity and inspiration. His efforts have helped raise tens of thousands of dollars for Camp Sunshine by running ridiculously long distances and collecting innumerable donations with his never say quit attitude. His help and encouragement to struggling runners of all ages is usually anonymous. His quest for a fast time takes a back seat when he encounters a hurting runner in need of support to the finish line.

Thank you, Mike, from runners young and old, from here to everywhere, for the gifts you bring to marathoning.

Mike's Comments: Larry is jealous of me being younger and much better looking than him. Smile. Larry is an amazing guy. Doing well over 100 marathons a year and still working full time is truly amazing. I think I have run about 100 marathons/ultras with Larry. I have probably repeated the same stories and jokes to him about that many times also. Jim Simpson and Larry have a lot in common when it comes to being tough mentally and physically. No matter how bad they are hurting neither one will quit. I don't think they know how or when you should. Don't tell Larry but I really do enjoy his company at races.

Moore, Blaine

- Life-Long Runner with over 40 Marathons and Ultramarathons
- Running Coach and State Representative for Maine in the Road Runners Club of America
- Race Director for 15+ races per year
- He ran the 1-More-Mile fundraiser for Camp Sunshine (1 more mile every day than the day before, 1 on the first, 2 on the second, 3 on the third all the way up to 31 on the 31st) - took 2 tries to succeed, but managed to complete it in 2012.

Mike's comments: Blaine also helped me when I did the Ten Day Race for Camp Sunshine by creating a place online where people could check my progress or lack thereof every day. Blaine donates countless hours helping runners and is deeply involved with the sport.

I also did a good size marathon that Blaine was in. When I saw Blaine at the finish line I asked him how he did. All he said was, "I won."

"You won your age group, that's great!" was my response.

Then Blaine said "No, I won the race." I have been in a few races with Blaine and the only time I see him are on the out and backs. I am on the way out and he is on the way back.

Paquette, Ron

- Born 1941; affectionately known as "Dad"
- Ron has been running for 37 years and has completed 215 marathons and ultras. He was inducted into the Running Hall of Fame in 2012 and has completed the 50 States twice

- In general, he brings up the rear with Mike
- Husband of Donnajean Polham
- "Sharp as a Marble"

Ron confesses: Let's face it - there is only one Michael J. Brooks! He is proud to be that person and openly displays it on his license plate and his email address, MJBRUNS. Those of us who have run with him could not ask for a better person to share the road with. There is not a pretentious bone in his body or his head. With Mike, what you see and hear is what you get. This quality makes him a great running companion.

While I was running the older version of the Maine Track Club 50 Miler in Brunswick, Mike was tending to the 2 mile aid station. He promptly jumped in and ran a loop with me.

Mike, who can easily talk to anyone, began describing some of his running plans and what he had already done. He rattled off stories about trail ultras and his plans to drive across the country and run marathons.

He also brought up the 50 States Marathon Club. His enthusiasm and contagious excitable spirit hooked me into setting new goals. Could I do a 100-mile trail race and travel to far off places doing marathons? Run back to back marathons in the same weekend traveling from one state to another?

Little did I know the great adventures that were to follow. Thus began an incredible friendship and an odyssey of unknown ventures that would encompass this beautiful country and its splendors, one step at a time!

Polham, Donnajean

Donnajean's been running since 1980; she actually started running to spend time with hubby Ron Paquette.

She's a member of the Central Maine Striders and Maine Track Club, and has directed and volunteered at many races. She completed marathons in all 50 states in 2012. In addition, she spent many hours crewing for Ron and Mike at marathons and ultras.

She is the "voice of reason"...although Ron and Mike don't really listen all that well.

Prescott, Kendel (formerly Kendel Melin)

- Originally from Minnesota, currently resides in Georgia
- Marathon/ultra total - 380+
- Ultras total - 80+
- Finished a marathon in all 50 States six times (first and only female)
- Completed a marathon in all 7 continents
- Completed a marathon/ultra in 12+ countries
- Completed a hundred miler at Umstead 100 Mile Endurance Run
- Finished 4+ Ironman Triathlons and 30+ triathlons of various distances
- Qualified for and ran the Boston Marathon
- Olympic Torch relay runner during the 1996 Atlanta Olympics
- Member of 50 States Marathon Club, 50 States and DC Group, Marathon Maniacs, Marathon Globetrotters, Georgia Ultra Trail Running Society (GUTS), Darkside Running Club, and others

Prescott, Walt

- Originally from New Hampshire but currently resides in Georgia
- Marathon/ultra total - 360+
- Ultras total - 106+
- Finished a marathon in all 50 States five times
- Completed an ultra marathon in all 50 states
- Completed a marathon on all 7 continents
- Completed a marathon/ultra in 15+ countries, including Comrades Ultra marathon in South Africa
- Completed more than 12 one hundred milers including Western States
- North American coordinator for World Megamarathon Ranking 300+
- Completed an Iron distance Triathlon
- Through-hiked the Appalachian Trail from Georgia to Maine
- Hiked 1000+ miles of the Pacific Crest Trail
- Hiked numerous international trails including the Camino de Santiago across Spain and the Milford Track in New Zealand
- Hiked the 48 "Four-Thousand Footer" mountains of New Hampshire
- Olympic Torch relay runner during 2002 Salt Lake City Olympics
- Member of 50 States Marathon Club, 50 States and DC Group, Marathon Maniacs, Marathon Globetrotters, 50 States sub 4 hours, Georgia Ultra Trail Running Society (GUTS), Darkside Running Club, and others
- Walt met his wife, Kendel, at the starting line of the Bismarck, North Dakota, Marathon in 2004.

Walt recalls: When Mike Brooks has that smirky look on his face, it's hard to believe a word he says, and this one was hard to believe. We were at the starting line of the Cincinnati Flying Pig Marathon when Mike told me that the "Old Man of the Mountain" had come tumbling down the side of Cannon Mountain in New Hampshire during a storm the night before the race.

Being a New Hampshire native son and living there all my life, I was shocked. The "Great Stone Face" was the symbol of our state; it appeared on our license plates, our highway signs, and even on the New Hampshire state quarter. Mike, who lived in Maine, took great joy in letting me know the details of the Old Man's demise, as I shook my head in disbelief while we lined up for our second race of the weekend. The day before, our gang of running buddies had run the Indianapolis 500 Half-Marathon, and today we were back for more.

I'm not really sure when or where I first met Mike but it was probably at the starting line of a marathon somewhere. Was it at the Badwater Ultramarathon where we both crewed and paced our running friends so they could finish the grueling event in Death Valley? Was it at the numerous Florida marathons we had run to escape the snow and ice of New England winters? Or was it at one of the 100 mile races that our mutual running buddies had suckered us into running?

The initial introduction most likely happened while we were both running races around the country in pursuit of finishing a marathon in all 50 states. When you see the same faces at the same running events week after week, you develop an immediate, strong bond with each other, and you take heart in knowing that you're not the only fool out there.

And Mike Brooks was one of the biggest running fools there was on the running circuit. He seemed to be unstoppable, having completed hundreds of running events from 5k's, hundred milers, and numerous multi-day events.

He has slowed down a bit since I met him more than a decade ago, but he will always take the time to help out a first-time marathoner or to pace and crew one of his friends to help them achieve their goals...like the time he paced me to finish the Western States 100 miler. I could not have done it without Mike's help.

Mike's running resume reads like a Hall of Famer.... finishing a marathon in all 50 States five times and completing more than 400 marathons/ultras all over the world. I've been fortunate to run close to a hundred of those races with Mike, from the Great Wall in China to the Grand Canyon.

We've shared rides, car rentals, hotels, and other travel expenses. We've stayed at each other's homes on numerous running occasions. Mike was there the day I met my future wife, Kendel, at the starting line of the Bismarck Marathon. I was there the day Mike finished the climb up to the

Whitney Portals and completed the Badwater Ultramarathon. Mike is one tough runner.

Mike has a very quick wit and he doesn't hesitate to share his worldly wisdom and repertoire of jokes and stories learned during his years as a fireman. It's always fun to run races with Mike and our group of running buddies, because the banter is nonstop. It's a party for 26.2 miles. When Mike realized that the fate of the "Old Man of the Mountain" was something that concerned me, he was relentless in needling me (in a friendly way) about it. One time when our group was driving in Texas from one race to another, Mike took out one of the New Hampshire quarters with the "Old Man" on it and scraped the face off the coin. He then proceeded to throw the coin out the window, somewhere between Huntsville and Dallas. I still think about that coin and the Old Man every time I'm in the area. I've also received New Hampshire toll tokens in the mail from Mike with the "Old Man" scraped off. Lord knows how he can sleep at night after inflicting such a sacrilege!

But I've found a method to settle the score with Mike in a bizarre sort of way, and it all comes down to a bar of soap. Several years ago, after a particularly muddy trail race in Kentucky that we ran together, Mike let Kendel and me use the shower facilities in his hotel room before we dashed off to the airport for a flight. Mike saved extra towels for us but pointed out that there was only one bar of soap, and he had already taken a shower. He let us know exactly where that bar of soap had been. Because of that brief conversation, and the unfortunate mental picture that Mike painted for us, since that day we have always thought of Mike every time we're in the shower and washing our butts with soap. It's the absolute truth that Kendel and I mention Mike almost every morning in the bathroom....and I've since told Mike of this connection many times with the same type of joy that he had when he first told me of the collapse of the "Old Man."

Mike is a great guy and has been a true friend of mine. He doesn't hesitate to do anything he can to help out his friends, and has raised considerable funds for his charities through his running events. As a runner, he is steady and stubborn, and a "never-give-up" kind of guy. As a person, Mike is fun-loving, honest, hard-working and a true-blue Downeast-Yankee from Maine. It's too bad he isn't from New Hampshire.

Mike's comments: No more Delta companion tickets for me now that Walt married Kendel. Walt is one of my original gang of ultra runners. I have stayed at his home in NH and his present home in Georgia. Kendel is a sweetheart and someone I have also run with. I can't say enough about how much fun all three of us have had together. BTW Kendel is the best thing that ever happened to Walt.

Rueden, Henry A.

- Henry lives in Wisconsin.
- He's completed well over 900 marathons and more than 100 ultras and has done the circuit of the states at least 13 times; he has also done an inaugural marathon in every state.
- In addition, he has completed all 50 states in a year, as well as all territories and provinces in Canada, all continents, an ultra in every state, and a marathon or ultra-based on the letters of the alphabet A-Z.

As Henry tells it: I can't remember when I first met Mike and the various individuals he crewed/ran with over the years. I seem to be always behind Mike when the race is completed. I always could run but never fast. I was in a reserve unit and had to be somewhat in shape. It helped that I was born and raised on a farm. My first marathon was back in 1988. Several reserve unit members were going to run Chicago so I ran it just for fun and finished around 4:45. I would run every Chicago until I was deployed overseas in 2004. In 1989, I ran 6 marathons. In the early years some races had a 5 hour cut off. I finished one in Texas that would give you the finisher shirt for finishing, but the time was not recorded. In the early years many of the races did not even give medals. Some of the early medals were generic; today there are lots of races that try to outdo each other with the biggest, largest, most moving parts, parts add onto a series etc.

In my early marathon career, we were advised that doing one a month is best. More might lead to medical problems. Over the next several years, I averaged around 13 or so. I ran my fastest one in South Bend in 1991. In 1993, I had signed up for one in Lake County, IL, that started in Zion, IL. I heard about another nearby marathon, the Drake Relays in Des Moines, IA. I figured with a little luck I could do both. I did not get a lot of sleep that night because the drive took about 6 ½ hours but I completed both races. I did not do another double unit I returned from military duty in 1996.

When I started running, I did not have any long range goals. I did not have a lot of time, so I did many local marathons, including a unique one in Wisconsin that started in Marathon City and finished in Athens. I had run into some individuals doing all the states. I figured if I did a few a year, I would get done someday. In the fall of 1995, I completed my 100th marathon and my 20th state.

In civilian life, I am an accountant but I had taken some computer classes in college. Finding marathon or ultras in the early years was not easy. You would have to write the race director for an application and enclose a letter so it could be mailed back. You would include postage; otherwise you might not see the application. I worked with databases so I could track the various races. In the early years, maybe 300-400 would be listed. I would look forward to the race listings in Running Times, Runners World, and Ultra Runner and would try to keep my database updated.

When I returned from military duty in 1996, I figured I should try and complete the states. I looked at my race database to determine which states would be the hardest to finish. I finally finished the 50 states and D.C. in 1998.

Over the years the number of marathons I did increased to around 20, then 30, then 40. I reached 50 a year in 2002 and maintained that number for a few years. I retired from the reserves and that gave me more time to race. I completed the states a few more times around. In 2004, I was recalled to active duty with deployment overseas. I had planned a few races in the fall of 2004 but did not make any. I had time in July to try and get to Wakefield, MA, for a race. I did not realize how bad traffic was from New York to MA on a Friday night. Mike was running the race. I waited to see him; Mike did not recognize me because I had shaved my beard. We talked a little as I had to return to duty the next morning. Mike was one of the last runners I saw before departing for overseas duty. I had completed 396 marathons/ultras before leaving for duty.

One of my goals was to do an initial marathon/ultra race in every state. Finding them has not been easy. It can be difficult and somewhat costly. I had entered the NH/ME double and found a new marathon in WV. The new one in AK was the day before Chicago. I saw snowflakes in AK before I left for the overnight trip to Chicago. I made it to the start in time. With the current security, that most likely would not happen.

Doing the 50 states in one year took a lot of planning and luck. Back when I planned my list, I started with the states sorting by least number of races to the most, choosing dates and looking for a backup date. I came down to the last state being the only choice having to go from the east coast to the Midwest. Today it is fairly easy, there are races held during the week. If someone wanted, they could do the 50 states in less than 6 months. Someone told me I should write a book about all the places and things I have seen; maybe someday I will when I no longer get to the finish line before everyone goes home. But at least there are some timed events like 6, 12, 24 hour races that are available. I would like to thank Mike and all the various runners, supporters, volunteers, friends I have met over the years.

Savage, Chuck:

I started running in the Air Force when I was 25. I ran about 10 miles a week and thought I was doing high mileage. I was 40 when I ran my first marathon. (I always say it took me 15 years to screw up the courage.) My first marathon was "Trails End" on the coast of Oregon. (The name refers to Lewis and Clarks Expedition to the west coast.) The weather was so bad I thought it would be my last marathon. We ran in a gale with 50 mph gusts and real cold rain.

For years I only cared about how fast I ran a marathon, but now they are mainly social events for me because I am so slow. I remember lately saying to Mike, "If we speed up a little, we can break 8 hours!" I have run 367 marathons so far and I will probably run a few more.

I put on a race series in New England each May called "The New England Challenge." It is 5 marathons in 5 states in 5 days. I saw the need for such a race for members of the 50 States Club since for someone living on the west coast, flying to New England 5 times would be very expensive. I also noticed that these states were so small and close together that driving each day would be only a short drive (about 100 miles at most). So 2015 was the third year for this series.

The main thing about running for me is the friends I have made and all the wonderful people I have met because of running. They are my best friends.

Mike's Comments: Running with Chuck is always a pleasure. He is very knowledgeable on just about any subject and always has plenty of stories and jokes to tell. I hope to have half the energy that he has at 75.

Simpson, Jim

- Born December 1941
- Jim is modest and humble so he will not brag about all his accomplishments but he is an admirable athlete.

Mike's Comments: Jim has completed over 1,300 marathons/ultras and has finished all 50 States 11 times.

Those are not misprints: 1,300 marathons/ultras and all 50 states 11 times is amazing. I have known Jim since 2001 and he was traveling the country in his camper equipped pickup truck which he continues to do. Jim does over 100 marathons a year now. His home is usually the camper in a Wal-Mart parking lot. I told him he should get a job as a Wal-Mart traveling greeter. Smile. Always enjoy running with Jim and I see him at many races, kind of have to since he does so many.

Smith, Mike:

- Mike is from Fishers, IN. He has completed:
- 89 - 100 milers
- 30 - 50 milers
- 8 – 100k runs
- 215 - marathons
- 50 State marathon finisher 2001
- Badwater
- Comrades Marathon
- 3 Rim to Rim to Rim Grand Canyon Crossings
- 2 Baton Rouge to New Orleans Mississippi River Levee runs

I can't remember the first time Mike and I ran together, but I'm sure I met him while we were working on completing marathons in the 50 states. We've done the same races dozens of times, often with a group of our friends.

I think I've probably run every race distance there is with Mike. In addition, we've done most of the timed race alternatives (8/12/24 hour) together. We've been to elevations over 14,000 feet (Pikes Peak) and we've been below sea level (Death Valley).

I can only hope to be running the kinds of races and distances that Mike is doing at his age. I also admire the fact that Mike has taken a pretty selfish endeavor, running races, and turned it into an opportunity to support charitable causes like Camp Sunshine.

I'm looking forward to continuing to run races in the future with Mike and hope we have the opportunity to crew for each other too.

Mike's comments: My brother Walter and I have stayed at Mike Smith's house several times. Andy, Walt, Bob Wehr, Mike, and I used to run together all the time. As I get slower he seems to get faster so now it is just a fun race once in a while. By the time this book is published he will probably have done over 100 100-mile races. He is not slowing down. We still keep in contact and all of us planned a reunion race in early 2016 with our spouses so we can participate in part or all of the Dopey Challenge.

Spear, Howard

- First road race was a 5 miler in 1987
- 23 marathons
- 3 Goofy Challenges and a Dopey Challenge
- 6 time Mt. Washington finisher

I've been a member of the Maine Track Club since 1993 and served as equipment manager, clothing manager, and race committee and board member. I've been selected volunteer of the year, MTC Lifetime Achievement Award, Comeback Runner of the Year, John Fyalkia Award Winner, Race Director: 3 years Patriots Day 5 miler, 3 years YMCA Back Bay 5k, 15 years Portland Sea Dogs Mother's Day 5k, 5 years Portland Sea Dogs Father's Day 5k and 15 years Maine Marathon, Relay & Maine Half Marathon.

I did not qualify for Boston Marathon but got a waiver, finished, but second time quit at mile 25....did not feel well; Helped raise almost $3.5 million for cancer research and local nonprofits that help Maine children. I think Mikey Brooks is the craziest runner ever, nice guy but crazy.

Mike's comments: I first met Howie in 1996 and have done a few races with him but know Howard mostly as a race director and for helping me with Camp Sunshine fundraising. I was on the Maine Marathon committee for years where he is still the race director along with Bob Aube. Howard refuses to accept any money for being the race director and keeps them as all volunteer events with proceeds going to nonprofits.

Wailes, Bettie:

- First marathon January 1993
- 100th marathon March 2011
- 200th marathon January 2014
- 300th marathon January 2015
- Ran 102 marathons in 2014, 12th American overall, 4th American woman to run 100 or more in a calendar year. 5th woman in the world to run at least 100 in a calendar year.
- Published "Running in the Back of the Pack: a Memoir of My Running Life" in 2014.

Wehr, Bob

According to Bob, it's hard to put into words a story of a friendship that spans so many miles and years. Such a journey has many great times and happenings but a few are especially memorable.

Mike Brooks has been known as Old Mike for a long time. It started as a way to know which Mike we were talking about whenever several of us were together with Mike Brooks and Mike Smith. Mike Smith is a dozen or so years younger than Brooks, our Old Mike. While I had known and run with Old Mike for several years, I really got to know him when we crewed for Mike Smith at Badwater.

Old Mike and I were one crew of his 2-crew team with Walt Prescott and Andy Velazco making up the other. Badwater is a 135-mile extreme endurance race that goes from 280' below sea level to finish at Mt. Whitney Portals at 8300' elevation. Running across Death Valley in the middle of summer makes Badwater one of the toughest races in the world.

It's a hot, tortuous, grueling race for the runner but it's also very draining on the crew. Every crew member spends 4 hours or so at a time caring for the runner, driving to a hotel to nap for a couple of hours, then getting back to the racer for another 4-hour shift. The cycle is repeated day and night for 2 or more days. Finishing Badwater is a huge accomplishment for the runner and extremely tiring for everyone.

I was still exhausted when Old Mike, Andy Velazco, and I drove back to Las Vegas in one of the support cars. Thankfully, Old Mike volunteered to drive the car and his slow weaving pace along the curvy roads soon lulled me to sleep. Within 15 minutes Mike was also dozing off and said he couldn't drive and still keep us on the road. I was grateful that Andy was wide awake and quickly volunteered to drive. That gave Old Mike and me a chance to sleep. But our prior 30 mph restful drive suddenly turned into a harrowing 50 mph twisting turning speedway. After the first squealing curve my droopy eyelids opened wide. It was clear that Andy really knew how to straighten out a road. I couldn't tell if our knuckles were white from fear or from the tight grip we used to hold ourselves upright. Andy was able to use all of the road as well as some of the gravel on each side. At each turn we craned our necks to see who or what was coming next. We always knew that Andy was an orthopedic surgeon. What we didn't know was that he was also a former race car driver. I never found out who or what Andy was racing that day, but I'm pretty sure we won.

Old Mike was always a better runner than me but it was common for him to slow his pace so we could talk for companionship. I have great memories of running with Mike on the Great Wall of China in 2006 when he again thankfully was going at a very slow pace and so it was easy to talk.

After a while I noticed that not only was it easy to keep up with Mike but also that I was leading the pace. I felt great that my running had improved so much that now I was the one who had to slow down so that Mike could keep up as we plodded through the beautiful Chinese countryside. We had plenty of time to talk as we walked and I soon learned the details of the Self Transcendence Race that Mike had just finished. He had just completed running 320 miles in 6 days. It turned out that with little rest Mike was lucky to be able to walk and he found it almost impossible to run. There went my hopes of ever really being a better runner than Old Mike. We managed to finish the marathon with 15 minutes to spare and so avoided being DQ'd from the race. We had a great time.

Most of my running friends have run much harder, faster, and longer than me. I feel fortunate to have many friends who have accomplished such incredible feats of endurance and will. The focus and dedication it takes to run hundreds of marathons, ultras, and endurance events in all kinds of weather is monumental. The old mantra is that running is simple. You put one foot in front of the other and repeat. But those simple steps help you gain some incredible friends along the way.

Mike's comments: Bob did not mention that after having both knees replaced at the same time he ran an 8 hour ultra. Bob also completed a 15k, 5k, and marathon to finish the Gasparilla Challenge in Tampa, FL. Bob is a veterinary surgeon and I think he must have replaced his knees with those from a greyhound.

White, Marsha 'Bookladywalker'

I did my first race, a half marathon, at the age of 59 and since then I have completed 221 marathons/ultramarathons (and counting) plus lots of half marathons. Although I have never won a race, and probably never will, I occasionally place in my age group. I love to do timed races (12/24/48/72 hour races) because the pressure is off.

I try to volunteer whenever I can and I especially like to stay and cheer on the last people to finish (I've been there!)

I can't remember exactly where Mike Brooks and I first crossed paths but we see each other a lot at races - we usually keep a similar pace. I hope to keep racing as long as I can!

Mike's comments: I do not remember where I met Marsha either but I seem to see her more often lately. The thing that impresses me the most about Marsha is her volunteering. Even though she was not doing any of the Savage 7 races she volunteered all day at one and had to travel a distance to do so. I mentioned to her that I was going to write a book and without me asking Marsha volunteered to help me. She is an excellent writer. I was doing an article for a running magazine and on two occasions the editor referred to articles she wrote saying more or less that is how I should write my article. I told him "I am no Marsha White." She is a much better writer than me.

Velazco, Andy:

- Born 3/22/1948
- 28 years running
- About 400 races including:
    321 marathons
    72 ultras
- Done 50, 100 milers and Ironmans
- Best distance 50 miles

I met Mike in 2000, a retired fire fighter from Maine. It was at dinner in a gathering of the 50 States Marathon Club in Tulsa, OK. I had traveled there to run their marathon and knock out Oklahoma. I had just joined the club and was a newby, with 20 or so marathons run. I happened to have dinner with several runners, one of whom was Mike. It was that event that led me into running ultramarathons. After introductions and during dinner, I listened to this group of runners. They were talking about running marathons every weekend, marathons back to back (Saturday-Sunday), 50 kilometers, 50, and 100 miles. I was overwhelmed, but also realized, that these were regular people who had families and jobs but nonetheless were able to run these tremendous distances. I was told that several of them were driving to Kansas City after the Oklahoma Marathon to run the Gobbler Grind Marathon. They encouraged me to do it. They told me they would look after me. So, with trepidation, I changed my flight back to Atlanta and decided to follow them.

That's how I met Mike Brooks, Mike Smith, and Walter Prescott, all people who would become friends and would become very important in my future running life.

I managed to finish my first back to back marathon weekend without any problems. Then Mike encouraged me to run Olander Park, in Ohio. My new buddies had entries for it already, and I was told that I should run it. I signed up. I did not mention that it was the Olander Park 24 Hour run. My argument, that I had never gone beyond 26.2 miles, was not important to Mike. He told me to run a mile, walk and eat a little, and repeat. The Olander course was a 1.1 mile around a lake.

Zielinski, Mike:

I was born in 1959 in Mount Prospect, IL. In my younger years, running more than a short sprint was a chore. I never would have guessed that by age 45, I would make it to each of the 50 states plus Washington, D.C. to successfully complete a marathon. Of course I never could have done this without the support of God, two loving parents, my younger brother's family, and numerous runners and volunteers from across the country (including Mike Brooks). How lucky I was to accomplish this but it was also the loneliness of the long distance runner.

It made me realize how most humans and other earthly creatures suffer in some way like my parents (my father was sent to faraway places with the Civilian Conservation Corps and the Navy and later tried to hold a job with my mother worrying about raising a family). Other heroes would include sick young folks (like at Camp Sunshine) and the pains of old age. The American people have been blessed with a beautiful country and I would like to think when much is given, much is expected. Americans should set an example with hard work, eating good, staying away from harmful substances, and getting proper exercise.

Mike's comments: I have run several marathons with Mike the last one probably ten years ago. We stay in touch by email. Mike is a big supporter of Camp Sunshine and that is very much appreciated. Mike has started running more and hopefully we can do a marathon together soon.

Disney post-race dinner at Texas Roadhouse:
Mike, Anthony, Joey, and Sandra Smith,
Denise and Mike Brooks,
Nancy Walton, Carl Hunt

Disney's Dopey Challenge:
Laurie Nicholas, Jan Gagnier, Howard Spear, Bonnie Topham, Mike

Chuck Savage, Frank B, Jim Simpson, Mike, Nellie

CHAPTER 3: DENISE BROOKS:
SHE DESERVES HER OWN CHAPTER

What follows is in Denise's own words:

A few years ago Mike told a reporter that he was lucky to have an understanding wife. As I look back over the years to write about "what traveling with Mike and being a part of his running has meant to me" I have to ask myself, how much do I really understand?

I am 14 1/2 years Mike's junior (not 15 mind you but 14 1/2). Never in these past 32 years have I ever looked at him as older than me. Most people wouldn't understand that but I figure I have always been older than my years and I suppose he has been younger than his. Whatever the reason, it has worked for us.

Mike and I first met on a Wednesday night in 1983. He was with some friends and I was with my sister. Mike loves to tell the story of how he came to the table to ask my sister to dance and he "ended up "with me because another man had asked her before he got there. The rest as they say is history!

Mike and I had both been through a divorce. I was enjoying being single and focusing on my nursing career. Mike was newly single and getting used to not living with his 3 daughters. He had quit smoking and had lost some weight by doing some recreational running. One of my memories of those early years is of a weekend morning when I was to meet him after he had gone for his morning run around Lake Auburn. It was in the winter and I remember thinking "People run this time of year? Voluntarily?" When Mike returned from his run he had icicles hanging from his moustache and I thought "this guy is crazy!" -- Little did I know then that I was going to see even more crazy antics many years later!

After about a year he started smoking again and slowly gained back the weight he had lost. At some point (it is mostly a blur now) Mike started doing some biking, skiing, a little golfing, and, oh yeah, running. Most of these activities were sporadic and short lived -- except for the running, which I believe will continue, in some form, as long as he can put one foot in front of the other. Mike is a very disciplined individual; he sets goals for himself, does research, reaches out for help and then achieves (most) of his goals.

Initially I went to almost all of his races, since they were usually fairly local and short 5 or 10k's. Once the marathons started the traveling to more distant locations began. Once Mike latched on to his goal of running a marathon in every state, I decided to have a shadow box made so Mike could display his 50 medals (actually 51 with D.C). I thought "there, all of his medals would be in the same place and on display." Fast forward 20 years and those 51 medals are just a mere sampling of all the ones he has collected. Fast forward to several years later, Mike's running and traveling to reach his goals has been great for me because it has given me the opportunity to do the same. I have seen more of this country and the world than I had ever thought I would. One great advantage to that is that it helps me answer some Jeopardy questions!! Through our travels I have met some of the nicest people from all walks of life. Once they put on running shorts and a bib number they are all the same.

I have dabbled in running but have never developed the love for it that Mike has and now with 2 bad knees and facing 2 knee replacements in the future my running days are over. I have, however, still been able to join him on many trips, and we often joke that if there is a casino, a beach or a mall nearby, then I'm going on that trip! Recently Mike's brother Walter asked me "why do you go to Hawaii and Florida and I go to Kentucky and Ohio?" My answer to that is "I'm not stupid!" Of course there is nothing wrong with Kentucky or Ohio but I do like warm weather and beaches!

I have been with Mike at his lowest points, like when his mother died the day before a marathon and he struggled with whether or not to run. After talking it over, he decided that his mother would be the first to tell him to run — so he did. Another low point was when he had his first DNF (did not finish) at the Vermont 100. I learned through that period of time that the phrase "I'm never doing that again" is really just a reaction and not a true statement!

I have also seen Mike at his highest point—when that impish grin turns into a full blown smile. For instance, when he did finish the Vermont 100, after he completed "Badwater" with the added joy of raising money for Camp Sunshine, and when he finished the 50 States for the first time in Alaska. Oh, and by the way, he was "never doing the 50 states again" either and he has now completed them 5 times and is on his way to the 6th time.

I do understand, I understand him, I understand that it is not all about the running, his passion is with the running community, the social aspect of the running events, and the sense of accomplishment that he feels when he reaches a goal. I understand that while he sometimes shows a rough exterior, he is honest, kind, thoughtful, generous, and loving. He loves me, his children, his grandchildren, Nellie (our dog) and most of all doing the right thing. He has a special place in his heart for children, especially those with special needs or illnesses, so his connection with Camp Sunshine just "makes sense" in so many ways.

So there you have it – a combination that just works -- a crazy thoughtful man married to an understanding woman!

Mike's comments: I was told our marriage would not last because of the 14-year age difference. We got married anyway, that was 30 years ago. Denise has been extremely supportive. Her favorite saying is " do it while you can."

It does not matter if it is a 5-week cross country trip or a marathon in Africa. She does not worry about the cost and takes care of things at home. If it was not for her support, I don't know what I would be doing. As she said, we have had some great trips together and she enjoys traveling as much as me.

We are as much in love today as when we first got married.

Mike and cousin George circa early 1950s

CHAPTER 4: THE EARLY YEARS

Growing Up in Somerville

I spent the first 19 years of my life in Somerville, Massachusetts. This city is known for its rich history, dating back to before the Revolutionary War. When I lived there, 1945 to 1964, it was a mostly working-class city of over 100,000 residents, squeezed into 6 square miles, the most densely populated city in New England. It is also known as the home of the Winter Hill Gang. A rivalry with another gang resulted in about 40 murders. "Whitey" Bulger was the last leader of the gang. He was on the FBI's most wanted list for over twelve years and was finally captured in 2012.

Growing up, the only sports I played was what we called sand lot. These were football and baseball teams formed by neighborhood kids. Stick ball was played in the streets. The only time I ran was when I was playing these sports or someone was chasing me to do harm. I also ran home for lunch when I was going to grammar school. If I ran fast enough, I could do the pledge of allegiance to the flag and toast it with a glass of milk with uncle Bob on the Howdy Doody show.

My mother stayed home to take care of my two brothers and me until my youngest brother was in his teens. My dad worked as a crane operator at the Watertown arsenal where he poured molten steel to be made into cannons. Later he worked at a steel warehouse. We lived in a three family home that my parents owned. We shared our bathroom with the people on the third floor, which my mother did not like. When they moved out, the third floor was converted into bedrooms for my brothers and me.

My aunt Evelyn lived on the first floor with my grandmother Wallace. My grandmother died in 1959 and was waked at home, the custom back then.

Our home sat on a small lot surrounded by apartment houses. We did have room on one side for a driveway. There were two coal furnaces that my brothers and I kept going in the winter. Milk was delivered to the house and in the summer I would sneak onto the milk truck. A piece of ice from the truck was a treat that would cool you off on a hot day in the city. Our neighbor had a truck that he used to deliver kerosene in 5 gallon cans and ice in blocks. The kerosene was used in stoves for heat and cooking. The ice was used to keep food cold in iceboxes, the forerunner of refrigerators.

Luckily we had coal to heat and a refrigerator. I can remember my mother using a washboard to do laundry. We had a bath tub, but no shower. Saturday was the only day we kids took a bath. I can remember how dirty the water would be! No phone meant we had to use my aunt's which was a pain for her and us. She would yell up the stairway when one of us would get a call.

When we were young kids there were times when money was tight. My father was laid off several times. There were strikes, injuries, layoffs, and other problems. My mother did not have to tell us to "finish what's on your plate" and lots of times there were no seconds. I can remember one time my mother just had a quarter she could spare for one of us to go to the movies. I won the coin toss and was supposed to tell my brothers about the movie when I got home. I was excited to be going to see the horror movie; I think it was "The House of Wax". On the way to the movie I was flipping the quarter and it went down a sewer! What to do? I went to the Somerville Theater and stood outside until the movie was over. I asked friends who were leaving to give me details about the movie. Never telling the truth about what happened I told my brothers what a great movie it was and told them all about it.

Another time a neighbor who worked at Tufts College brought us to see Santa at the school. This was for poor kids and I guess we qualified. Every kid got a toy and talked to Santa. It was a thrill this young kid has never forgotten. A roll of pennies for penny candy and a plastic pistol that shot suction cup tipped darts was what Santa brought one Christmas. I was the happiest kid to get these great gifts. When I was a young kid I never thought I was poor.

There were plenty of good times. My parents would bring us to the ocean beaches on Cape Cod and Revere Beach. My mother saved me from drowning one time when I got caught in a rip tide. I loved to fish and we would fish off ocean piers and once a year go on a party boat to catch mackerel. Another treat was going for ice cream out in the country at a place called Kimbal's. They had dairy cows there and excellent ice cream. Dad always let me sit up front so I could look for turtles. As a kid I had turtles and snakes for pets along with a dog at one time or another. My keeping snakes in the house came to an abrupt end with a loud scream. I told my mother one of my snakes had escaped. A day or two later we heard a loud scream from Aunt Evelyn and my mother said "I think we found the snake." Evelyn went to pick up her milk delivery in the back hallway and when she reached down for the bottle, she noticed the snake curled around the bottle!

I started working when I was about 8. My first job was in a commercial laundry. I do not remember much about this job except for diluting very strong bleach with water to use in cleaning. My next job was selling newspapers on a corner in Davis Square. The Record American was 7 cents; I kept 2 cents and if someone gave me a 3 cent tip I was one happy kid. On Sundays I would take the subway into Boston and find out where I would be selling papers for the day. It was always at a traffic light where I would walk between cars stopped for the light, yelling "get your Record American " and fumbling with the 3 cent change of a dime. I would hope the car would take off and not wait for the change when the light turned green. Cars would zoom by me as I waited for the light to turn red again. One day my mother and dad saw me out in the traffic. I thought my mother was going to have a heart attack. They were not happy to say the least. The dream newspaper delivery route was Massachusetts Avenue in Cambridge. There was a bar on almost every corner and that is where the tips were. Around Christmas time a lot of them would put out tip jars for the paperboy and he would make what was a small fortune to him. I also sold newspapers in a shopping center for a few years.

After that it was on to a big time job. When I was 14 I lied about my age and got a job working after school and summers at a tomato packing plant in South Boston. The year was 1959 and I was making $1.60 an hour, which was excellent pay for a 14-year-old. I think I was the only one working there that wasn't Italian until my friend Johnny McCormick started work. We took the subway to work and sometimes put in long hours to get orders done. One 4th of July I went to work thinking I would be working a full day of overtime. This was the day I always went mackerel fishing on a party boat with my parents. It was a stupid decision to go to work instead. After a few hours of work, we were told the orders were up and work was done for the day. I ran to the subway station hoping to get home in time to go fishing. I got home just after my parents had left, what a bummer! I did get laid off for a short period of time and got a job at the "Wrinkle Krinkle" paper company, honest. It was embarrassing cashing the check.

When I turned 15 I really didn't like doing things with my parents but dad would let me drive the car so I would go on trips just for that reason. We kids never asked our parents for a ride. Transportation for us was buses, trolley cars, the subway, bike, hitchhiking, hopping trains, or jumping on the tailboards of stopped trucks at traffic lights. I had been smoking for a few years by now and my mother gave up trying to stop me. Back then the health consequences were not known. She knew I was smoking because as soon as I got home I would brush my teeth so she would not smell the smoke. Not putting the cap back on the toothpaste was the giveaway she later told me. When I turned 16, I immediately got my license and loved to drive. One school day, on a Holy Day when Catholics were supposed to go to Mass, I got permission to use the car. After attending Mass like a good Catholic, I was eyeballing this good looking girl, and smashed right into the car in front of me. The front end and radiator were damaged. Keep your eyes on the road is something I learned that day.

There were plenty of groups or what you could call gangs of kids in Somerville when I was a kid. Most were from what are known as squares. These are usually areas with pool halls, bowling alleys, bars, and restaurants. I hung around Davis Square in Day's pool room mostly. My brother Walter, 4 years older than me, hung around different guys known as the "Greeks."

If we wanted to have a few beers or play cards we would go down to the railroad tracks, simply known as "the tracks." Cities around Somerville also had gangs. If you went to a party in Somerville and a bunch of guys showed up from another city there was usually a fight before the night was over. I never got in any serious trouble as a kid. Worst things I ever did were break some windows and swipe copper from the Edison power company barrels. I think the copper was being thrown away because it was small pieces wrapped around glass insulators. Power company workers would chase me but I always got away. Maybe they let me? I would break the glass off the copper and burn the insulation off the copper in my backyard. When the price was high I would sell the copper.

From High School to the Military

I hated school but my mother use to tell me "you are going to graduate from high school no matter how long it takes. I don't care if you have a long beard!" Just working at school as little as possible I graduated on time at 17 in 1963. Brother Walt was in the National Guard and told me I should join to keep from getting drafted. So at 17 I was off to boot camp at Fort Dix, New Jersey. On the bus ride there you heard some horror stories about how you are going to be treated but luckily the stories were exaggerated.

Being assigned to Frontier Company could be the worst or best thing that happened to me. This was definitely the toughest run company that I know of on Fort Dix. The company commander was a 23-year-old captain who, if I remember correctly, had been to Vietnam. The war in Vietnam had not really started but this guy had been there. We ran early every morning while the other companies were still asleep. We would make sure that we made enough noise to wake them up singing songs about going airborne, girls from Mass. with dimples on their ass, we proud, we tough, you can't push us enough, and other such ditties. All the other companies would ride in trucks to the rifle range but we ran and marched. The captain did everything we did so I thought he was an alright guy. Going into basic training you are tested to see how fast you can run a mile along with doing pushups, chin ups, grabbing rung after overhead rung, and a few other things. At first I could not do any of these things. Running a mile in 8 minutes was one of them. Being overweight and out of shape changed in 8 weeks of rigorous training. At the end of basic training I passed all of the tests and was off to a month of training to be a cook and then 3 months as a cook.

Getting out of the service, I quickly got out of shape. Smoking two packs a day did not help. I trained to be a welder and went to work in the Quincy shipyard building submarines. I met my first wife at Old Orchard Beach, Maine, and was married in 1966. Later that year I became a father of a beautiful girl just a week after my 20th birthday. Thinking back to those days I realize how immature I was and how I could have been a better father and husband. In 1967 I was in a motorcycle accident just weeks after Massachusetts had passed a helmet law. Fortunately, along with my tank top and shorts, I was wearing a WWII German helmet. My friend was driving the bike when we had the accident. I slid down the road long enough to feel the skin peeling off me so I rolled over to finish off the other side. The German helmet saved serious injury to my head. My friend had similar injuries.

A New Career as Firefighter

While I was recuperating from my motorcycle injuries at Old Orchard Beach, I saw an ad for firefighters in my wife's hometown of Auburn, Maine. After talking with my wife and mother-in-law I decided to try for the job. Moving to Maine would allow my wife to go back to college and my mother-in-law agreed to watch our baby, Kelli. I took a really easy written test and passed. The physical went something like this: "how many fingers do I have up?" My answer: "two"' Response: "Good, you passed the hearing and eye test." I got the job and walked into a firehouse for the first time in my life to report for work. I was shown the back of the truck and the bar I was to hold onto.

Back in 1967, the only training you got was on the job. The newbie cleaned the toilets, did errands for the other firefighters, and always helped the most important guy on the shift, the cook. Part of my initiation was being told that this certain firefighter was gay and that he would be visiting me tonight. Being wide awake I could see someone undressing at the foot of my bed. Then a voice said, "Are you ready?" I responded: "No, get the hell out of here!" Laughter filled the station, as all the other firefighters listened for my response. Another stunt they would pull is to tell a firefighter it was against the rules to play with yourself. The bed springs had no covering so they would string a rope to them that would make a squeaking noise when pulled. The proby firefighter would go to bed and someone would pull the rope to make a squeaking sound. "Stop playing with yourself," a voice would yell, and the proby would deny doing anything. This would go on for a time with the other firefighters listening until everyone broke out in laughter. To test a firefighter, they would put you on the front of the fire hose with no breathing equipment and push you right up to the fire. Being a firefighter is a lot like being in the military. You eat, sleep, and do combat together. Your life can very well be in the hands of another firefighter. The pay was about a third of what I was making at the shipyard, but other than that I loved the job.

Back in my early years as a firefighter we went to many more fires than when I retired. Some towns around us had little or no fire protection and called us when a fire was first reported. Better firefighting, more sprinkler systems, better house construction, and more smoke alarms helped reduce loss of property and life over the years. We seldom used self-contained breathing apparatus the first ten years or so I was in the fire department. We would use a mask that filtered the smoke to some degree but, of course, could not supply oxygen to breathe with. Almost every fire ended up with a few firefighters going to the hospital with smoke inhalation. The Occupational Safety and Health Administration (OSHA) rules now make it mandatory to wear proper breathing apparatus and created other rules that greatly reduced injuries and deaths to firefighters.

Spending 33 years as a firefighter provided me with many memories, mostly good, some tragic. Firefighters are notorious for pulling practical jokes. When I first joined the fire department, we had lots of spare time on our hands since we did not train much and did very few medical calls. Usually things that happen in the fire station stay in the station, but I can share a few stories. One involved an Auburn cop who used to stop by Engine 2 station. He was always pulling jokes on us like getting behind your car and hitting the siren and lights. While he was in the station one of the guys sneaked out, put a garden hose in the cruiser window and let the water flow. After about ten minutes someone said "hey Porky (his nickname), is that water pouring out of your cruiser?"

Another cop who was known to be extremely jumpy was showing off his hand gun when one of the firefighters sneaked up behind him, smashing a cookie sheet on the table which sent the gun flying and everyone ducking. An ex-Auburn firefighter turned State Trooper stopped by this same station while on duty. He was telling us a story about when he was training an instructor, he took his cruiser to teach him a lesson about leaving the keys in his cruiser. I guess he didn't learn his lesson well. One of the guys sneaked out and took his keys. It was funny listening to this trooper trying to get his keys back.

The funniest story I ever heard was from our neighboring Lewiston fire department and involved water and gasoline which don't mix. A private was told to gas the chief's car up. This private did not like the chief. He put water and gasoline in the gas tank. A short time later the chief took off and ended up walking back to the station. The private was the first person he saw. The chief said, "I don't know what happened, the car just conked out." The private said, in a serious tone, "maybe you got water in the gas, chief."

One of the best ones I can tell you about involved an overweight captain. A new station was built in the early 70's that had tiny windows that you could open and an air handling system that did not work properly. There were no air conditioners and the station got hotter than hell in the summer time. This captain would shower twice a day and use baby powder. A couple of the guys replaced the baby powder with flour and we all waited to see what he would say. After his shower he came in the kitchen and said "it's so f**king hot the baby powder is balling up". Everyone managed not to laugh. This went on for a couple of showers until he finally caught on. He was pissed but we laughed and nicknamed him the Pillsbury Doughboy.

Enough with the firehouse humor . . .. It took me over ten years to get promoted to lieutenant. Firefighting had changed by then, with a new chief who was big on education, so I went to night school and got an associate's degree in fire technology. I still thought the most important aspects to being a good firefighter were having some balls and common sense. I still do except substitute balls with guts since there are some excellent women firefighters today. Without these things a degree means nothing. I did get promoted to captain while going to school and platoon chief later. That was in the early 80's and I was a two pack a day smoker weighing in at 235 pounds on my 5'9" frame. I also had three daughters whom I loved dearly but I was having marital problems.

It was the spring of 1983 when I decided to try to run. I made it exactly one block. Each day I ran a little farther. I do not know if I tried to run because I was planning on getting a divorce or what the reason was. One of the toughest things I ever had to do was talk to my three daughters, one at a time, telling them I was leaving home. In the process of getting a divorce I decided I would run from where I was now living around Lake Auburn and back without stopping. I was to do this on my 38th birthday Nov.17th, 1983, the distance was 14.7 miles. I quit smoking and lost a lot of weight. The running and no smoking lasted about a year; then it was back to my old bad habits.

I got remarried in 1987 to a much younger woman, almost 15 years my junior, and was now a platoon chief. My duties were being in charge of a shift and training. I was still in the union, Local 797, and enjoyed my job. I had my own office, bedroom, bathroom, and car. The chief was excellent to work for and never took over a fire from me. I got along with everyone on my shift. The guys really helped me with training and they all followed what I thought were the most important rules: never lie to me, no alcohol or drugs on duty, and if you make a mistake own up to it. There was nothing physical about my job so I was not in great shape.

CHAPTER 5: I START
TRAINING AND RUNNING

The Multiple Sclerosis 150-mile Bicycle Ride

In 1992 a bunch of firefighters were doing a 150-mile bike ride to raise money for multiple sclerosis research. The ride was called the MS150. A firefighter's wife had MS and this is what got the firefighters interested in doing the ride. I trained, did the ride, and that Christmas morning started running again. I kept running, stayed off the cigarettes and lost weight.

Training for Boston

I was running with 2 friends in 1995 and they mentioned there was a running club in nearby Lewiston. The three of us joined and I did my first race, a 5 miler, in April of that year. I went out too fast but loved it. I was hooked on racing. Bob Brainerd was the coach and he was the head of the Hilltop Running Club. I told him I wanted to qualify for the Boston Marathon and run it next year, the 100th anniversary of the race.

Bob set up a training program for me to qualify. I did my first marathon in October 1995, a month shy of my 50th birthday. I ran a 3:38 but needed 3:30 to qualify. The Boston Athletic Association let me in when I explained some problems at the start of race, no chip timing, I started way in back and narrow street. Yes, I did a lot of whining. A month later I did the NYC marathon, my favorite big city race. The crowds are great; each ethnic neighborhood is different. Loud music, people cheering and it is a day you can go through all the boroughs safely. I was supposed to run NYC with my friend Linda L'Heureux, but she was injured. She died years later and her obituary said that two things she wanted to do and never did were run the Boston and New York City marathons. Do it while you can.

In April 1996 I did the 100th anniversary Boston Marathon. This was the largest Boston ever with about 38,000 runners. I was still recovering from an iliotibial band injury. It was a fun race to do with the huge crowds and thousands of runners. Denise and daughter Heidi were supposed to meet me at the finish but they were not there. I had enough money on me to take the subway to my mother's where Denise and Heidi finally showed up. No cell phones in those days. In August I tore cartilage in my left knee while doing a marathon in Canada but it did not bother me until after I finished. The torn meniscus required arthroscopic surgery. I chose to have a spinal and watched the procedure on a monitor. I was drugged up and kidded the surgeon that it was like getting a haircut as he trimmed the meniscus. Five weeks exactly after the surgery I ran the Thanksgiving Day 4 miler in Portland, Maine, and was very happy to be back running.

From a 5 Miler to Ultramarathons

My first injury-free year was 1997. In that year I did my first triathlon; the hardest part for me was a one mile swim in a river with a tidal current. Having come very close to drowning three times made me a little anxious in my swim training . . .. The swim started with a jump off a pier and when someone landed on top of me, I almost lost my goggles. Then I swam way too far out from shore and had a hell of a time getting back to shore a mile away. I did survive and had a pretty good swim time. The 25-mile bike and 10k run were much easier than the swim for me.

I did 16 marathons by the fall of 1998 and I did my first ultramarathon, a 50 miler, on October 17, 1998. The ultra was a learning experience. I ran 8:58:52 and puked instantly after crossing the finish line. My mother was in a nursing home in Massachusetts and was dying of colon cancer. My two brothers and I met there to see her. My mother always liked seeing the three of us together. I had a tough time fighting back the tears seeing her lying there knowing she may have just a few more days to live. Leaving the nursing home, I headed to Rhode Island to do a marathon the next day. My brother Paul called me at 4:00 am that morning to tell me Ma had died in her sleep. He said there was nothing for me to do and to go ahead and run the marathon if I wanted to. I did the marathon with mixed feelings. My mother did not like me running long races so I hoped she did not mind me doing this one. As sick as she was, it was a blessing that her pain was over.

More Marathons and Ultras

On November 21, 1998, I did my second 50 miler, the famous JFK trail race. Then I did the Virginia Beach Marathon in March of 1999. This was a marathon I will never forget. Denise and I drove down from Maine and my back was killing me by the time we arrived. I believe I had a pinched nerve. I could not bend down to tie my shoes race morning and Denise did not want me to run. My response to this was "I did not drive down here to not do the race." Starting in the very back every step felt like someone sticking an ice pick in my back. A little way into the race my sister and brothers-in-law along with Denise saw me. Denise said I was as white as sheet. About mile 10 I started running with Bill Whipp. After he told me about his back and knee problems, I felt like a wimp for whining about my back. We stayed together to about mile 18. At that point I saw Denise and my in-laws again and their cheering gave me a much-needed boost. By now my back was much better and I started passing runners, 200 to 300. I finished before anyone thought I would and had a few beers waiting for them. I watched as they looked for me to finish. When I walked up behind them laughing and asked" where the hell have you been?" they were surprised to say the least.

By August of 1999 I was ready to try my first 24-hour race. This was the 24 hour Around the Lake in Wakefield, MA. It started at 7:00 pm and by 10:00 pm there was lightning and pouring rain. During the storm I tripped on a crack in the concrete sidewalk we were running on and had some heavy bleeding from my left knee. The knee was sore but I could keep running. Twelve hours into the race I had 55 miles in. The sun was out by now and the heat and humidity were two more things I would now have to deal with. My wife Denise and daughter Heidi crewed for me and kept my spirits up. About 1:00 pm Denise told me I was in 3rd place! She also said that someone told her there was another runner in 4th who usually finishes strong. I was feeling terrible by now but wanted to hold onto third.

I never took more than a minute or two breaks during the entire race. By now I could barely walk but I stayed on my blistered feet and finished 3rd with 98.9 miles. Don Allison, publisher of Ultrarunning magazine, told me if I did another 1.1 miles he would put me in the yearly listing for a 100 miler finisher. The race only counted full 5k laps so the 1.1 did not count for the race. That was the most painful 1.1 miles I have ever done. Taking my too tight shoes off exposed blisters and black toes with missing toenails. After the race director handed me my award and took a few pictures I fell to the ground puking and laying in goose shit. I was shaking from dehydration also and the race director came over and handed me a towel to clean myself off. The only thing he said was "you can keep the towel." Lessons learned: stay hydrated and when your feet swell during long races be sure to have larger size shoes available. My feet swelled so much I permanently damaged the big toe on my left foot. I did the Mount Pisgah 50k in New Hampshire 5 weeks later and was still hurting from this 24 hour race. I went to a podiatrist and he told me because of the damage to my big toe I should never run more than 6 miles at a time or I would end up in a wheel chair. I was devastated at first but started thinking "heck, it is only a big toe." After talking to Bob Brainerd, he suggested going to another podiatrist in NH 120 miles away. After a very thorough exam and treadmill session the doctor gave me the news. "I am going to make you some orthotics that will get that toe to move and you can run any distance you want." This was the first of several times I have been told not to run or stop doing long races. Solution: Find another doctor.

The Vermont 100 miler in July of 2000 was to be my first 100-mile trail race. The race started at 4:00 am with the owner of the property playing Chariots of Fire on a grand piano located on his porch while he was dressed in a tuxedo. I felt pretty confident that I would finish the race, maybe even under 24 hours to get a buckle. It was raining and the trail was a little slippery but not that bad. I met up with a friend, Jim Sullivan, and we ran the first 22 miles together. He was running faster than I wanted to, this was my first mistake. The rain continued, pouring most of the time. When I got into Camp 10 Bear at mile 44 I was exhausted and Denise and my daughter Heidi could see how tired I was. By the time I reached 10 Bear the second time at mile 68, it was 18 hours into the race and still pouring.

I would now have a pacer, Bill Rice, and having 12 hours to go just 32 miles I thought I could make the cut off of 30 hours. At the mile 82 aid station I started puking just as a couple arrived. Seeing me vomiting they decided to skip the food there. I felt a little better after emptying my stomach and taking a dump in the woods. I had fallen into a pile of cow manure before a barn where they check your weight and blood pressure. Denise and Heidi were there and my spirits were high even though I soaking wet and covered with cow shit. My weight and BP were ok so after having some chicken soup, we left quickly so as not to lose any precious time. All I could do now was barely walk and both knees were hurting big time. I also could not bend my legs. Going up Blood Hill I would take two steps forward then stumble one back.

Finally, I told Bill I was done. He tried everything to keep me going; we walked a little further to Blood Hill aid station at mile 88.6. I managed to go a few hundred yards after that, but then could not go another step. A van stopped and picked us up and I was out of the race. When I got to the finish first aid station, I was wrapped in blankets and two massage therapists worked on me for about an hour. I was shaking uncontrollably and the therapists said I was hypothermic. It had rained 6" during the race, it was probably in the 50's, and all I had on was a tank top and shorts. I was so out of it I did not feel cold during the race. I never thought I would drop out of a race, so this was a humbling experience. My wife said she would never go to another 100-mile race with me after seeing the condition I was in. I told her not to worry I will never do this again. About two weeks after the race I made up my mind that I would go back and finish it. Dropping out I thought had some positive points. I needed to be humbled and knocked down a notch or two.

My big race for 2000 would be the US Track and Field 24 Hour Championship Race held in Olander Park, Ohio. It was an excellent course, asphalt, almost flat, looping for 1.1 miles around a lake. The weather was perfect, in the 50's and 60's, sunny, with no wind. I had diarrhea for a couple of hours but managed to get in 57 miles in the first 12 hours. I was glad they had 3 bathrooms on the course. My goal was 100 miles and I ended up with 103. That was good for 3rd place in my age group, but they gave the award to someone with fewer miles. I missed getting a hug from Sue Ellen Trapp and some recognition at the award ceremony. Afterwards I told them they made a mistake and they apologized. Sure did miss that hug.

Another Busy Year: 2001

I retired from the Auburn Fire Department in February of 2001 after 33 years of service. I told Denise that when I retired we would go wherever she wanted to celebrate. She picked Hawaii and I immediately started looking for marathons there (she had no idea).

By now I was trying to complete the 50 States and I decided to do the Los Angeles marathon on the way there and then the Maui marathon. Denise still was unaware of these plans. In California we visited all the local attractions including Hollywood and Beverly Hills. A day trip brought us to Coronado Island where the Wizard of Oz was written, Denise's favorite. We had met two of the Munchkins in Nashville. Denise has a room full of Wizard of Oz stuff.

After the marathon in Los Angeles, our next stop was Oahu. We booked an ocean view room at the Hilton Hawaiian Village which has 23 acres and 2,500 rooms. Our room was not ready when it should have been and they apologized. I told them it was not a problem we will just go to the outside bar. Being nice about it paid off big time. We ended up in a top floor oceanfront suite corner room in the Rainbow Tower which is right on the beach.

We spent a few days there hiking to the top of Diamond Head, visiting the Arizona and just sunning ourselves on Waikiki Beach. Then it was off to Maui and the marathon. The road to Hana was beautiful. It is not recommended to take a rental car on it, but we did anyway. The road is narrow with many turns. You go through the jungle, see many waterfalls and ocean views. There are turnoffs to get out and enjoy the views. Whales can be seen from shore or you can take a whale watching trip this time of year to get even closer. We could see them from our hotel room. Another option is to take a snorkeling boat trip and you will see plenty of whales. My wife and I did both the whale watching and snorkeling cruise. Both were out of the small town of Lahaina, our favorite place to stay on the island, and it is the finish line of the Maui marathon. The last island on this trip was the Big Island, the island of Hawaii. This island is loaded with things to do: volcanoes to visit, Black Sand Beach, waterfalls, jungles, beautiful ocean views, and much more. Kona had a microbrew festival while we were there and it was excellent.

We stayed in Kona this trip but liked Hilo better. You can spot the sea turtles from a bridge near Coconut Island. I have also done the Hilo to Volcano 50k here and the Maui marathon the next day. One year the Hilo Marathon was the site of a 50 State reunion race; in this race, the first half is much nicer than the second. Visiting the volcano one time, I did a very foolish thing. I wanted to see where the lava flowed into the ocean and went into a very well-marked restricted area. A few hundred yards in, my feet got hot, and I realized lava was flowing underneath me. Not sure how to get back to safety, I walked like I was in a minefield. I was very happy to get out of there unharmed and promise never to try that dumb stunt again.

Another trip was to the island of Kauai. This island does not have the hustle and bustle of the Waikiki area which was what we were looking for on this particular trip. My brother Paul and his wife Barbara shared a condo with us. It was within walking distance of a nice beach where you could snorkel and see plenty of fish and large sea turtles.

Another not too bright thing was snorkeling behind a turtle, and ending up on a coral reef. The waves pushed me into the coral, cutting my hands. If I had rubber gloves on, I would have been okay. I escaped with minor cuts.

Like the other islands the scenery is beautiful and there is plenty to do. The food and entertainment at Smith's Tropical Paradise Luau was excellent. The Kauai marathon was hot, hilly, and humid with showers but the hula girls and volunteers were great. Another race I tried on Oahu was the HURT 100 miler. I did not finish (a DNF) this very tough 100 miler. Lots of mountains through a jungle full of rocks and banyan tree roots are some of the things that make this one of the toughest races in the country.

My First Long Road Trip

In May 2001, I did my first long drive from Maine to do marathons. I will never forget seeing the Rocky Mountains for the first time, awesome! Between Cheyenne and Laramie is where I did the Rocky Mountain Double Marathon. From there I drove west and on the top of a mountain road got my first glimpse of the Grand Tetons. They were spectacular! I spent a few days exploring the Grand Tetons and Yellowstone National Park. Looking back, it is kind of funny when I thought it was a big deal seeing an elk and some buffalo. I ended up seeing hundreds of elk and even more buffalo but never got tired of watching them. I also saw 2 grizzlies, deer, a coyote, and several other animals. On May 31 I drove through Bear Tooth Pass, elevation 10,947' and the snow drifts on the side of the road were 20' high! The scenery made me think there must be a God, how else could all this be possible?

My next marathon was the Governor's Cup in Helena, MT. Visiting the museum at the Capitol, I was impressed with everything there especially the stuffed white buffalo, a sacred animal to Native Americans. The race was point to point starting in a ghost town and ending in Helena. It was mostly downhill and easy. I left the morning after the race and headed for Glacier National Park. It started snowing just after leaving Helena and did so for about 100 miles. Glacier National Park was beautiful, plenty of wildlife, glaciers of course, and spectacular views. What I liked most was watching a grizzly crossing a snow field into the woods. A minute later a large grizzly was running across the snow being chased by a smaller one. Male grizzlies will kill grizzly cubs. My thought was this was a mother grizzly chasing a male away from her cubs. What do you think?

My next race started in Storm Lake, Iowa. I took in many attractions on the way there. It was a very scenic ride with lots of historical sites. This race was called Marathon to Marathon and was a flat easy course from Storm Lake to the small town of Marathon. I ran almost the entire race with Paula Boone whom I had run with at the Rocky Mountain Double. This helped make the miles go by faster on this rather boring course. After the race, I took a shower at a school and upon returning to my car I could not find my keys. A boy about 12 or 13 saw me trying to get into the locked car and went to the school returning with a coat hanger. Using this he managed to unlock the car. I offered him $20 for helping me but he would not accept it. Looking at him I realized $20 to him was a great deal of money. I told him in a stern voice "where I come from it would be considered an insult not to accept this money." He finally accepted it and I believe he was one happy kid.

Then it was time for the long ride home. I tried to get in as many miles as I possibly could and was so exhausted that I pulled out directly in front of an ambulance that was not on a call, barely missing it. One of the EMT's came over yelling at me. What could I say? I apologized. I told him I was extremely tired and should not be driving and was going to check into the closest hotel I could find. The rest of my ride home was uneventful.

My Second Attempt at the Vermont 100

In July of 2001, I would make my second try at the VT 100. I had trained hard since the beginning of April. I did an 8 mile run/walk both before and after the Oklahoma City Marathon on a very hot and humid day for a total of 48.2 miles. Another race I did to get me used to the climbs and get 52 miles in was the Rocky Mountain Double Marathon on May 27th, as mentioned earlier. The race started at 8,600' and the lowest point was 7,500'. It rained, hailed, and was very windy at times during the race. Steve and Paula Boone, members of the 50 State Club, drove up to me and asked if I needed anything. I said no and when they asked if I wanted to get warm in the car, I told them it was too temping and I might not want to get out. By the time I finished the race I was so cold my hands were shaking badly and I had a hard time getting the key in the car door. Then on June 19th I did a 12-hour hilly training run which consisted of 5 10-mile loops near my home. With the race 4 weeks away coach Bob wanted me to start to cut back on my miles and take it easy. Before the race, the VT 100 volunteers weigh you and take your blood pressure. They weigh you again during the race and if you lose too much weight they can take you out of the race or make you eat and hydrate until your weight is satisfactory. I did not eat for 8 hours before the weigh-in, but then really chowed-down after. I gained 6 pounds eating and drinking at the pasta dinner!

I had a tough time sleeping before the race due to being nervous. No way did I want to DNF (did not finish) again. I met Bill Rice, who had paced me last year, and coach Bob at the 4:00 a.m. start. Once the race began I was not nervous anymore. The temperature was in the 50's and felt cool. I ran the first 25 miles or so with Bill and felt good. Bill was going a little slower than I wanted to so I went ahead. I walked all the steep hills with the only goal of just finishing. Getting a belt buckle for finishing under 24 hours was not even considered by me. My crew, which consisted of my daughter, Heidi, sister in-law, Debbie, and Denise were meeting me along the course and cheering me on. Bob was also there making sure I was staying conservative. By mile 40 it was in the 80's and humid. By the time I got to Camp 10 Bear at mile 44 my stomach was bothering me and I had to wait 20 minutes for my crew to show up and I was pissed. Agony Hill was my next challenge. The climb tired me out but I was still moving. At mile 55 I met my crew, changed socks, and took a 5-minute break. I met Helen around mile 60, her boyfriend dropped out a few miles later and she wanted to stay with me mostly so she would not get lost at night. Coach Bob was now pacer Bob as the 3 of us left 10 Bear at mile 66. Helen was slowing me down a little but neither Bob nor I wanted to leave this 55-year-old lady from Ontario alone in the woods at night. After climbing a tough hill, we met some other runners who were slowing their pace and Helen joined them. Denise and Debbie missed me again at mile 83 so I just left after waiting 10 minutes. By the time I got to the top of Blood Hill I was sure to finish unless I broke a leg. Denise showed up at mile 90 with everything I needed. I was surprised and very happy. Bob and I were enjoying the race and each other's company. We were talking up a storm, kidding around and happy we had just 10 miles to go. The sun came up about mile 92 which is always nice. Heidi met us at mile 96. I was feeling great with only 4 miles to go and I think those last 4 miles were my fastest in the race! About a half mile from the finish, Bob and I kept picking up speed to maybe a 7-8 minute pace. It felt great to finish in 27:31:54!

Denise, Debbie and Heidi were at the finish along with Bill who had dropped out at mile 48. At mile 96 in front of some volunteers I said to Bob "this is fun." I was starting to believe that and decided right then to come back and do it again.

CHAPTER 6: SOME LESSONS LEARNED

The following stories are a few of Mike Smith's recollections of running with Mike Brooks:

In 2002, Mike was one of the first people I wanted on my crew for Badwater. We really had no idea what we were doing, runner or crew, but somehow we got through it. Mike ended up running it in 2004 too and I had the opportunity to crew for him. Mike was raising money for Camp Sunshine, and the Finish Line Youth Foundation (I was working for Finish Line) made a contribution in Mike's name. I remember one of Mike's friends had provided him with some sports drink mix, for free, and he was using it at Badwater. Unfortunately, it wasn't agreeing with him after a while and he had some stomach issues, resulting in some unscheduled toilet breaks in the middle of the desert. During one of these, Mike lost control of some used toilet paper, and I spent some time chasing it across the windy desert floor, providing some much needed entertainment for runner and crew.

(Lesson learned: Badwater and ultramarathons in general are not good places to experiment.)

That reminded me of a similar experience I had at my first 100 mile race, Umstead, where I decided oatmeal, since I liked it so much, would be a great pre-race meal. One serving probably would have been, but the three servings I ate had me spending some significant time in port-o-lets for the first 50 miles.

(Lesson learned: You can get too much of a good thing. Fiber during an ultramarathon is probably one of those things.)

Mike ended up finishing Badwater and crewing for both Andy Velazco and Carl Hunt. Those Badwater years really tested our commitment to one another in a very extreme environment and through a grueling race event, but I wouldn't trade them for anything.

In another example, Mike Smith remembers running with Mike at Umstead (which I have done 14 times) and even a year where he completed the 100 miles faster than me. In fact, it wasn't unusual for Mike to run the same or even a faster pace than me when we first started running together. Often during longer events, you just want someone else out there to share some of the ups and downs. The most competitive runners would probably disagree, but I enjoy running with friends, sharing experiences on the trail, and catching up with each other's lives while running longer races. A cautionary note, Mike and I have probably been lost together too many times to remember.

(Lesson learned: Keep an eye on those trail markings as you talk to other racers.)

Speaking of Umstead, Mike and I were doing it with some friends one year and after we had finished, I was driving us out to an aid station to pick up our drop bags. I was having a hard time staying awake after running all night and apparently was drifting off while driving. It definitely made for an interesting ride and I don't think they ever let me drive after a race again.

Mike and I were doing Sunmart one year, when I needed to hit the port-o-let before the race. As usual before a lot of early race starts, it was still dark. Unfortunately, someone using the port-o-let before me didn't have very good aim and I sat down on the seat before realizing it.

(Lesson Learned: If you are going to use the port-o-let before a race in the dark, bring a flashlight.)

Mike also ran with us on a Rim to Rim to Rim crossing of the Grand Canyon. I remember he turned his ankle on the way down the south side and needed to turn back at that point. While most people would have been disappointed about the run and only focused on the negative of the injury, Mike was very upbeat when we met with him later and described how much he enjoyed the hike out of the canyon and some wildlife sightings on the way.

I remember running the Tahoe Triple one year with Mike. One of our other good friends, Walt Prescott, was also there. Walt and I were finishing up the last marathon in the series and very close to the finish line when he took a bad fall. As he was being attended to by the first aid folks after the finish, Mike, always the concerned friend, came over to briefly check on him and immediately liberate Walt's unused beer ticket. Mike has never been one to let a beer go to waste...

This is what a friend like Mike will do for you. He invited me to join him at the Jay Mountain Marathon in 2006. At that point, I had done quite a few marathons as well as ultras and thought a scenic marathon in Vermont wouldn't be so bad. That's when I got there and found out the marathon was really like 31 miles (now they honestly list it as a 50k). Not only was it 31 miles long, but you run in creek beds, not across them but in them. You need a rope to cross one river. Black flies are attacking you. At one point we ran down a double black diamond ski slope. The temperature can be in the 80s. As I finished, Mike was waiting (probably beer in hand) and let me know he had dropped down to the shorter distance option that day. I always check the race details now when Mike invites me to run.

I was able to get some measure of revenge by inviting Mike and a couple of other friends to run the HURT 100 with me one year. At that point, I had not successfully completed the 100 miles, but had done the 100k a few times. Since, I have been able to finish the 100 miles a few times, but mostly I have 100k or 80 mile finishes. The year I invited Mike, he and Bob Wehr managed to complete one 20-mile loop (I think before dark) and were more than happy to call it a day and head back for the beach. I don't think either of them has forgiven me to this day.

Mike Smith concludes by stating "I can only hope to be running the kinds of races and distances that Mike is doing at his age. I also admire the fact that Mike has taken a pretty selfish endeavor, running races, and turned it into an opportunity to support charitable causes like Camp Sunshine. I'm looking forward to continuing to run races in the future with Mike and hope we have the opportunity to crew for each other too."

Another close runner friend, Ron Paquette, volunteered the following tales about adventures with Mike Brooks:

Mike surrounds himself with a large group of like-minded runners who would support and encourage each other and I got to take advantage of their experience. Meeting, traveling, and running with the likes of Mike Smith, Walt Prescott, Andy Velazco, and Carl Hunt gave me the confidence that I could reach even greater goals.

In October 2001, I did two trail 100s - Umstead and Vermont. Both were major endeavors for me but Mike and all the others were so supportive and encouraging that I was able to complete both races. They will always remain two of my most unforgettable accomplishments. The first race that the whole group of us did together was the Bataan Memorial Marathon in Las Cruces, New Mexico. Carl Hunt and his wife Fay went down a bit early and scouted out a visit to Mexico. Mike and I joined them on an excursion "across the bridge" for a look see and some fine Mexican food. Back in New Mexico, Mike and I stayed a couple extra days and took a road trip to Carlsbad Caverns.

Next was a trip to the upper northwest. We flew into Seattle and drove over the mountains to do the Yakima River Marathon. Touring the wine country of that region was special. After finishing the marathon, we drove to Whidbey Island to run a marathon the following day. The next morning we left early and took the car ferry over to Olympic National Park. That's when I learned that Mike had a thing for trees, especially big ones. It was a thing to behold as Mike wrapped his arms as best he could hugging those giant trees. I won't mention the other things he did; just suffice it to say the trees would never be the same!

The next road trip was undoubtedly the greatest of our adventures. We flew to Denver, drove to Choteau, Montana, to do the Grizzly Marathon, spent the week there, and then hightailed it to Idaho for the Mesa Falls Marathon. After that, it was on to Leadville Colorado, to explore the probability of doing the Trail Marathon there at a later date. You are probably familiar with the saying "what happens in Vegas stays in Vegas." Well, a lot of what happened in the North is still echoing in the mountains. I will relate a couple of our misadventures. After the Grizzly Marathon we drove up to Glacier National Park. I had brought a tent so we could camp in the park, as I truly enjoy being out in nature. However, Mike is not what you'd call "a happy camper". But being a good sport, he agreed. We set up and we immediately were told "Stay aware, there are bears in our area." Large, real life big bears. That night Mike swore he heard what sounded like hungry bears around our tent. He made me sleep near the door figuring if they could, they would unzip the door and get me first. I wasn't worried because Mike has a lot more body fat and they probably would smell him from a distance and prefer him to my scrawny butt. Anyway we made it through the night and got out early to head to the popular local eatery, the Park Diner about 10 miles away. On the drive, low and behold, we saw 11 bears lurking in the foothills as we sped by. We were ready for anything at that point, or so we thought. We decided to see if we could go across the Road to the Sun. When we got to the visitor's center, we found the road was closed due to rock slides. It was a beautiful day so we decided that if we couldn't drive we would hike the road to explore the area. After quite a distance, we came upon a roadblock. A park ranger saw us and immediately stop us; he interrogated us as to the whys of our being there and didn't we see the roadblock?? We almost got ourselves arrested for violating park rules. We started hiking back and got hit with a severe rain and ice storm. Of course, we were not prepared. I mean, what could we possibly encounter? We pretty near froze all our extremities. A lesson well learned the hard way. Thus ended our camping trip to Glacier.

After driving to Mesa Falls and doing that marathon, we headed for Yellowstone. We once again ventured too far and were pelted with a frightening hailstorm. When Mike went nose to nose with a buffalo, we decided it would be best to get out of the woods for a while. We finally ended up in Colorado and drove up and over Independence Pass. We both made the comment that we were surprised we had not seen any mountain goats or sheep. While descending the Pass, we nearly got driven off the road on a tight curve by a herd of sheep. I swear, one even jumped over the hood of the car. Thankfully that was the last of our wildlife encounters on the trip. That day ended with a nice bike ride through the mine country of Leadville. Next day, back to Denver and the flight home. What a trip!!!!!

We did get to do another camping trip as we signed up for the Cranberry Island 50k. We took the ferry over to the Island from Southwest Harbor and pitched our tents in the field near the start/finish line of the race. The race was a 4 mile out and back with a Guinness stocked aid station (way to pick 'em, Mike!) and the lobster bake was a blast but the all-night party was a bit rough keeping us up beyond our usual early bedtimes! I did learn from Mike that fried clams & onion rings with a few beers is a great pre¬race feed.

In 2014, I discovered a unique race to be held in Florida in Feb. Knowing Mike is always up for something new, I ran it by him. How about we jump out of a plane and run a 50k right after it? Well, we did it! Mike had skydived before but I had not. I nearly pissed my pants as I leaped out of that plane. What a rush! Mike took it in stride even though due to race logistics, we ended up running 9 miles before the jump and the rest of the 50k distance after, much of it in the dark.

These are but a few of the Brooks and Paquette Amazing Adventures. There are many more as we have run and traveled together in 40 of the 50 states, many of them more than once! As an added bonus, on some of those trips my wife, Donnajean Pohlman, (the voice of reason), joined us as she worked on her quest for the 50 State Marathon goal.

Donnajean has this to say about Mike Brooks:

Who was this guy my husband, Ron Paquette, spent so much time with? Who was this person who could talk nonstop about all things running: training, races, toe nail maintenance, rehydrating (Guinness anyone?), and other important topics? Who always seemed ready for a long distance adventure, whether an ultra, run and sky dive, or whatever? Mike Brooks was in for the long distance, hmmmm? Was he the follower or was he the instigator?

I finally met Mike it seems like "forever ago." It turned out that we were "kindred spirits" sharing the same astrological sign, Scorpio, and in fact the same birthday – November 17, although he is older, a lot older than me, at least 5 years anyway!

Ron and Mike were instrumental in my decision to complete a marathon in all 50 states. The tales of their travels around the country made each trip sound like a unique and fun experience, and I am sure, knowing Mike and Ron as I do, there was no embellishment of the "truth" - coming face to face with wild animals, almost freezing to death in a tent, the sleet and wind on a course, the hair-raising drives in the dark to the start of an early morning race, and of course all the flying/airport delays, and so forth. The actual runs were mostly wonderful, if not adventuresome. When we had the opportunity to run together Mike would share his stories and observations, helping to keep me entertained and motivated.

Although there are many memories, two races in particular come to mind. These cannot be forgotten (although I have tried!). My Kentucky state marathon was "Hatfield and McCoy Marathon" in June 2011. Getting to the race wasn't easy (remember those flight delays) and the hotel was far from the race start, but we made it on time. It was a beautiful day – humid, sun peeking in and out, gentle rain showers, then hot. The course was varied beginning with a nice tour of the countryside and onto a cart path that started through the local golf course. Up ahead was a narrow swinging bridge (barely two carts could pass each other) over a small river. Having difficulty with heights and bridges, let alone narrow SWINGING bridges, I froze – there was no way around! Looking panicked, because I was, Mike and Ron firmly said "close your eyes" and each grabbed an arm and literally dragged/carried me over the bridge. Thanks, guys!! I couldn't have done it without your understanding, quick thinking, and muscles! The finish line photo with Mike and me and his brother Walt, who was along on this trip, with Mr. Hatfield and Mr. McCoy in period costumes holding their shotguns, was a perfect and safe ending.

The other "memorable" race is one Mike will not let me forget. One year at the Cape Elizabeth "Winter Classic 10 Miler" we all ran fairly close to each other, back and forth as we often do. When we neared the finish line I "sprinted" to finish ahead of them, or so Mike says, taking advantage of the "old guys"!

In the running community, I believe there are many "kindred spirits" who share a bond because of an experience that has drawn them together – either the same experience at the same time or two separate experiences similar in nature". But the same birthday??

Mike's response to Ron and Donnajean's stories:
Ron is the person I have run the most races with. He is also the person I have taken the most trips with, not counting my brother. From 5k's to 100 milers we have managed to finish every race we started together and had a good time doing them. Even though some involved severe back pain, bug bites, falls, diarrhea, vomiting, getting lost etc. we were always glad at the end of the race we did it. Ron is really an amazing guy to be doing what he does at 74.

Donnajean is the best thing that ever happened to Ron. She has run all over the country with him, crews when not running, and also paces him in some races. She usually packs a few snacks for Ron and me when we go on trips. After doing all these things for Ron he still picks on her. Ron is 6'3" and DJ is 4'11" so Ron is always saying she is "vertically challenged. " She might be short but she is a lot smarter and better tempered than Ron. She teaches anger management classes which is a good tool to have with old grumpy men. BTW Donnajean's mother is in her 90's and still does 5k's. Ron told me that when the two of them are walking together he has a hard time keeping up.

CHAPTER 7:
THE BADWATER YEARS BEGIN
2002

Umstead - April 2002

My first Umstead 100-mile trail race would be my best. I flew into Raleigh, NC, with friends Ron Pauqette and Bill Rice. Once there we met up with Mike Smith and Walt Prescott. I would run almost the entire race with them. The course at this time was ten mile loops (more or less), with 8,000 feet of elevation over 100 miles.

This is one of, if not the easiest, 100-mile trail runs around. A few weeks before the race I was in pretty good shape and maybe I could break 24 hours. The three of us started off together, Walt, Mike, and me. We started out a little too fast and slowed in the later miles.

By mile 90 Mike and Walt said there was no way we would break 24 hours. I talked myself into pushing by telling myself "you trained for this race and if you don't break 24 you're going to have to train even harder to do it next year." Push I did.

Hurting pretty bad, I kept moving as fast as possible, trying to have a few minutes "in the bank" in case I slowed. This last lap I saw friend Jerry Sullivan, he was walking on a badly sprained ankle and dropped out of the race. I asked if he wanted some help and he said he would just walk the 3 or 4 miles to the finish line. I came in at 23:50:15.

Mike, Walt, and Ron all finished 100 miles with Bill dropping to 50 miles as he had planned. This race proved to me what I have always thought, running ultras you have to stay mentally tough.

Another theory I have is the more ultras you run the more brain cells you kill. The more brain cells you kill the dumber you get and that is why you want to do more ultras. On the way back to the motel Mike Smith fell asleep driving which added a little more excitement to the day.

The Vermont 100 - Again

July 2002 would be my third attempt at the VT 100. I kind of talked my friend Ron into doing it by telling him "it's not that hilly." Well, 14,000-15,000 feet up isn't that hilly, is it? I decided to camp this year near the start. Being a city boy and not a camper I went to Wal-Mart and bought a real cheap 2-person tent. Ron and Bill laughed when I started to set it up. It was a 2 kid tent! I could barely fit in it and all the campers had a good laugh. When I got up at 3:00 am the tent had leaked, my clothes were wet, and my shoes were full of water from being up against the tent. Not a good way to start a 100 miler.

My next mistake was leaving my hat that had my name on it next to a pile of poop I left around mile 20. We were told to carry out everything, leave nothing behind including poop or you would be disqualified. I was running with Jeff whom I had met earlier when this happened. I realized about a mile later that I had left my hat but told Jeff I wasn't going back for it. Jeff dropped out at mile 44 and went back got my hat and brought it to Denise! What a nice guy for several reasons. It must have been difficult to find his way back to the trail, it must have stunk pretty bad, and how did he locate my wife? Next mistake was forgetting to pick up my flashlight from my drop bag. I had to go back at least a mile to get it. This let Ron and Bill get ahead of me. I caught up to Ron around mile 55; Bill had left him to keep up with Celia even though he said he would stay with him the entire race. We picked up pacer Bob at mile 68, 10 Bear.

As I headed up a steep trail, I was climbing over a tree that had fallen when I slipped and ended up in some branches that felt like a hammock. Bob and Ron thought I was hurting but it was really comfortable. They finally had to pull me out and we continued up the steep trail with Ron yelling at me "I thought you said this wasn't that hilly." I had a bad spell at the top of the hill. Feeling really dizzy, I thought puking and diarrhea were about to happen. This passed quickly. By this time Ron was leaning badly to the port side and looked like an old ship getting ready to sink. Bob worked on his back and pumped 800 mg of ibuprofen into him. Ron was moving again but it was not pretty. He did have enough strength to swear at me as we went up the hills. To really piss him off, I told him there were no more hills just before we came into sight of one Monster Mountain we had to climb. "Gee Ron can't you take a joke?" At mile 98 we came upon Bill on the side of the trail; he could not move. Ron wanted to wait for him. A runner who had been following us for most of the race decided to wait also and we all went across the finish line holding raised hands in 28:26:47. We were a bunch of happy runners and Ron was so glad I told him "it wasn't that hilly."

After the race I took an ice cold shower with a garden hose, ate 2 hamburgers, had a beer and headed to Logan Airport for a flight to Vegas. The next morning I picked up an SUV and Andy and I headed for Death Valley. Our job would be to crew and pace Mike Smith for the 135 mile Badwater race. The race starts at Badwater in Death Valley 280' below sea level, goes across the desert where the temperature reached 124 degrees in the shade, and ends 135 miles later on Mt. Whitney, the highest mountain in the continental US. Bob Wehr and Walt Prescott were already there so we had two teams to assist Mike. Forty-five hours and 12 minutes after starting Mike finished the race. Blisters covered his feet and a wide grin covered his face.

Lone Pine Surgery

Andy Velazco Remembers Crewing for Mike Smith at Badwater:
Usually I always carry a small suture surgical pack in our running trips. As the doc, I usually want to be prepared in case of an emergency, especially when out in the boondocks. Well, I had the opportunity to use the kit during our Badwater crossing of 2002. Mike had developed a severe case of "trigger finger" on his middle left finger. He soldiered on with his duties as pacer and crew chief, but he was suffering. The diagnosis was easy, and we talked about taking care of the finger once the run was over. Mike Smith finished his Badwater crossing, and we retreated to our rooms in a motel in Lone Pine. We all had to rest, but especially Mike Smith. At the hotel, we talked about the finger again, and Mike decided that he wanted his finger fixed. So with some local anesthesia, sitting in a chair, and using another chair for a surgical table, Mike had a tendon release. He never flinched during the procedure, but agreed that he felt a little queasy, seeing his tendon moving his finger.

Next year would be Andy's turn to do Badwater.

On August 18th, 2002, I would do my first Pike's Peak marathon. Mike Smith did the "Pike's Peak Double Challenge" which is the ascent on Saturday and marathon on Sunday. This is one of my favorite races and I will write more about it in another chapter. It is one of the toughest marathons in the country. In September of 2002 I was back at Olander Park for the US Track and Field 24 hr. championship race. This year Mike, Andy, and Walt were also there. The elite were plentiful. I sat next to Roy Pirrung on the plane to Toledo. He holds several age group records in 24 and 48 hour races and is a late bloomer as far as running goes. The greatest ultra runner I have ever seen, Yiannis Kouros, was there along with John Geesler, and Mark Godale. Running a 24 hour race on a 1.1 mile course is great because you get to see the best runners in the world during the entire race.

The race conditions sucked, high 80's, very humid, with thunder and lightning storms. My goal was 100 miles and I was hurting big time. Telling Mike this he paced me so I would get 100 in. Walt finished a few minutes ahead of us which is kind of amazing when you consider we ran for 24 hours. I was hurting after the race but wicked happy to have done 100 miles thanks to Mike.

The 50 mile Sunmart trail race in Huntsville State Park, Texas December 14, 2002, would be my last long race for the year. If I remember correctly, the course was four 12.5 mile loops on trails. I ran the first 2 loops with Mike and Andy. On lap 3 Andy was close to me but we were not together until near the end of the lap. Andy was hurting now, I think it was his ankle. Figuring it might get dark before we finished I grabbed a flashlight and advised Andy to do the same. Seeing how Andy was hurting I decided to stay with him for most of the last loop.

Our motto has always been, "leave no man or woman behind." I had a goal of breaking 10 hours at the beginning of the race and now had changed it to 11 hours. When it started to get dark I pulled out my flashlight but Andy did not. He figured it would not get dark on this last loop.

I was kind of pissed because if I stayed with Andy to the very end of the race I would not break 11 hours. If Andy had a flashlight he could have walked by himself the last mile or so and I could run ahead and break 11. Being the mean person I was, it crossed my mind to leave Andy and break 11. This thought was just for an instant, honest Andy. We crossed the finish line together to the cheers of Mike, Layne, Henry, Steve, and Paula Boone. Boy am I glad I did not leave Andy. When I returned home from Sunmart, there was a package from Andy that he had mailed before going to Sunmart, a Christmas present. In it was a professionally framed picture of Walt, Mike, Andy and me taken at the Olander Park 24 hour race. Along with the picture was a card with some kind words about how he liked running with me. Can you imagine what an ass I would have felt like if I had ever left him on the last mile or so of Sunmart?

2002 Totals

- 54 races
- 16 marathons
- Two 100 milers
- One 24-hour race (100.6 miles)
- One 50-miler
- One 50k

I set a PR for a 100-mile trail race, 23:50:15. There were no injuries that kept me from running. My back and neck bothered some along with patella tendonitis. But what does not kill you makes you stronger and pain is just weakness leaving your body. Right?

CHAPTER 8:
THE BADWATER YEARS CONTINUE: 2003

Umstead 100

I decided to drive to Umstead for the 100 miler and do 2 marathons the week before. My first marathon would be in Ellerbe Springs, NC, on March 29th. It would turn out to be a hot, humid, and hilly race. I started the race with Paula Boone and around mile 6 we were joined by Larry. I was feeling pretty good so I went ahead but still took time to talk to runners I was passing. I thought the heat was the worst part of the race and I did get a little sunburn. I waited for Paula and Larry at the finish, took a shower, and then headed for the next day's marathon 240 miles away in Abingdon, VA. When I woke up race morning I could not believe that it had snowed during the night! Eighty degrees yesterday, now in the 30's and 4" of snow on the trails! The roads were so hot the snow melted on contact but the trail I would be running on was covered with snow. I had an excellent time running the Virginia Creeper marathon. It felt so good to have my sunburn covered up and be cool instead of, to me, boiling hot. I actually ran this second marathon faster than the first one.

With Umstead 100 six days away I had time for some sightseeing and a visit with friends DonnaJean and Ron. We met at a brew pub in Gatlinburg, TN, just outside of Smokey Mountains National Park. The next day the three of us did about a 5 mile easy run inside the park. It was very scenic with lots of deer around. I spent two nights at their condo then headed to Raleigh, NC. Once there I met up with Walt, Mike, and Andy. It was about 70 at the start of the race. A heavy shower, blisters, and being tired from last weekend's marathons gave me something to whine about to Walt for the first 60 miles.

Maybe that is why he dropped out at 60? Hurting big time both physically and mentally I was very happy to see the finish line 28 hours 2 minutes and 43 seconds after the start. The ride home was memorable. It was raining when I left Raleigh, and the rain continued all the way to Baltimore. The fun started there with freezing rain and a snowy mix with lots of accidents. It turned to all snow until I got to MA. Then it was light snow from there to my home in Danville, ME. It took me 17 hours to finally get home. I wanted to get a motel but a couple tried to screw me on the price so I said the hell with it and just drove straight through, something I will not do again.

Finishing the 50 States

In June I would finish a marathon in every state plus DC for the first time at the Mayor's Midnight Sun marathon in Anchorage, AK. This is an okay marathon, but there are some in AK I like better and will write about them later. What was nice about this trip is two of Denise's sisters along with their husbands came up for a vacation and to celebrate my finishing. What I also liked besides finishing the states was my chance to go halibut finishing .This is something I've wanted to do since I was a little kid. As luck would have it I got the biggest fish of the day, a 55 lb. halibut. The best part of it is I caught it just as the captain was getting ready to pull anchor. I also caught it on a spinning rod with a light test line that nobody wanted to use. It took me 30 to 40 minutes to haul it close enough for us to harpoon and gaff it. Luckily the line did not break. This really made my day I have to say. Once the fish was on board we headed to port.

Mount Desert Island 24 Hour Race

The July 12th and 13th Mount Desert Island 24 Hour Race is one I will not forget. I drove three hours from my home to the high school in Bar Harbor, Maine, where I thought there was supposed to be a 24-hour race on a quarter mile track.

When I arrived, I met with the race director, Gary Allen. He asked me where my team was. I told him I did not have a team. He then informed me this was a relay race and asked what I was planning on doing. I told him "run for 24 hours." Next question, how far, "My goal is 100 miles."

He had no problem with that so I set up my chair and table. Gary would also be running and he broke a North American 45-49 age group record for 20 miles on a quarter mile track that was held for many years by legendary ultra runner Ted Corbett. It would be a tough race for several reasons.

First, I had never run for 24 hours on a quarter mile track. Second, I could not change directions on the track to balance out wear evenly on my body. The race started at noon and knowing Gary was going for a record I gave him the inside lane and stayed out of his way. It was a hot and humid day but Gary finished his 20 mile record breaker in 2:08:41. About 4 hours into the race I started having diarrhea. It was a good distance off the track to the bathroom. I know this because I made plenty of trips to it. I kidded Gary that I wanted the distance measured and him to count it towards my total mileage.

In addition to this, I was feeling dizzy and was puking every once in a while. When I puked I did it leaning against a fence as far away from people as possible and making like I was stretching my calf muscles. I did not want Gary to make me stop running. One time when I was puking he sent Evan Graves over to check on me. He asked if I was all right and I told him "I always puke like this in 24 hour races." Running on a quarter mile track was taking a toll on my 58 year old left knee. Since I could not change direction to make for even fatigue on both knees I ran the straightaways and walked the curves. There had never been anyone run for 24 hours on Mount Desert Island so runners and a reporter came to watch not only Gary's record breaker but the old man circling the track. With people watching and me telling Gary my goal was 100 miles I felt like I should put on as good a performance as possible. Peter Palmer, who once held the fastest time for finishing the Appalachian Trail, was counting my laps, his wife making sandwiches, and Gary helping me out. When I could not bend over to change my shoes to a larger size because of my swollen feet, Gary did it for me.

The Crows were gathering as the race continued lap after lap after lap. The Crows are from the Crow Athletic Club which Gary heads. When I got to 100 miles at 22 hours, 52 minutes, and 15 seconds, they had a tape across the finish line. They thought I was done at 100 miles but I told them I was there to run 24 hours. At 23 hours 59 minutes and 30 seconds, they had the tape set up again. I told them I had 30 seconds left and kept running. Kind of a show off, I guess. I asked them to measure the distance I covered in the 30 seconds and add it to my 416 laps with a big grin on my face.

I immediately collapsed into a chair so happy that I did so well in a race that I came in dead FIRETRUCK last but also won. Puking, diarrhea, stomach cramps, pain in every joint in my body, and I could not be happier.

Another reason I was so happy was I had met some people in the last 24 hours whom I will not forget because of all they did for me; I consider some of them friends to this day.

An example of this friendship would be when I emailed the Mount Desert Island marathon telling them I was doing a 50k the day before the race and could not get there in time to pick up my race packet and asked if I could pick it up the day of the race. This is usually not allowed. I got an email back from race director Gary Allen saying "let me know what motel you are staying at and I will drop it off." I joined the Crow Athletic Club and have been a member ever since.

Caw! Caw!

Andy Does Badwater

This year, 2003, would be what Andy called "the hot year" for Badwater. July 22 and 23 would prove him right. The temperature reached 133 degrees, one degree away from a world record. Andy trained hard for this year's race as his son Alec can attest. He could hear Andy pounding away at night on his treadmill with the heat turned up. Mike Smith, Walt, and I returned to help Andy finish Badwater. The two rookies on his crew were his son Alec and his brother-in-law, Jeff. Alec was 16 and seemed like a nice kid but we wanted to test him a little. To make sure everything would work according to plan several of us would run the first 17 miles of the race with the other guys crewing. Alec was invited to join us and he did an excellent job. He passed the test. I had done 97 marathons/ultras by now and to prove my theory of killing brain cells in long runs I must tell you the first thing I did after running the 17 miles was jump in the shallow end of a swimming pool head first. The only thing that saved me from breaking my neck was my outstretched arms. Another thing that backs up my theory is having my big toenails permanently removed. I did this so I would not get black toenails from running. Do you know if you drop something on a toe with no toenail it hurts like hell? Same thing if you bang it in any way.

Well, Andy started the race strong and was running well despite the heat. By the second day he was showing the effects of the extreme heat and fatigue of so many hours on his feet. I fell asleep in a chair while crewing for Andy and thought I was dreaming of a loud train bearing down on me. Startled, I woke up with a fighter jet a few feet overhead. I had to check my pants after that. As time went by, Andy started leaning more and more. By the time he started the climb up Mt. Whitney, mile 122, I practically had to hold him up he was leaning so bad. He also had a terrible back ache. I took a break from pacing Andy for about an hour then returned to find Andy angry and grouchy. This is out of character for him. Pacing him the last few miles I put a trekking pole in his hands and told him to just follow that. He was bent over so much he could not see straight ahead. When Andy finally finished, a big smile came over his face. Two things he said after finishing I will never forget. The first was "I might have quit but I did not want to let you guys down." The second thing he said to me was "you did things for me my wife would not do." The second comment had me wondering if he had some kind of sexual hallucination. Walt, Mike, and I had all finished a marathon in every state, so Andy gave each of us a gold 50 States finisher's ring he had designed. This was for us helping him in the race. Andy was selling these rings for $500 each. I always wanted to buy one but never did. Thanks to Andy I now wear it proudly and frequently tell the story of how I got it. Andy and Mike both finished Badwater; hopefully next year will be my turn.

The Pikes Peak Double

Mike Smith tried to tell me that doing the Pikes Peak Double is no harder than doing the marathon, yeah right. Two things you must know about Mike: don't believe everything he says and, well, I better not mention the second one. Deciding to try the Double I flew into Colorado Springs the day before the Ascent on August 15th. Both races start at a little over 6,000' and go up to 14,300 plus. Flying in the day before a mountain race for a flatlander is not recommended. This is one thing you can trust me on. When I started the ascent I was almost immediately gasping for breath in the thin air. By mile ten, you are at tree line and tough rocky single track trail with lots of Z switchbacks. I was still gasping for breath when I crossed the finish line. Feeling dizzy and like I was going to puke, I wondered how I was going to do this again tomorrow plus the descent. There is a 10 hour cut off for the marathon and they will pull you off the course. I made up my mind no matter what that I would finish the race. If they tried to pull me off the course I would take my race number off. They cannot stop me from using a public trail! I had chest pains that I figured were from breathing so hard and expanding my chest so much that I stretched the muscles in between my ribs.

On race morning I was nervous and pissed at the same time figuring they might DQ me. At the start I felt about the same as the day before but as I climbed the mountain I actually felt better and could breathe more easily. The only explanation I can come up with is that I was finally used to the deep breathing and my chest muscles were stretched out a bit to allow for better breathing. Once I got above tree level I was enjoying a Rocky Mountain high taking in the scenery on this clear day. I reached the top of the mountain faster than the day before and felt confident now about finishing under the final cut off time. Starting back down I would encourage runners still climbing until I got to a point where I knew the runners would not make the turn around cut off. Those runners I just smiled at but said nothing, it was kind of sad. I was doing great going down the mountain until I stumbled and almost went head first into a vertical rock. Luckily I got my hands out just in time. It was something like the swimming pool incident. I finished strong with Andy and Mike already done and waiting at the finish line for me. I hate to admit it but Mike was right as far as I am concerned; the Double is not much harder than the marathon.

My 100th Marathon/Ultra

The United States Air Force marathon on September 20, 2003, would be my 100th marathon/ultra. A local Maine newspaper told the race it was my 100th and they made a big deal out of it. I was on the front page of the USAF marathon newspaper and they announced my name all through the race. When I finished, the base commander shook my hand and congratulated me. The press wanted to interview me after the race but we had to drive to St. Louis for another marathon the next day. I told them I did not have time for the interview, sorry. I felt kind of funny refusing but Mike, Walt, and Andy wanted to get going.

The Tahoe Triple

Denise traveled with me to the Lake Tahoe Triple marathon. We flew into Reno, NV, spending one day there before heading for a day of sightseeing around the lake which straddles the borders of California and Nevada. These are 3 of my favorite races. The distance around the lake is 72 miles which you cover when doing the three races. The scenery is awesome and there is gambling in NV plus plenty of other nearby attractions. The first race was on October 9, 2003. Walt, Mike, Andy, Ron Vertrees and I took a race bus to Inspiration Point for the start of the first race. It was about 35 degrees at the 6,800' above sea level start. The first two miles are downhill and the next 11 pretty flat. I ran these miles with Ron and Walt. Ron carries two bottles with him. He has a prostate problem, so he drinks out of one and pees in the other. I would walk in front of him so no one could see him shove the bottle under his shorts. This worked great unless he got the bottles mixed up. Walt was still hurting from being sick and having run from one rim of the Grand Canyon to the other and back with Mike the weekend before. I went ahead of the two of them and managed to get lost which added a little distance to the race. There were no aid stations, just a Jeep that would show up now and then with water. This might have been the first year they had the Triple. The last 13 miles are very hilly with the race ending at 7,000' and me dehydrated, having missed the Jeep when I got lost. The start was in California and the finish in Nevada.

The second race starts at the finish line of day one. It was in the 30's at 7,000'. The first 11 miles are mostly downhill. After the Half marathon finish is where you hit the hills. It warmed up to the 50's and was a sunny day. At about mile 22 there is a hill about 2 miles long. The last few miles are easy and the race ends in Tahoe City. I ran most of this with Walt and he was feeling much better. This was the easiest of the three races. There was about 3000' of downhill and 2000' of uphill. BTW Denise had been busy at the casinos in Stateline, NV, while we ran the races. She had developed quite a bicep muscle from pulling the handle so many times on the slot machines. Staying at the Horizon Casino Hotel might have been a mistake.

Race 3 started on the golf course in Tahoe City. All three races were on asphalt roads and bike trails. This is the marathon that had many more runners than the other two combined. It was the coldest morning with the temperature around 30 degrees. I ran a few miles with a guy who had brain surgery about 30 days before he started the Triple. He was a Los Angeles firefighter who had a few good stories to tell as we ran. This is the toughest marathon. The first 15 miles were a mix of roads and paved bike paths with just a few hills. Mile 15 is where the "Hill from Hell" started at 6200' and climbed to 7000' over little more than a mile. It was then about a three quarter mile downhill to Emerald Bay followed by a mile climb up to Inspiration Point. Spectacular scenery along with a two mile downhill from Inspiration Point made this part of the race a little easier. The last 4 miles are flat which makes for a nice finish for the Tahoe Triple. After crossing the finish line, I found out Walt fell just a tenth of a mile from the finish at this, his 100th marathon. Walt hobbled to the finish line and then right into the first aid tent. I went in the tent and he was laid out on a cot with some minor scrapes and bruises. Each runner has a tag attached to his race number for a free beer. As he laid there I grabbed his tag and told him "no sense wasting a free beer." Walt did not complain about me grabbing the tag, I was his ride back to Reno. If you want to visit Lake Tahoe and do a race there are many to choose from. There are half marathons the same time as the fulls, an ultra, and other races.

Across the Years Ultras

The Across the Years ultramarathons include 24, 48 and 72 hour races that start at the end of one year and end at the beginning of the new year. I chose to do the 48-hour race since this would be my first multiday race and 48 hours was about how long I thought it would take me to do Badwater.

I had done the Sunmart 50k and next day the Dallas, TX, marathon 2 weeks before and was still recovering from them when I started the race near Phoenix, AZ, on Dec. 30, 2003. The course was a 500-meter oblong loop on packed gravel. The race was chip timed. A huge tent sat inside the loop for runners to set up smaller tents inside or just a sleeping bag and gear. It was cloudy and cool at the start. I ran some laps then started a walk run routine. The first 24 hours I only stopped once to get a massage. My goal was to get in 90 miles the first day and night and then 60 miles during the second 24 hours. I struggled but managed to complete 93 miles. At the end of 24 hours I changed socks and shoes and got another massage. At 11:00 AM I went into the tent and stretched out in my sleeping bag with feet elevated. I was shaking from the cold and it was so noisy in the tent there was no way I could sleep. This was a real low point for me in the race. I felt like saying the hell with my 150 mile goal, just find some place warm and some sleep. But I didn't. Even walking was now much more difficult.

I stopped for another massage at 3:00 pm, changed my shoes and socks, and popped a few blisters. I had been walking and running with Ron Vertrees off and on. I was having stomach problems at one point and Ron gave me some ginger which really helped. Ron saw that I was limping and asked what the problem was. I told him my knee was bothering me and I had blisters; he insisted on treating my blistered feet. Ron spent about 20 minutes draining new blisters, wiping feet with wet wipes, and applying blister block dressings. The cause of the blisters, I think, was my feet swelling more than I thought they would, causing the shoes to be too tight.

Ron was doing the 72-hour race with a goal of 175 miles and he took 20 minutes out of his race to help me. What a nice guy. This is what ultra running is all about. It was now 2:00 am. I walked a few laps with Ron until my feet got use to the blister block. Now with just my knee hurting some I started a run/walk routine that would be about 4 miles an hour, a 15 minute pace, that was good for me this late in the race. I got my 150 miles in by 8:00 am and another three miles more by race end. This was 492 laps. What made me really happy was Ron reaching his 175 mile goal. I made a few more friends during the race and saw some great runners as they lapped me. I also learned a lot about running multiday races and my body.

One runner, whom I talked with several times during the race, died shortly afterwards. Mark Heinemann, 46, was the defending champion. He went to sleep after the race and was found dead the next day. He finished third and really pushed hard. I believe he had pneumonia and his lungs filled with liquid.

2003 Totals:

- 26 marathons
- 6 ultras
- 71 races
- Total race miles: 1,306

Umstead:
Andy V, Mike S, Jim Sullivan, Walt P, Jerry Sullivan, Carl H

Sunmart 50 miler/50K friends (Left to Right):
Me, Gene DeFonzo, , Brent Floyd, Carl Hunt, Walt Prescott, ,
Layne Riebel, Alex Velazco, Andy Velazco, Mike Smith,
Jerry Sullivan, Ron Paquette

CHAPTER 9: MIKE BROOKS SMITH AND CAMP SUNSHINE (AS TOLD BY MIKE BROOKS SMITH)

"Mike Smith, hey its Mike Brooks, I have Mike Brooks Smith on the line"

That is the actual introduction to a phone conversation I had with Mike Brooks Smith in April of 2004. It was just a few months before the Badwater Ultramarathon and Mike Brooks was introducing me, Michael Brooks Smith, Camp Sunshine's Director of Special Events, to Michael Smith his Badwater crew leader. Alright, so bringing together some common names may not be that ironic, but it certainly was an amusing way to start my adventures with Mike Brooks.

Camp Sunshine is a national retreat for children with life-threatening illnesses and their families. Located on the shores of Sebago Lake in Casco, Maine, our one-of-a-kind program addresses the impact an illness has on every member of the immediate family. Luckily, Mike Brooks was very familiar with our program when he approached us in what would later become a decade of fundraising.

I remember our first meeting about Badwater and what went through my head as he described the challenge ahead of him. He talked at length about the uncertainty of actually being able to finish, the pain, blisters, toe nails falling off, uncontrollable vomiting from dehydration, oh and let's not forget the hallucinations. First impressions were easy ... this guy is certifiably nuts!

Running on the Sun as we referred to the Badwater Ultramarathon was really one of the first opportunities that Mike had to share his story with the world, and people took notice. From an overweight, two pack a day smoker, to a marathon man was an alluring story. Add to that his career as a firefighter (pre 9/11) and he was the poster child for amazing - and the press ate it up.

Soon, everyone in the community became his supporter, and Camp Sunshine benefitted.

By the time July rolled around, Camp Sunshine was buzzing with excitement; after all, Badwater was such a unique event. Let's face it, unless you are part of an elite running circle, chances are you'll never meet another person that has taken on Badwater, and that is what made it so much fun and inspirational.

Driven was the man who ran on a treadmill in the sauna to ensure success. I will never forget how proud I was of Mike when he completed the Badwater Ultramarathon. I was impressed that he did it for so many families and children he had never even met. As a result of running Badwater, Mike raised in excess of $20,000; because of Mike ten more children with life-threatening illnesses and their families could now come to Camp Sunshine! However, Mike's goal was to raise $25,000, and as was the case with his running endeavors Mike simply refused to come up short.

More About Camp Sunshine

Most families tell us that having a child with a life-threatening illness leaves them physically, emotionally, and financially exhausted. That is why our goal is to provide a place where families are able to regroup, reenergize, and restore hope for the future. Our unique program continues to attract families from around the nation - and the world. Since its inception more than 43,500 family members from 48 states and 22 countries have attended Camp Sunshine. There is never a charge to participating families thanks to the often Herculean efforts of supporters like Mike Brooks.

In 2014, Camp Sunshine was pleased to celebrate its 30th anniversary. The crossover from one decade to the next is always a major milestone for any individual, and for an organization as unique as Camp Sunshine, its historic magnitude is amplified by the thousands of lives that have been positively affected over the years.

While at Camp Sunshine, activities abound for all family members. Our 23-acre campus includes: a sprawling family activity center, complete with a heated indoor pool; arts and crafts rooms for both children and adults; tot lot and nursery, full of everything imaginable for the little ones; teen center, loaded with unique and fun games; fully-stocked library; and a computer learning center. Outdoors, families have access to a wide range of areas and activities, including: an 18-hole, handicap- accessible mini-golf course; sports field; archery range; amphitheater with outdoor movies and snacks; climbing wall; ropes course and nature trails; a basketball court; and so much more.

The waterfront offers kayaking, canoeing, paddleboats, swimming, a club-house, and a non-denominational chapel. Thankfully for our constituents, fall, winter and spring programs have been added, making Camp Sunshine more readily available and convenient to families at times when they need us most. Winter recreational activities such as ice-skating, snowshoeing, and sledding are enjoyed.

But while this recreational component is important, the program would only be half as effective were it not for Camp Sunshine's psychosocial pro-gram, one of Camp Sunshine's greatest strengths. These sessions may be the first opportunity the family members, including the children, have had to share their fears and frustrations with others who can genuinely identify with the same experiences. Workshops provide a forum where family members can learn from each other how to manage the needs of their children in the midst of the child's illness and, should the child fail treatment, during the end stages of life.

If we could play back the laughter, the stories, the love-cup trophy win-ner announcements, the wish boat ceremonies, and the end-of-week slide-shows, the colors and emotions would be more magnificent and powerful than any masterpiece painting, song, or stage play. Here at Camp Sunshine, the moments and emotions of real life are powerful.

Mike Brooks Continues His Crusade

In May 2005, Mike Brooks was back at it, preparing for a 24-hour race in Minneapolis, MN, with hopes of raising another $5,000 for Camp Sunshine. In a letter to his supporters he stated:

I'm back to actually finish what I started! I made a promise to myself and Camp Sunshine that I would raise $25,000 and as we near the anniversary of my Badwater run I'm back to meet that goal.

Once again, I will challenge myself by competing in a 24-hour race and I'm challenging you to help me raise the remaining $5,000 for Camp Sunshine. After raising just over $20,000 in 2004, I know that this will be a walk "in the park" or in this case "around the lake." On the morning of June 4th in Min-neapolis, Minnesota, I will begin the first of many 2.4 mile laps around Lake Nokomis.

That's how Mike worked. Anyone else would have been happy with rais-ing more than $20,000 for Camp Sunshine. Not Mike. He set a goal of $25,000 and if it took him 10 more events to reach his goal, then that is what he would do! Thankfully, he did meet his goal and we were all able to move on to the next big fundraiser.

6 Days to Celebrate 60 Years

Mike would once again challenge himself by competing in the grueling Sri Chimnoy Self-Transcendence Six Day Race in an attempt to raise another $6,000 (in celebration of his turning 60) for Camp Sunshine.

After raising over $20,000 in 2004, and another $5,000 in 2005, this should be a another "walk in the park" as Mike said about the Minneapolis race. This time the park was Corona Park in New York City. On the morning of April 30th, 2006, Mike would began the first of what he hoped would be 300 miles over six days. Quick math – that was six 50-mile days or two marathons a day for 6 straight days.

We discussed strategy briefly in a meeting prior to the run – it was simple. Mike said, "I will run until I can't run anymore, then I will sleep, wake up, and run until I can't run anymore. If I can do that for six days, we should be in good shape!"

The end result was another $7,000 windfall for Camp Sunshine.

Why not 10 Days?

Apparently, six days was too easy! I was shocked when a banged up Mike Brooks said after the six-day Sri Chinmoy that perhaps some day he would do the ten-day race. I was even more shocked when the phone rang in 2009 and he exclaimed he was registering for the summer race.

Back to work we went reaching out to friends, family, fire departments, and track clubs. This time his goal was to do the ten day race to reach a $10,000 goal! I named the constituents we solicited because it is important to remember we were often times reaching out to the same supporters for each event and each time they unequivocally responded favorably. What ultimately led them to continue to make Camp Sunshine the recipient of their generosity was that Mike continued to up the ante with each event.

Once again, with Camp Sunshine volunteers stopping by to cheer him on, Mike entered Corona Park for the challenge of a lifetime. At Camp Sunshine, children and families attending sessions would track his progress. Each day, we would post Mike's mileage and people were amazed and inspired by his efforts on their behalf. I always say that even after 15 years working at Camp Sunshine that I cannot imagine what it would be like to have a child diagnosed with a life-threatening illness. I would never pretend for a moment to know what it is like to walk in their shoes and the same can be said for Mike Brooks. It is impossible to fathom what it must be like to run for ten straight days – again I won't even try.

But together, we would raise another $11,000 for Camp Sunshine.

For Mike's sake, I'm often thankful that Sri Chinmoy didn't think a 100-day run was a good idea!

A Decade in Perspective

Here we are, so many years later, it's almost crazy to think how many times I've given a tour of our campus, stopped in front of Mike's framed Badwater jacket and belt buckle, and said, "This gentleman here ... this is Camp Sunshine's own Forrest Gump." If I've said it once, I must have said it a thousand times, and it couldn't be more true.

Every time I think Mike is done, like a bearded Tom Hanks reaching a new coastline, he just turns around and starts running again. Mike has been a blessing to Camp Sunshine, an inspiration to children, and a beacon of hope to families. Thanks for all the memories, and being in it for the long run!

Tish Caldwell, a Camp Sunshine supporter, remembers:
I truly cannot remember what year I first met Mike Brooks but realized as I read Mike Brooks Smith's story about Mike Brooks and his fundraising for Camp Sunshine that time truly does fly by. It was probably in 2000 when I first met Mike at the Auburn Lewiston YMCA where I worked at the time. He attended my yoga classes at the Y. Mike swore that these classes helped to keep his injuries at bay as he continued to pound the pavement running his marathons and ultra-marathons. For me and the other yoga class participants, Mike's stores made us laugh. He was a true storyteller; we all enjoyed his tales of adventures as he traveled the country seeking out marathons and ultra marathons, and we relished his tales about all of wonderful people he met as he traveled across the country and the world. He captured our attention and we couldn't wait to hear about each new adventure when he returned from another journey.

The YMCA and its staff supported Mike in whatever small way we could, beginning with first major fundraising effort running Badwater for Camp Sunshine. Mike is passionate about running and even more passionate about helping those who want to run. Even though I worked in the health and fitness field, I never considered myself a runner. However, in 2007, I made a promise to a dear friend that my first 5k would be Emily's Run in memory of this man's daughter who died tragically in an automobile accident in 2004. I was determined to do this and with the support of Mike Brooks, I and a group of runners from the YMCA successfully finished Emily's Run, our first 5k!

Now I am a runner, but I am not fast, really more of a social runner, kind of like Mike but with much shorter distances. Mike inspired me to begin helping encourage others to run, and that led to a group of us meeting on Saturday mornings to run up and down Spring Road, a beautiful, lakeside dirt trail. At the end of each run, Mike would always bring a wonderful selection of craft brewed beers.

Another result of running my first 5k was the creation of the Triple Crown 5k Run/Walk Series. Mike was instrumental in helping to develop this race series in 2008; it consisted of three local races, the Y Fit Fest, Emily's Run, and the Lewiston-Auburn Bridge, one in June, one in July, and the last in August. Mike Brooks was one of the original committee members helping to get what continues to be a very successful event with well over 2000 participants. Mike helped recruit the Auburn Fire Department and its Children's Local Charity Fund as sponsors to the Triple Crown Series and implemented the Auburn Firefighter's Local 797 Kids Fun Run, which encourages kids to get active via running. Because of Mike's passion, the Auburn Fire Fighters' Local 797 also sponsors the Dempsey Challenge, an annual run/walk cycle event, the primary fundraiser for The Patrick Dempsey Center for Cancer Hope & Healing. The Dempsey Center, located in Lewiston, ME, provides FREE support, education and integrative medicine services to anyone affected by cancer. The Dempsey Challenge is the fundraising experience for the Dempsey Center; 100% of funds raised by participants directly benefits the Center. The Dempsey Center believes that well supported children are an integral part of health, hope and healing for all involved. With this in mind, The Healing Tree Children's Program is committed to providing the highest quality of cancer education, support, and wellness services to enhance the quality of life of children, families and communities touched by cancer.

And here you have the fundraising recipe, Mike Brooks, the AFFL 797, the Auburn Lewiston YMCA, the Dempsey Challenge, Positive Tracks, a treadmill, gymnasium and a whole lot of kids ... Mike Brooks & the AFFL 797 12 Hour Run/Walk at the YMCA for the Dempsey Challenge. Mike run/walks for 12 hours, (only stopping to take potty breaks) and throughout the day the youth at the Y are encouraged to run or walk with Mike and help him fundraise. As members and community members drop money in Mike's firefighter boot and donate online, all funds raised are matched by the firefighters and then again by Positive Tracks (a national youth-centric nonprofit that partners with the Dempsey Center), so it looks like this; $20 becomes $40 which becomes $80. To date with matches included, Mike has raised well over $16,000 for the Healing Tree Children's Program of the Dempsey Center!

It has been an honor and a privilege to know Mike and his wife Denise (who is a SAINT by the way) and I look forward to many more runs together.

Mike responds: Tish has helped me raise funds for nonprofits, taught me yoga, and is a good friend. Some of our best times together have been the Spring Road runs and meetings for the Triple Crown 5k Series with a kegarator to keep our glasses full. Always ready to volunteer or help a friend and Tish is someone special.

CHAPTER 10:
MY TURN FOR BADWATER: 2004

This was the year I was to do Badwater. As part of my training I did the Wyoming Double marathon on May 30, 2004. I had done Double before and figured it would be good training for Badwater. The race is hilly and starts at 8,600'. The course is an out and back on paved and asphalt roads. If you are doing just the marathon, which is what 90% of the runners do, they do the course just once.

For the Double you do it twice. It was in the 20's at the start. I was planning on using trekking poles at Badwater so was using them here for the first time. I did a 45-mile fundraiser 5 days before so I started tired. The fundraiser was part of my effort to raise $25,000 for Camp Sunshine. Being tired was good; it made the race tougher and helped prepare me for the big one. I was with Gene Bruckert from miles 12 to 24. It was extremely windy blowing my trekking poles sideways and almost tripping Gene several times. Gene, Ron, and Carl were all doing the marathon. Layne Rieble was planning on doing the Double but decided on the marathon instead. Starting out on the second marathon was tough.

I was already tired and the wind was blowing so hard it made my eyes water even with glasses on. A lot of runners dropped out of the Double or did not finish, DNF. It got awful lonely doing the second marathon. The finish is at the top of a steep hill that seemed twice as steep the second time around. None of my friends were there when I finally got done. I came in 11th which was good for Dead Firetruck Last. Brent Weigner, the race director congratulated me and gave me my belt buckle finisher's award. Well what does not kill you makes you stronger as the saying goes. More brain cells gone . . .

On to Badwater and the Mt. Whitney Summit

After crewing and pacing for Mike and Andy it was now my turn to try Badwater. Since I'd been to Badwater twice I had a pretty good idea of what to expect. My first goal was to finish, second was to buckle. Buckling is when you finish the race in under 48 hours. My third goal was to summit Mt. Whitney. The race starts at Badwater in Death Valley, California, 282' below sea level, the lowest place in the western hemisphere, and ends at 8,400 ' on Mt. Whitney, the highest mountain in the continental US. If I summited Whitney, I would have gone from the lowest point in the Western Hemisphere to the top of the highest mountain in the continental US.

Badwater is a very expensive race to do. Mike and Andy paid for all the crew expenses once they arrived in Las Vegas, including hotels and meals. Vegas hookers and gambling were not included. Hey wives, only kidding . . . They also had to pay for renting two SUV's, gas, ice, coolers, etc., plus the entry fee. I figured it was going to cost me $4,500 to $5,000 to do it right. Spending this much money on myself seemed kind of greedy. Raising money for Camp Sunshine would serve several purposes. One, I would not feel like I was spending this money on just myself. Two, I would be helping children with life threatening illnesses. Three, what a motivator this would be for me. No way could I go around collecting pledges for Camp Sunshine and not finish the race. I would not accept any money towards my expenses with two exceptions. Mike said if I finished Badwater in under 48 hours he would pay for both SUV rentals. If I finished in over 48 he would pay for one and if I did not finish he would pay for nothing. A firefighter said he would only donate money to me and maybe make a separate donation to Camp Sunshine. The most interesting donation I got was from Bob Wehr. Bob said he would donate $100 per mile for the last ten miles. This is the toughest part of the race and he knew it. Bob wanted me to think of that $1,000 donation as an incentive to finish the race and bust my balls at the same time. Thanks Bob.

First thing I had to do was get accepted into the race. Badwater only accepts 80 runners out of hundreds of applications each year. The application is like a résumé. I listed all the ultras I did and explained that I had run over 100 marathons. You could get into the race without qualifying if you donated a certain amount of money to the race director's favorite charity. On my application I told him if I got in I would raise money for Camp Sunshine instead.

Once I knew I was in I asked the people who would be my two "dream teams" if they were in also. All agreed without hesitation. My next step was to start training harder and to meet with Mike Smith from Camp Sunshine about fundraising. When I talk about Mike Smith from Camp Sunshine I will put CS after Mike's name. Mike's full name is Mike Brooks Smith, not to be confused with Mike Brooks or Mike Smith the runner. I was going to put Mike BS, for Mike Brooks Smith but thought CS might sound better.

Everything was falling nicely into place as the race drew closer. After finishing the Wyoming Double, I started heat training. I used saunas, a steam room, plus drove around with my heater on full blast. Bob and I drove to Walt's home because it was closest to the Manchester, NH, airport which we would fly out of the next day. On the drive down we had the heater on for a little more heat acclimation preparedness. As we pulled up to a toll booth the attendant must have thought we were crazy when he saw I had gloves on and could see us sweating heavily.

Once in Las Vegas the dream team was all together and ready to head for Death Valley. But first we had a huge shopping list to fill. I call this the dream team because if I could pick any group of people to be on my team it would be these very close friends who had the talent, patience, and perseverance to get me through the race, up the mountain, and back down again. Another very important thing was I knew that they would work together well. The team consisted of Mike Smith (2002 Badwater finisher, crew -pacer 2003), Andy Velazco (Badwater finisher 2003, crew-pacer 2002, and orthopedic surgeon, which came in "handy" another year), Walt Prescott (Badwater crew- pacer extraordinaire 2002 and 2003). The two Badwater rookies were Bob Brainerd, professional coach, trainer, physical therapist, and tri-athelete and Carl Hunt, ultra runner and Badwater wannabe. The crews would be with me for 135 miles and two of them for another 22 plus miles from the Mt. Whitney portals to the summit and back. They would put up with my vomiting, diarrhea, and hallucinations. They also kept me motivated, taped my feet to try to prevent blisters, treated the blisters I did get, changed my shoes and socks, etc. This incredible team gave me the confidence I needed to take on Badwater and summit Mt. Whitney.

The dream team and I left Las Vegas on July 10, 2004, for Furnace Creek, Death Valley. After checking into our motel rooms Mike supervised the two teams on how to set up the SUV's for the race and once again went over some basic rules. Get ice whenever possible, keep the gas tanks full, and don't leave keys in vehicle. Two other important rules were: don't run air conditioners, vehicles might overheat, and never put your hands on the ice, use a ladle. Sticking your hands in the cooler for ice and you could contaminate it. Running out of gas, ice, or locking your keys in a vehicle could mean the end of the race. Rules of the race say you must have one vehicle close to the runner at ALL times. I have seen runners drop from Badwater because they only had one team instead of two like I had. One runner dropped because his crew was not keeping up with him. My team had all heat trained for Badwater. I have heard that some years more crew people have ended up in the hospital than runners. There are no aid stations on the course because of the danger from the extreme heat so beware, crew people.

The day before the race it is mandatory that all runners and crews attend a race briefing. During the meeting, race director Cris Kostman went over all the rules and added a new one. No trekking poles. I had been training with poles figuring it would help prevent or help with the back pain I often get in ultras. Well that sucked, but he is the race director and there was nothing I could do about it.

I had been nervous about everything going as planned. Someone not making it, me getting sick before the race, almost anything that could go wrong I thought of. But now it was race morning and all those worries were disappearing. I had the 8:00 am start on July 12th. There were three starts, 6:00 am, 8:00 am and 10:00 am, each consisting of about 25 runners. The faster runners started at 10:00 am, slower 6:00 am, and mid-pack 8:00 am theoretically. When the race started most of my worries disappeared. Knowing I had two excellent crews that would take care of any problems that arose, all I had to do was put one foot in front of the other and stay healthy. It was close to 100 degrees by the time I got to mile 13 and I was already in trouble suffering from the "runs." My crew figured out the sports drink I was taking was too sugary for the large amount I was drinking. Furnace Creek at mile 17 was a short real bathroom break with just a couple of minutes in a chair. Taking in just water and food the diarrhea stopped after about 6 hours. There is no place to conceal yourself while taking a desert dump except by your vehicle. Opening both passenger side doors I would hold onto the door frame hanging out of the SUV. The first time I went, I looked back and saw Mike chasing the windblown toilet paper across the desert; only a good friend would do that.

By 28 miles the temperature in the shade was 123 degrees and much hotter on the asphalt road we were on. BTW there is no shade in the desert. At mile 42 I would take my longest break of the race at Stovepipe Wells. I spent about 15 minutes in the pool trying to cool my body down. I then had a pasta dinner as Andy partially re-taped my feet. You can tell Andy is a surgeon by just watching his method of taping feet to prevent blisters. Using 2 different types of tape and spray adhesive he carefully applied such and snipped the slightest crease that could cause problems. I never got a blister until leaving the portals for the summit. In less than an hour, I was back on the course starting up a 5,000' climb for 18 miles. Around mile 53, I puked out my pasta dinner and whatever else was in my stomach in front of my crew. Another disgusting display for my crew, but they are starting to get used to it. I never should have forced myself to eat so much but I felt much better after expelling it. By nightfall, the desert had cooled to the 90's. Around mile 59 we reached Town Pass summit and I knew I had the hottest part of the race and one of the mountains done. Next was an 8 mile downhill where I started running to Panamint Springs. I ran very little the first 59 miles saving my energy for the many miles to come. I have had a pacer with me every step of the race since mile 17 and the crew within sight almost constantly. During the hottest part of the race I carried two water bottles that my crew would fill with ice. Holding the bottles in my hands helped cool me and the ice melted quickly and I would drink the water. The pacer had a spray bottle that was also used to cool me. From head to toe I was dressed in white even wearing long pants to protect me from the sun and heat.

I tried to sleep in the SUV at Panamint but gave up after about 10 minutes. At mile 70 or so, I started another climb to Father Crowley's of about 3,400 ' reaching mile 90 on July 13th at 2:00 pm, 30.5 hours into the race. I had climbed 2 mountain ranges and descended a long downhill to find a flat stretch of road ahead of me. This would bring me to mile 122 where I would start another climb up 8,400' to Mt. Whitney portals and the race finish line. Darkness arrived around mile 112, about 36 hours into the race. It was about then that I started having hallucinations. I was seeing things that were not there and there were miles I have no memory of doing. A golf course in the desert, really! The hallucinations were brought on by a combination of things. I seemed to hallucinate more at night, brought on by about 40 hours with no sleep and extreme fatigue. I know when I am hallucinating most of the time and it is not a scary experience, just weird. With Bob pacing me starting at mile 122 the hallucinations were in 3-D. I saw giants coming out of a tent. The best one was when I peed on the asphalt road and the pavement turned into what looked like a black lava flow. The only worrisome part of hallucinating was that it was often accompanied by dizziness and I was afraid of losing my balance and falling. What I did was focus on Bob's shoes and I followed them up the mountain.

Mike was always close by encouraging me from the SUV and Bob stayed in front of me. I knew now that as long as I kept moving I would get the coveted Badwater belt buckle with time to spare. Forty-six hours and seventeen minutes and 135 miles after starting at 282' below sea level, I was at the 8,400' finish line with all my 5 person crew. Exhausted, filthy, and happy as hell we celebrated by taking a few pictures with the race director and calling my wife at work. We then headed back to Lone Pine for a shower and about 4 hours of sleep. Three of the crew, Mike, Walt, and Andy headed for Vegas and a plane ride that afternoon. They all did the Vermont 100-mile trail race that weekend and they all finished.

I had not told many people about my plans to climb the rest of Whitney after the race but now Bob and Carl picked up our permits which you needed to order ahead of time. After the awards ceremony we started climbing from the portals which is 11 miles each way and a 6,200 ' climb to 14,400'. An hour after we started the bad news was we took the wrong turn somewhere on the trail and we had to backtrack. The first part of the trail was easy with many Z switchbacks and brook crossings where the worst thing that could happen was slipping off a log and getting your feet wet. My training with trekking poles paid off now as I used the poles to maintain my balance and take some pressure off my aching knees and back especially when jumping off rocks. There were a few places where you could take a wrong turn but we had no problems staying on the trail in the darkness. When we would stop to eat or drink we would turn off our headlamps and look at the millions of stars that were visible because of the lack of any ambient light. This was spectacular and something I will never forget. As the sun rose we were surprised to see the many drop offs about 500' or more. This is not a technical climb but you must be careful. As we were traversing the 96 switchbacks to trail crest we saw Marshal Ulrich and Art Weber descending the mountain. They too had done Badwater and summited Whitney. Weber did so to write the name of a fellow Badwater finisher who had died in the log book on the summit. Marshal had climbed Mt. Everest a month earlier and must have thought this was a piece of cake. Art though was hurting and looked in bad shape. Marshal mentioned it had been a "tough night on the mountain," glancing back at Art.

The three of us continued our climb totally exhausted, at least I was, but enjoying the spectacular views now that the sun was out and shining brightly. We were now at 12,000' of altitude and there were large areas of snow. This was quite a contrast from the desert below. As we reached trails crest we thought we were almost to the summit but then saw an "8" painted on a rock which meant we still had three miles to go. The next three miles did not have much climb but there is over 14,000' altitude and it is mostly single track trail and only wide enough for one hiker. There were also plenty of sheer drop offs. The drop offs and lack of oxygen had me worried that one of us might tumble down the mountain. With about half a mile to go to the summit, we reached a snowfield 50 to 60 yards long that was easy to pass through because other hikers had been through already. A short time after crossing this, I almost lost it. I bent over my poles totally exhausted, both mentally and physically. I had a moment of self-pity and felt very humbled by the mountain. I promised myself if I ever do Badwater again, I will never climb Whitney afterwards. I then straightened up and followed my crew to the summit, arriving at 10:15 am, 13 hours and 45 minutes after starting our little jaunt. We celebrated our summiting halfheartedly knowing we had to hike back. We signed the log book, ate, rested, and headed back down after 45 minutes.

The skies were now cloudy and all I could think of was " we do not need a violent thunderstorm now, especially above tree line!" I was a sorry sight descending the mountain. I noticed other hikers staring at me and wondering whatever must have happened to that old man. Without asking, one of my crew would say, glancing my way, "he just did Badwater." This is all it took to answer their stares.

Going downhill was supposed to be easier but I was moving very slowly trying not to trip. I did start to fall a couple of times but either Bob or Carl would catch me. I did have one pretty good face plant, maybe a 7 on a scale of 10. Worrying about needing to be helicoptered out passed as we finished the 96 switchbacks. I did one more gross thing on the switchbacks and while passing through a campground but I ain't gonna tell you. No more gross stuff, promise. The last three miles seemed to go on forever. It got dark again. Bob went ahead of us and spotted a bear on the trail. A short time later we got to the trailhead. It was 9:20 pm and Bob said the car was gone. I could not go another step. Carl and Bob found out the car had been towed to a lower lot because there was some kind of event where I had parked. They had posted no parking signs after we had already parked there. Exactly 85 hours and 20 minutes after starting Badwater I was done with all my goals except one. I eventually did raise more than $25,000 for Camp Sunshine thanks to lots of individuals, businesses, police and fire departments. Fifteen families went to Camp Sunshine because of all this generosity.

Of course none of this would have been possible without my having the best crews at Badwater. Thanks Andy, Carl, Mike and Walt. Next year was Carl's turn.

Rim to Rim to Rim of the Grand Canyon in Fall 2004

This was Mike and Walt's idea. They had already run from the south rim of the Grand Canyon to the top of the North rim and then back to the top of south rim. We all met at the Phoenix airport on September 22, 2004, rented an SUV and drove to our motel, located a mile or so from the trail, the day before starting. The rim to rim to rim was not a race, just something we all wanted to do. Walt, Mike, Andy, Carl, and I all started down the Bright Angel trail at 3:00 am to get ahead of mules and hikers that would be using the trail later. I tried just using a headlamp but it did not illuminate the trail that well. I decided to put my trekking poles in my back pack so I could use a hand held flashlight. The trail is narrow with many switchbacks and drop offs. Near the bottom of the trail, about 5 or 6 miles in, I rolled my ankle on a rock and fell. I got up immediately and tried to run. Going a few 100 yards the ankle gave out and I felt a sharp pain shoot up my leg. I thought I had broken my ankle but Dr. Andy said it was just a sprain and offered to turn around with me. I told Andy that with the help of my trekking poles, I would be okay so Andy continued on with the other runners. I was at the bottom of the canyon now and it was sunrise. Moving slowly with the support of the poles I came within 20' of four mule deer and two does with their fawns. What a beautiful sight, the deer, sunrise and canyon made. After watching the deer for a minute I started up Bright Angel trail. A park ranger asked if I was okay and if I had seen the condors. Answering yes, I was OK, and what condors not knowing there were condors in the canyon. They were in the area but I missed seeing them. I slowly made progress and the closer I got to the top the more hikers and people on mules I saw.

Once out of the canyon I went back to the motel, showered, and slept for a few hours. Next I went back to the paved trail along the canyon top and walked a little with poles and took in spectacular views. Later I returned to Bright Angel trail. Andy and Walt had called me to say they were ready to be picked up. They made it to the base of the north rim and turned around thinking it would take too long to do the ascent and descent. Mike and Carl finished about 10:30 pm, a little less than 20 hours. I believe the distance is about 45 miles. We were all back at the motel around midnight and on the road shortly after 3:00 am for the ride back to Phoenix. At my age and ability, I will never try this again. Maybe I'll do the rim to rim but only during daylight hours.

Across the Years 72 Hour Race 2004

I was back at Across the Years on December 29, 2004, to January 1, 2005, for the 72-hour race. This year my goal was to be 200 miles. Carl picked me up at the Phoenix airport. His wife Fay and two grandchildren, Anthony and Joey, were with him. It rained for a lot of the race and the conditions were pretty miserable. The volunteers spread sand over low spots so the puddles were not too bad. The company at the race made for an enjoyable experience. Sixty something year olds, Ron Vertrees and Don Winkley, did many laps together swapping stories and that made the race go by more quickly. I don't think I ever met a nicer runner than Ron. Don is a character who drove his stainless steel Delorian up from Corpus Christi, TX. Don has completed some of the toughest ultras all over the world. I got in 86 miles the first 24 hours.

It stopped raining on day 2 but I now had blisters that were treated by one of the runners who also volunteered from time to time during the race. He used a large syringe to drain blisters which worked well but I had to go back again when new blisters developed. I only got in 39 miles on day 2 and knew I would not reach my goal of 200 miles. John Geezler's goal was the 300 mile belt buckle which nobody had done before. His first 24 hours produced way over 100 miles. On day 2 he did terrible, but on day 3 his 300-mile goal was completed well before 72 hours!! John's performance bordered on unbelievable, especially seeing him hurting so badly on that second day.

Fay and the kids came down several times to see Carl and maybe me. It was fun walking a ways with them. Carl and I also did lots of laps together and celebrated New Years by walking a loop sipping fake champaign and watching fireworks that the race set off. Happy New Year!! The last few hours of this race amazed me. All the runners were out on the course going harder than ever to get in as many miles as possible. The closer to race end the harder they went. I ended up with 581 500-meter laps for 180.5 miles. A little disappointed that I did not reach my goal but happy that I did the race and learned several things. I gained 8 to 10 pounds during the race because you go by the aid station every 500 meters and I was eating far too much. Also I was taking too many electrolyte caps and retaining too much water. I learned that whenever I felt a hot spot, I needed to treat it before it became a blister. I also learned that I needed to take more breaks if I began to go so slowly that it simply did not make sense to stay on course. Another important thing I learned was to smile more - nobody really gives a shit how many miles you do, only you.

2004 was a very good year.

- I raised lots of money for Camp Sunshine
- Had no major injuries
- Did a total of 57 races:
- 20 marathons
- 5 ultras
- Total race miles: 1,164

Badwater T-Shirt

The Crew:
Andy V, Bob B, Carl H, Mike B, Mike S, Walt P

Mike and Andy

Mike on the road

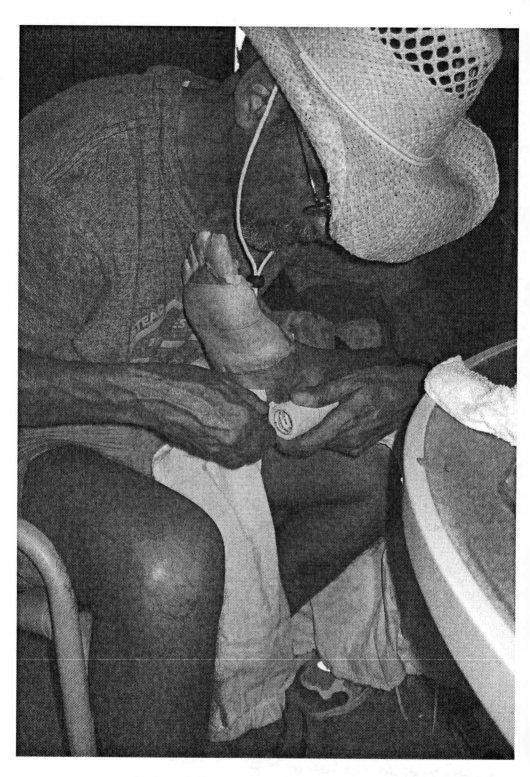

Andy on blister prevention at Badwater

Nearing the Finish Line

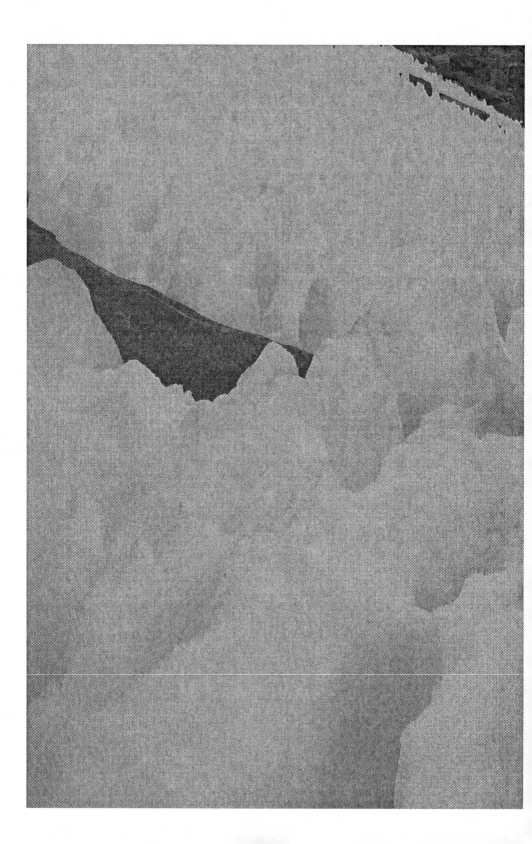

CHAPTER 11:
2005 WESTERN STATES AND MORE

At a cookout at my brother Paul's home, I told my nieces Kristie and Kerrie, along with Kristie's husband Jim, what a great time we would have if we did the Walt Disney World marathon. They fell for it and shortly thereafter started training for their first marathon.

I also figured it would be a good time for my granddaughter Madison, who was 5, to make her first trip to Disney World as a surprise. I had a condo with room for the three of them which made for an easy time to get to the race together.

We all started in corral F which is near the back. We ran a few miles together then Kerrie went ahead. Kristie, Jim, and I continued together until about the half marathon mark, then I went on ahead. We all met at the finish line and were happy with the results. The three newbies finished in tired but good shape and I survived after doing the 72-hour race 8 days earlier.

I have done the marathon many times and the Goofy Challenge twice. The Challenge is the half marathon on Saturday followed by the marathon on Sunday. In my opinion it is a nice destination marathon and also a good race if you want a flat course with a lot of bells and whistles. It is overpriced but all races sell out each year including the Dopey. The Dopey is 5k, 10k, half marathon, and full marathon on 4 consecutive days.

My daughter Katie and granddaughter Madison flew into Orlando the night of the marathon. Madison did not know where she was. I had asked her months earlier where she would like to go and she said she wanted to go where she could swim in the winter.

We also discussed Mickey Mouse. I told her he was a rat, he had to be since he was so big. She told me he was definitely a mouse. Picking them up at the airport I drove into Disney World until you see the water tower with the huge Mickey Mouse hat with the ears. She saw it and said "Mickey must live around here." I turned around and told her we would look for him tomorrow. We found him the next day and had a ball doing it.

Carl Touchstone 50 miler

Ron Paquette and I flew into Jackson, Mississippi, and met up with Andy, Mike, Walt, Carl, and several other friends at the host hotel of the Carl Touchstone Mississippi 50 mile/50k trail race. The race was on March 12, 2005. The 50 mile course was all wide trail with hills and water crossings, nothing technical and 12.5 mile loops. I ran most of the race by myself and managed to trip and fall a few times. I also got lost on the 2nd or 3rd loop. How did I manage to do that? I was having a tough time and was concerned about the 12 hour cut off. The last loop a few miles from the finish line Mike jumped out from behind a tree yelling "you'd better hurry up or you won't make the cut off." By this time I knew I would make it. I did finish in 11:51:59. They had run out of belt buckles and wanted to give me a gym bag instead. "No way, I want a buckle, that's one of the reasons I did the race." They agreed and mailed me one. I felt so bad I could not eat or drive. Ron drove back to Jackson and we flew out the next day. I went back a few years later and did the 50k. One of the volunteers on the course looked up the race number I was wearing and said the race director wanted to see me when I finished. Walking up to him I told him who I was and in a very serious voice he started in on me. "You are one of those Yankees I see. Your Carpet Bagger relatives came down here after the Civil War and cut all our yellow pine. They missed one tree and that is where this wooden bowl came from. You might as well take it like your ancestors took our other trees. Here, take this shirt too." He handed me an excellent button up shirt with an alligator and Mississippi 50 embroidered on the back and the bowl. With that, a big grin appeared on his face and we all had a good laugh.

In 2005 my friend Carl Hunt took over the Jack Bristol Lake Waramaug ultras as race director in CT. Ron and I volunteered along with Mike Smith to help and we also ran the race. The races are a 100k, 50 miler, and 50k and are held in late April. These are some of the oldest ultras in the country and if Carl did not take them over they might not have continued. The courses wind around Lake Waramaug in New Preston, CT. Each loop is 7.6 miles and there are several hills. It is all asphalt roads, some narrow and scenic. Almost every year Ron and I go down together to put up race packets, get food ready for aid stations, and help at packet pickup. We do a few other things and once in a while I help cook, making my famous chicken parmesan at Carl's home. We stay at Carl's and leave together race morning like a caravan, trucks loaded with food and other supplies and a car or two. This is one of my favorite races because of the camaraderie and the excellent job Carl, his family, and the volunteers do. Great food on the course and after the race BTW. Ron and I always do the 50k and see many runners we know every year. The races have grown from about 35 the first year Carl took over to about a 135 now.

Another fundraiser I did for Camp Sunshine was the FANS 24-hour race in Minneapolis, MN on June 4-5, 2005. This was my 150th marathon/ultra. At the start of the race I was already in trouble, with inflamed sinuses and on antibiotics. Denise had dropped me off and left with the car and her friend Nancy. They are both shopaholics and were headed for the Mall of America never to be seen again until the end of the race. The course was 2.48 mile loops around Lake Nokomis. The only "hill" was 20' high on a short grassy stretch. The rest of the course was asphalt and concrete sidewalks. Race day brought a mixture of weather with pouring rain, sun, humidity, and then more rain. I saw Andy on a few laps but did not know anyone else there. I stopped four times during the race to get massages and took another 30-minute break. I only managed to get in 74 miles but I did the best I could. I was pissed because Denise never showed up during the race but that dissipated quickly when I saw she had some Sierra Nevada Pale Ale for me at race end.

On June 25th the Western States 100 mile trail race started and my job here would be to crew and pace. This is the oldest 100-mile race and started with Gordon Ansleigh. It was supposed to be a horse race but Gordon's horse was injured so he asked the race director if he could run it. And that, my friends, is how 100-mile trail races started. Andy, Mike, Walt, Carl, and I were here. Mike and Walt were the runners. I crewed through the day and started pacing with Walt around mile 78 at 2:00 am. There is a bench on the course placed there in honor of a woman runner killed by a mountain lion. Shortly after passing the bench Walt had to take a dump. He started to walk into the woods when I told him I saw two big eyes with my flashlight (not true). Walt decided to take a dump right next to the trail. A little further down the trail we heard music and saw some male volunteers dressed up in hula skirts and coconut bras alongside a keg of beer. Keep in mind we are in the middle of the woods and some supplies had to be brought in by horse or mule. They offered me a beer and not to insult them I took it. No need to push Walt, he was ahead of the cut-off by a wide margin. The race finished on a quarter mile track where Walt's wife, Kendel, ran with him to the finish. Nice job Walt.

Badwater 2005

In July it was back to Badwater to crew and pace Carl. Andy, Mike, and I were back with two rookie Badwater friends of Carl's. Kyle was an experienced runner and had trained for the work ahead as did Ron. Carl did an excellent job during the race. No hallucinating and he kept up a steady pace, finishing faster than any of us had. There was only one problem. It only got to 118 degrees. Andy, Mike, and I did not consider it a true Badwater finish unless it reached at least 120 degrees. We told Carl nice going but you DNQ'd (did not qualify) and will have to come back again. All in fun of course. Walt, Andy, Kyle, Mike, and Bob Wehr climbed Mt. Whitney the next day. Walt and Bob flew in just to do that. They did it in 16.5 hours even with Walt suffering from altitude sickness.

On September 15th I met my brother Walter at the Salt Lake City airport for what would be the first of many trips together. I was not sure how we would get along since we had not been on a trip together for 30 years or so and he thought back then that since he was the oldest of the three of us, he could boss us around.

We drove to Logan, Utah, and did a few side trips from there. One was down a discontinued dirt road where I almost got stuck and another to Bear Lake where I would run two marathons around the lake on another trip. We got held up in traffic once. A large herd of cattle was being driven down the road and my brother was simply amazed. The race name was "Top of Utah" and it was a very easy point-to-point race with 1000' of altitude loss. After the race Walter and I went to a bar and shot some pool. I put him in his place winning every game so he supplied the beer and paid for the table. He talked to a guy at the bar and told him how I had done Badwater and was still raising money for Camp Sunshine. The guy ended up making a $20 donation. The trip went well; we got along just fine with the only complaint being his speeding all the time.

Heartland 100 miler

I flew into Kansas City, Kansas, to do the Heartland 100 miler, also known as the Spirit of the Prairie. The race was on October 8th and 9th. It is on dirt roads that are very rough in places. There were very few homes or ranches on the course and I don't remember seeing a vehicle for the first and last 40 miles. I made a couple mistakes before the race even started. First, the race is in the Flint Hills which should have told me it would be hilly. Second, it gets cold and windy in Kansas this time of year. The race goes out 50 miles and then comes back the same way. We started in Cassoday which is a very small town famous for being the prairie chicken capital of the world. The course had plenty of aid stations and good hot food at times. There was no need for a crew or pacer in this race. It was windy and about 40 degrees at the start. I ran with a friend, Kevin Hatfield, for about ten miles then he went ahead of me. I got to the 50 mile turnaround in 11:40 without twisting an ankle on the rocks on the course. I sat down there and had some excellent Mexican food. I was enjoying the scenery, runners, and volunteers up to now. I followed a skunk down the road for about a mile before getting to the aid station at mile 57.4. Kevin was in there all bundled up in blankets and getting ready to q-u-i-t. I told him that word should not be in his vocabulary. "You can walk the rest of the race and still finish in time. If you quit you will remember it the rest of your life. You are not injured so you have no reason not to finish." Kevin did get going and finished the race.

My spirits went downhill after dark and I began hallucinating. One reason for this was my eyes were screwed up from the constant wind blowing and the cold. Reflectors on fence posts looked like runners when lit up by flashlight. I only saw two runners the last 50 miles. They were Kevin and a runner who took a wrong turn. I yelled my head off to him before he finally turned around. He passed me awhile later and never said a word. No thank you for saving your ass? My goal now was to pass him which I did around mile 80. The sun came up with about ten miles to go. My feet were blistered and I was tired but feeling good as far as my spirits go. I usually don't hallucinate during the day but right around sunrise I saw a herd of buffalo on the road ahead of me. At one time there were over a million bison living in the Flint Hills. I kept getting closer and closer, then realized they were cattle. My second 50 miles was much slower than the first, finishing in 28:03. Got a nice buckle though.

Being a retired firefighter and my wife a nurse we are not poor or rich but middle income. To do all these races cost money so I try to save as much as possible on expenses. Since I retired I almost always travel with my brother sharing expenses with him. We split the cost of rental cars, gas, and hotel rooms. We also fly into the cheapest airport within a reasonable travel distance. My brother-in-law Bob drives us to the airport so we can save on parking fees. Thanks, Bob, that really adds up. Denise works so she goes to fewer places but always to Florida, Hawaii, and places that are warm in the winter. Walt Prescott worked for Delta and helped me get some good ticket deals. I also take out credit cards that offer big frequent flyer mile bonuses or points. I cancel the cards when the annual fee comes due. I also volunteer to get bumped from flights whenever possible.

2005 is the only year I kept track of how I paid for flights so here is a break down. All fights are from Portland, Maine:

- Phoenix -voucher
- Orlando - paid
- Orlando - paid
- Birmingham, AL -Frequent Flyer (FF) miles
- Jackson, MS – FF miles.
- Honolulu, HI -2 tickets – FF miles.
- Nashville, TN - paid
- Green Bay, WI – FF .
- Minneapolis - St Paul , MN - companion ticket with Walt - Delta employee deal
- Sacramento , CA - paid
- Las Vegas - paid
- San Francisco – paid
- Salt Lake City, UT – FF
- Moline, IL – FF
- Kansas City , KS – paid
- Louisville , KY – paid
- Baltimore- Washington , MD – paid
- Little Rock, AR – FF
- Charleston , SC – voucher

As you can see using 2 vouchers, being bumped, 8 frequent flyer tickets, and a companion ticket saved me a lot of money.

2005 Totals

- minor injuries only
- 56 races
- 15 marathons
- 5 ultras
- total race miles: 1,290

CHAPTER 12: LOTS OF RACES IN 2006

The Goofy Challenge

A bunch of us had always wanted to get the Donald Duck medal at the WDW half marathon but it was on the same day as the marathon which we preferred running. That all changed with the new Goofy Challenge. The Challenge is the half on Saturday and the marathon on Sunday. As soon as I heard of the Challenge I emailed my running friends saying we should all do it and bring the wives too. The response was great! Everyone I emailed showed up for the races with their wives, Carl brought his two grandchildren and Denise invited her friend Nancy.

All the men did the Goofy Challenge and the women the half. Kathy Velazaco might have done the Challenge as she could do it easily. This being the first Goofy we saw lots of runners we knew well. Both races were like moving parties. We did the races just to have fun, stopping to take pictures with Disney characters. I got in trouble when I asked Mickey, " why no kids with Minnie?"

Everyone finished the races, no DNF's. Lenore Dolphin, one of my favorite people, was handing out medals at the end of the marathon which made the perfect ending of the race for me. After the marathon most of us went to a steak house for dinner and pictures.

Everyone brought their medals to pose with them. Carl got into a peanut throwing fight with his grandkids and Lucas, Nancy's son. Carl lost. Hugs and handshakes ended a wonderful time.

Another Umstead 100 miler

I drove to Carl's home in CT and we left from there to do the Umstead 100 mile trail race on April 8th and 9th. I ran the first 50 miles with Bob Hilderbrant. I paced him for his first 50 miler and we became friends. Bob is from Fairbanks, AK, and a fellow Fifty Stater. Umstead is a 100 mile race but you can drop down and get credit for 50 miles if you want. That is what Bob was planning to do. If I had been smart I would have done just 50 and used it as a smart training run for my upcoming 6 day race. Of course I did not, even though my shins were hurting along with my right knee. Just before finishing the first fifty miles, a girl named Carolyn joined Bob and me. This was her 11th attempt at 100 miles with no success so far. She asked me to pace her last 50. A cold front moved through at night with rain and wind. Carolyn started to slow and get bitchy. She started talking about quitting, wanted to sit down, take breaks, etc. I figured the only way I would get her through the race was to keep her moving and get her so pissed at me she would put the pain and fatigue aside. I started in on her, " you gonna quit 11 -100 milers in a row?" "Keep moving, I don't care how slow you go but you are going to finish this no matter what." We did finish in 28:41. She never said a word to me after crossing the finish line. Guess she was really pissed at me but it worked, she got her first finish. Carl had a good time and a good finish. I also had a good time despite Carolyn being pissed. Saw lots of friends before, during and after the race.

Self -Transcendence 6 Day Race

The Self-Transcendence 6 Day race would be one of the few races I would do not knowing a single runner at the start of the race. By race end I had met some of the most interesting runners in the world, as well as a guru and his followers. This race would be another fundraiser for Camp Sunshine. Auburn firefighters' Local 797 has always been very generous when it came to my fundraisers. I told them I was doing a race to raise money for Camp Sunshine. The representative for the Children's Fund was very familiar with the nonprofit. He asked how much I wanted. I said if you donate $10 a mile that would be great. He agreed, and then asked how long the race was. I told him it was a 6 Day race, you run one mile loops, and do as many as you can. Looking a little puzzled since he'd never heard of a race longer than a marathon, he asked how many miles I thought I would do. "Over 300 I think" was my answer. Local 797 consisted of 64 firefighters at the time so $3,000 was a lot of money for them. Now he realized that maybe he should have asked that first and he wanted to change his mind. "This is for very sick children and you did agree on $10 a mile. How about I cap it at 300 miles - $ 3000? We had a deal. All I had to do is run around in circles for 6 days. A friend, Erik Boucher, set up a website, no charge, where donations could be made and he reported my progress or lack thereof daily.

I drove from Maine to Flushing Meadows in Corona Park, Queens, NYC, the day before the 6 Day race start. When I arrived the Ten Day race was on its 4th day. I met one of the race directors who showed me where I could set up my tent, the "dugout" area that is right next to the course where you can keep some of your gear. After setting up my tent I checked into a nearby hotel for my last full night's sleep.

The race started at noon with 22 runners under clear skies and about 60-degree temperature. The course was a one-mile loop on an asphalt path about 8' wide and open to the public. There was a makeshift kitchen on the course that served all vegetarian food 24 hours a day. Volunteers counted laps and recorded them on a large board visible to runners. I made a foolish mistake running 100 miles at Umstead 3 weeks before. I had sore knees and shins to start the race. I checked with a doctor at the Six Day race and he said my knee pain was muscle related and not torn cartilage like I thought. That was very good news.

Day 1: I had planned on running the most miles to get some "in the bank" since I am as rested as I will be. Getting 76 miles is 6 miles more than I thought I would do. I slept about an hour the first day. Visiting the doctor, eating, massages, bathroom stops, rest breaks, changing socks and shoes all take time but are necessary in a multi-day race.

Day 2: I am shooting for 60 miles today and that is what I do. The weather is nice and I received several emails that the volunteers delivered to me. The emails lifted my spirits and helped me keep a smile on my face. By now the volunteers who are counting laps are wondering why I say "Ca-Ching" every time I finish a one-mile lap. I explain to them about the Camp Sunshine fundraiser and that some people are donating by the mile. "Ca-Ching" is the sound an old cash register makes, I explained. Soon the volunteers are saying "Ca-Ching" when I finish a lap.

Day 3: My goal is 50 miles but I have a hard time achieving this. My feet are now swollen and blistered, my knees and shins are very sore and I have a hard time sleeping because of the pain. Yes, I am really starting to whine to myself.

Day 4: I try to tell myself that this race is mostly about being mentally tough and I am starting to be a real wimp. Everybody in the race is hurting like me. Think of the ten day runners. They have been out here twice as long as me. What about the kids at Camp Sunshine? They suffer much more pain than I am suffering and their pain does not end in 6 days. Talking to myself like this works and I put a smile on my face and start enjoying the little things I am experiencing. There are the ducks I see every loop during the day in the pond. Birds chirping, children playing, and all the different ethnic groups using the park. There are also the planes flying over constantly from La Guardia and JFK.

Brother Walter came down to see if I was still alive and tried to get me to drink an ice cold beer. You were not supposed to drink during the race and I did not know what would happen if I got caught. Besides to me drinking a beer or two would be like taking a performance enhancing drug. I always do better after a beer in a long race.

Americans are a minority in this race; there are lots of runners from the Czech Republic, Austria, New Zealand, Australia, Switzerland, Slovakia, and Finland. I enjoyed talking to these runners and with the Ten day runners. Dragan, a Ten Day runner from Serbia, and I talked for hours as we kept moving around the course. He has lived all over the world and is a follower of the Guru Sri Chinmoy who started this race. Dragan introduced me to "Shorty," a onetime professional actor who is in his 70's and in excellent shape. Shorty is also a follower of Sri Chinmoy. It is my understanding to be a follower you must be a vegetarian and neither drink alcohol or smoke. You can be any religion you want but you must believe in a higher power. Followers also believe that some day we will stop killing ourselves in wars over religion and power. This might take hundreds of years or even longer. Another belief is you should help other people in any way you can. Disciples believe these things. They are also celibate. My goal was 40 miles and I did 46.

Day 5: The weather changes to hotter and more humid with a few hours of rain. I am very tired by now and have abandoned my tent and moved into the large male runners' tent provided by the race. I could not get in and out of the small tent easily because I was so stiff and sore. I took longer breaks, which made it harder to move my stiffened 60-year-old body once I started moving again. Same story with my blistered feet. It would take them a couple of laps to get used to moving again and they actually felt better after a few laps. The same volunteers kept coming back day after day. They were all followers of the Guru and some of the nicest people I have ever met. They did not even mention their beliefs unless you asked them. Some of the volunteers sang and played different musical instruments. One played the drums and chanted as runners passed by. Others counted laps, prepared food, washed runners' clothes, and even ran errands for runners. The Guru lives in NYC and came down every day. They treated him like Catholics treat the Pope. They set up a fancy tent for him and followed him around holding an umbrella over his head. Sri Chinmoy handed out food, candy, and ice cream bars to the runners as they passed by and the runners thanked him. I looked forward to seeing him and the ice cream bars. There was only a handfull of runners in both races that are not followers of Sri Chinmoy so this was quite an event for them. My goal was 40 miles and I did 43. Having 275 miles I felt very confident of reaching my 300 mile goal since I had 24 hours to go.

Day 6: I was mostly walking now with a big smile on my face and talking to other runners. I promised myself to take a very long break when I attained 300 miles. Carl, Fay, Anthony, and Joey showed up and this really made my day. They walked with me, asking me how I felt and questions about the race. I told them I planned to reach my 300-mile goal and felt great mentally and have no serious injuries. They stayed for a few hours and planned to be back tomorrow. Some people associated with Camp Sunshine also showed up a little later. They were from the Bronx and Queens. Two of them volunteered at Camp Sunshine and brought me a $500.00 donation. This was another morale booster. What a great day. Don from Queens has also showed up at night to see if I needed anything and to make sure I was alright. I reached my goal of 300 miles at 12:30 am and headed for the big tent, sleeping bag, and long break. About 5:30 am I rose, had a little breakfast, and started doing laps. When there were only a few hours to go I decided to get in as many miles as possible and ended up with 320 miles.

The highlight of the race for me was the people I met. There was the oldest runner in the Ten Day race, a 62-year-old woman from Russia who was always smiling and often bouncing a ball. Rimas won the Ten Day race with 665 miles even though he only did 12 miles on Day 2. There was Dragan who at only 34 years of age has lived in Greece, Serbia, Portugal, India, and his favorite, the U.S. Glen Turner, Bob Oberkehr, Mark Dorion, and Romie Dzierlatka, the American runners I met, will be remembered for their toughness and persistence. They also had a great sense of humor when a little humor was needed. Sri Chinmoy and his followers did a great job at the race and made this event something special for me.

The top male in the Six Day finished with 420 miles and a women won the race overall with 450. I came in 6th and got a nice trophy handed to me by Sri Chinmoy. The volunteers had told the Guru about Camp Sunshine and he told me I did a noble thing running for Camp Sunshine. I may not be a follower but I felt honored when he said that to me. I considered myself lucky to have reached my goal as far as 300 miles was concerned. The weather was good for running most of the time. The course was easy, volunteers outstanding, emails cheered me, and the food was excellent even though I am not a vegetarian. Having a goal to raise $6000 for Camp Sunshine really motivated me.

I raised over $6,500 thanks to Erik Boucher for the website, Auburn Firefighters' Local 797, Mike Smith (CS) for all the effort he put in and the many donations from individuals and businesses.

Carl and Fay showed up to give me a ride to their home in CT. Going without beer for 6 days was something I had not done since basic training. Carl had a cooler of beer which solved that problem. I also went without dead animal food for 6 days. Greasy hamburger and fries never tasted so good. Thanks to Carl and Fay, I had a good night's sleep at their home before heading back to Maine. I cannot even imagine how many brain cells I killed in this race.

Great Wall of China Marathon

I had wanted to do the Great Wall of China marathon for a few years and when the 50 States Club made it a World Tour race I decided to do it with these friends. Denise and I flew out of Portland at 7:20 am on May 11th and arrived in Beijing the next day 2:30 pm their time. We met our tour guide at the airport and took a bus to our excellent 4-star hotel. We started our day the next morning with an excellent buffet breakfast in the hotel; we had a choice of both American and Chinese food selections. The hotel also served as a gathering place for runners to chat. Almost every day there would be tours we could take. A visit to Tiananmen Square, the Forbidden City's Imperial Palace, and the Temple of Heaven was the first tour we took. Another nice tour was a boat ride to the Summer Palace that also included lunch.

I did not want to go to China and not see the terra-cotta warrior excavation site. This is a burial site of a Chinese emperor; it covers 40 square miles and took 700,000 people 38 years to construct!! Only a small portion has been excavated so far. We flew East China airlines to Xian which was about an hour and a half flight. We stayed at a 5-star hotel for two nights and took in a play.

On Thursday, May 18th, we got our first look at the Great Wall of China where we would be running. A 3:45 am wakeup call enticed us to breakfast and by 5:00 am we were on our way by bus. About an hour into our bus ride we pulled over for a bathroom break. There are no bathrooms on the bus, bring your own toilet paper and find a bush. This is also where we met some more buses from Jixian and formed a 20 bus convoy. We stopped one more time for a bathroom break and then arrived at the Great Wall. This trip is mandatory for all runners so they will know how difficult this race will be. This is the time you can switch races if you want to do the half or 10k instead.

This section of the Great Wall is on the side of a mountain and has 1,800 stairs of various sizes. We run on them twice making for 3,600 uneven stairs. The highest elevation is about 4700' and there is a section where there is no wall and you have to hold onto a rope to traverse it.

This was going to be a tough race for me especially since I could hardly walk when I first got to China from doing the 6 Day.

We did a tour of a part of Beijing where people still live the old way. They are in single story homes crowded together with a community shower and bathroom. We rode rickshaws and visited a kindergarten class. This tour showed us a different part of Beijing and the kindergarten class was the best.

May 20th started with a 1:45 am wakeup call and by 3:00 am we were on the buses .The race started at 7:30 am and Becky and Denise were doing the 10k and all the 50 Staters the marathon. Bob Wehr was my pacer in this race. Without him I doubt I would have finished under the 8 hour cut off. The first mile or so was flat and on an asphalt road, next came 2 miles of uphill that we walked. Then it was onto the Wall for 3.2k where most people at the back where we were walk the stairs. It was the fear of falling down the very steep stairs that kept people from running. There is a rope that runners hold onto where the Wall has collapsed and there is a steep drop off. There was a backup of runners at this point and you had to wait your turn. Bob and I were now off the wall and back on flat asphalt, dirt, and concrete roads for a few miles. We then went through small villages that were the highlight of the race for us.

Children were handing us flowers and saying hi in Chinese or English and we answered back in the opposite language. They laughed and posed for our pictures. I prize a picture of an old man with a military coat who removed his pipe so he could smile for the camera exposing just a few teeth. These children and villagers lined the streets and were extremely friendly and excited to see us. Until mile 21 or so we were on a mix of rough dirt roads, concrete, and asphalt with lots of hills. At 21 you reached the Wall and headed uphill. The steps seemed endless and runners were stopping constantly to catch their breath. This and just before the Wall were the only places Bob and I passed runners. This part of the Wall seemed to go on forever but was only 2.5k. Finally off the wall we ran down a steep hill and then a flat section of road brought us to the finish. The cut off was 8 hours and we did it in 7:44:56. Unfortunately about 30 runners did not make the cut off. Two runners were disqualified for cutting the course. Thanks for pulling me through, Bob. A couple of cold beers, a Subway sandwich, and a great massage and we headed back to the hotel.

On Sunday, we went to the Beijing Hotel for a "Gala Party" put on by the marathon organization. The food, ice sculptures, and awards ceremony were all excellent and well worth going to. This was an excellent trip that the 50 States Club did through travel agent Kathy Loper. We had no problems at all and met some very friendly Chinese and many 50 Staters. One Chinese college student acted as our tour guide. He introduced himself and said he wanted to improve his English and could he walk with us showing us around Tiananmen Square. It was interesting to talk to him and we enjoyed his company. The air pollution in Beijing was bad and I did get diarrhea but other than those two things and a terrific toothache it was great trip. The diarrhea happened as we were delayed on the tarmac getting ready to take off. The flight attendant told me to get back in my seat. I told him I had diarrhea and he still insisted I get back in my seat. No way, I am not going shit in my pants and sit in it for 12 hours so I pushed by him. Oh, what a relief it is. Next thing I hear is the pilot threatening to go back to the gate if anyone else got out of their seat. Boy, did I get a lot of dirty looks as I walked back to my seat. We arrived home May 23rd and I had a tough 50k scheduled for the 27th.

Pineland 50k Trail Race

My friends Ian Parlin and Erik Boucher were putting on this first time 50 mile/ 50k Pineland Trail race about 10 miles from my home so I had to do it. Carl stayed over at my house with Fay and the kids. I picked up my race number and it was #1. I could hardly walk let alone run. Long story short I came in 77th out of, you guessed it, 77. There were kegs of beer at the finish. Figuring all the good brain cells I had killed doing the Umstead 100 miler, 320 miles at the 6 Day, and Great Wall of China I should kill some bad brain cells. It was explained to me that when you drink beer it kills these weaker, inferior brain cells. It is something like the survival of the fittest. The wolf attacks the weaker animals in a herd thus improving the herd's gene pool with the genes of the smarter and stronger animals. Beer does the same thing, killing the inferior brain cells which allows stronger and smarter brain cells to take their place. So that is why I drank so much beer after my races and continue to do so. I am still not very smart but would be much dumber if I laid off the beer.

Western States and Leadville Marathon

Brother Walter and I flew into San Francisco on June 21st where we met Carl. Our plan was to crew and pace Carl at Western States, then spend a week traveling to the Leadville marathon. Carl did not make the 22 mile cut off time by 4 minutes and was pulled from the race. The heat got to Carl and he was feeling very light headed and dizzy when pulled. Our only job now was to pick up Carl's drop bags that contained clothes and other items he would have needed in the race. A problem occurred when Walter did not take my advice to hydrate and bring a couple of bottles of water for our trip down to the Rucky Chuck river. It was downhill for about 3 miles to a drop bag and the further down we went the hotter it got. About a half mile before the drop bag location Walter was feeling the effects of dehydration. I told him to start walking slowly back up the hill, gave him some of my water, since he did not bring any, and told him I would meet him once I got the drop bag. Walter had collapsed on the side of trail by the time I got back to where he was and he could not move. I gave him the last of my water and continued to a Western State aid station. At first the person in charge of the station refused to help my brother saying he was not part of the race and had no business going into the canyon if he could not hike in and out on his own. Finally, after I told him my brother could die without help, he sent 2 volunteers on an ATV to get him out. BTW the volunteers were eager to help and did an excellent job helping Walter, taking him right up to where are car was parked. The asshole in charge gave me a hard time when I went to fill my water bottle for the hike out. I was so pissed I almost left without filling it but showed him my pacer number and filled the bottle. Walter was humbled by this event and from then on started listening more to the advice of a younger, smarter and wiser brother.

Next day Carl drove us to San Francisco where we picked up a rental car and went to Kings Canyon National Park and spent the night in a rustic cabin. I love big trees and this National Park had them. At the General Grant tree grove we saw the 3rd and 4th largest Sequoia trees in the world. Next was Sequoia National Park where we saw the General Sherman giant sequoia, the largest tree on earth. From here we drove to Las Vegas crossing the Mojave desert to Las Vegas where we spent the night. The drive from Vegas to Leadville was probably the most scenic and interesting one I have ever taken in just a 5-day period and would recommend it to anyone. We went to at least 7 National Parks, numerous State Parks and national monuments. Bryce, Zion, Capitol Reef, Glen Canyon, Natural Bridges, Arches and Canyonlands are some of the National Parks we visited. All of these plus Moab and much more are very close together.

Once we arrived in Leadville we met up with Carl, Ron, Andy, and Kathy Velazco. When we went to pick up our race packets I was admiring the finisher's medal. The race director asked if I liked it to which I replied yes. He said "you have to earn that" I asked him if there was a time limit and he said no. I then replied with a grin "I will earn that medal but you might have to wait awhile for me to finish." That night at dinner is when Kathy found out Andy operated on my hand in a motel room. She was not happy about it.

Leadville, CO, is the highest town in the US at 10,200', about twice as high as the mile high city of Denver. It is an old mining town that now relies partly on tourism. The "Race Across the Sky" marathon starts at 10,200' with about a half mile on pavement before you get on old mining and 4-wheel drive roads; some of these are EXTREMELY rough. There are a few miles of nice single track trail and a snowfield that we could easily do. There was 6,500' of elevation gain and loss. Mosquito Pass was the turnaround point at 13,185'. They have an award called the "Last Ass Through the Pass" and our friend Gene Bruckert got it for being last. Gene not only finished last but also won his age group since he was the only runner over 70 to finish what I think is the toughest marathon I have ever done, but also one of the most scenic. Walter spent the day with the town drunk and between the two of them drank all my beer. Walter and I flew out of Denver the next day.

Andy Velazco remembers the Leadville trip this way:
In 2006 we decided to meet in Leadville for the marathon. The idea was to see how the altitude affected us and to decide about the 100. So Mike Brooks, Ron Paquette, Carl Hunt, Mike Smith, and myself met in July 3 days early to acclimatize ourseves to the rarified 10,000' atmosphere. Leadville was a quiet mining town experiencing an economic slump due to the closing of the largest employer – the mine. The Leadville 100 had spawned a marathon, half marathon, fifty miler, and biking events. All this brought much-needed revenue to the area. The marathon started in town and headed straight up towards the mountain range. The half runners split at 2 miles, while the mara- thoners run for about 8 miles before both groups converge at the base of the trail to Mosquito Pass. The turnaround for both the marathon and half is at 13,300', a climb of about 1000' per mile.

It was very interesting how exponentially more difficult the trail became as we climbed up. Eleven thousand feet is easy in comparison to 12,000 feet. But from there every 100 feet is more difficult that the one before. The path was narrow, and the runners going up have to let the faster runners have right-of-way. We all climbed at different speeds, but we met on the trail, at about 12,000'. The air was crisp and clear and we could see for a hundred miles. We stopped to talk and take some pictures before some of us went down and some up. We got caught by a small thundershower on the way down. That is very typical of mountain running. Eventually, we all made it back to town and the finish line.

Leanhorse 100

Walter and I flew out of Boston and arrived in Rapid City, SD, and were greeted upon arrival with 106-degree temperature on August 23rd. We spent a couple of days being tourists. First stops were Lead and Deadwood, SD, where we visited a few casinos and the graves of Wild Bill Hickok, Calamity Jane, and Potato Creek Johnny. Wild Bill was shot in the back while playing poker in Deadwood and is buried next to Calamity Jane who claimed to be his girlfriend. Next was Devil's Tower in WY, site sacred to Native Americans. It is well worth the trip to see the Tower and learn the Indian legend about it. Back in SD we visited Custer State Park and saw plenty of buffalo, white tail deer, and pronghorn antelope and enjoyed feeding the wild burros that roam the park. There were many attractions near this part of SD including the Badlands, Crazy Horse, Mt. Rushmore, and many others that I have visited on other trips.

On August 26th at the start of the Leanhorse 100 miler the temps were in the 50's with light rain. The area was in the middle of a drought and 106 degrees one day to the 50's was quite a surprise for me. There is a 50 miler and 50k along with the 100 miler. This was a rails to trails race mostly and an out and back for the 100. The trail was gravel and crushed rock with long gradual uphills and downhills. It was very windy at times, stayed cool and rained almost constantly. I saw lots of runners I knew but most were doing the 50 miler or 50k with the exception of Tom Adair. Tom finished his first 100 miler at Umstead after many tries this year and when I saw him cross the finish line, there was a crowd of friends gathered and cheering loudly. Tom was the happiest guy at the race I believe. Tom was ahead of me and did finish his second 100 of the year. I got to the 50 mile turnaround in 13 hours even. It was dark by now and I was slowing down more every mile. I was cold from being soaked for so long.

At the race briefing we were told there were mountain lions in the area of the race. Going through the town of Custer at night there were deer everywhere. I must have seen at least 100. A light of my headlamp would light up many eyes on the side of the trail. I could not see what they were but wondered if one set of eyes was that of a mountain lion. This was probably payback from when I told Walt about the mountain lion at Western States. I passed at least 8 runners in the last 50 miles and saw more warming up at an aid station. As daylight came I could see runners moving ahead of me. Each time I caught up to one it turned out to be a fence post. How do fence posts move? Well anyway I was passing them like they were standing still. Once I knew what was happening I just grinned at the moving posts. Getting to the finish line the race director, whom I knew from running part of the Bataan Death March with, let out a big cheer. "Mike, I am so glad to see you!" That made me feel really good until he added the words, "you are last, now we can take down the finish line." Shaking like crazy I had the heater on full blast all the way back to the motel, then a nice very long hot shower. Only 51 runners out of 80 starters finished the 100 miler; I might have been last but I did finish. At the awards ceremony all finishers got a beautiful buckle gold plated with Black Hill's gold.

Equinox Marathon

Fairbanks, AK, was where I would finish a marathon in every state for the second time on September 16th at the Equinox Marathon. Denise and I flew into Fairbanks and stayed at the excellent 7 Gables Inn (recommended by Bob Hilderbrant, whom I paced at Umstead).

Denise and I went to the town of North Pole, the river boat discovery tour, and visited Denali National Park. Something we should not have done was drive our rental car on the Dalton Highway up to the Arctic Circle. The rental agreement specifically tells you not to go on this road which leads to the North Slope oil fields.

The Dalton Highway, also known as the Haul Road, is a gravel road with lots of rocks, some sharp, that can puncture a car tire or crack a windshield. If it is wet the mud sticks to your car like cement. It was not a scenic ride and we saw no animals. I was hoping for caribou. Once we crossed into the Arctic Circle we turned around. If I was to do this again, it would be with a rental car that allowed travel on this road.

I met Gene Bruckert at the start line and we ran the entire race together. The course was a mix of dirt roads, pavement, and single track trail. There was a lot of climb up to the top of Ester Dome. Part of the descent is down a very steep trail called the Alder shoot which I walked down sideways. This is a fairly tough race but Gene and I had fun doing it. Bob Hilderbrant and his wife Patsy met us at the finish line along with Denise. They had a nice dinner after the race that volunteers catered with homemade food. Denise got a phone call saying her father was very ill so she had to leave early. I followed a few days later.

On November 17, 2006, I would turn 61 and I found a race where I could run 61 miles on that day. This was the UltraCentric 48-hour race in Grapevine, TX. The race started at 9:00 am on the 17th giving me 15 hours to do 61 miles. The course was 2.4 mile laps on asphalt that was rough in places. The course was fairly hilly for a multiday. Well, long story short, I missed it by two miles. I finished the 48 hours with 131 miles.

When I was in Grapevine I filled out a short survey in the City of Grapevine magazine that has visitor's questions related to tourists. About 6 months later while I was away my wife got a call that I had won two plane tickets plus two nights in a hotel. She told me about it and I had forgotten about doing the survey and figured it was just a gimmick. Luckily they called back again when I was there and this time I believed them. UltraCentric 48 Hour 2007 here I come!

2006 Totals:

- No injuries I could not run with
- 53 races total
- 19 marathons
- 5 ultras
- 1 DNF 31.4-mile race, did not make cut off

Leadville Trail Marathon Finish:
Andy, Mike, brother Walter, Walt Schuttler, Carl H, Ron P

CHAPTER 13:
PACING, RACES, AND MORE IN 2007

H. U. R. T. 100 Mile Trail Race

Denise and I met Andy, Kathy, Bob W., Becky, Mike, and Sandra in Honolulu. The 4 boys were here to do the H.U.R.T. 100 mile Trail race on Jan. 13th. This was the toughest course per mile I have ever been on in an ultra. Bob W. and I decided before the race that we would stay together. The course is five-20 mile loops through the jungle on Ohau. The trail course had a tremendous amount of Banyon tree roots, rocks, and mud, and there is about half a mile of flat trail. There were places where I slid down on my butt rather than take a chance of falling. It rained off and on during the race. Bob and I only did one 20-mile loop. I was 61 and Bob 63 at the time and we both figured this was a young runner's race. The oldest finisher one year was 56. This year Mike was the only one to make it to 100k out of the four of us. Not to waste a trip to Honolulu we stayed for about a week and went snorkeling and enjoyed the beach.

Henry's 500th

Our friend Henry Reuden was doing his 500th marathon in Green Bay so we wanted to be there. Walter and I met Bob W. at the Minneapolis airport and headed to Fargo, ND, for the inaugural Fargo marathon. Walter drove about ten miles before getting a speeding ticket. At the start of the Fargo marathon on May 19th we met Andy, Kathy, Walt, Bob W., Gene, and Mike. I ran with Gene for a while, got some nice pictures of myself with some ladies in their 50's dressed up in Victoria Secret outfits. They were hot stuff, I tell ya. After we finished the race in the Fargo Dome, we all showered and piled into the car for the 520 mile ride to Green Bay, Wisconsin. Walter drove, Andy, Walt and Bob W. sat in the back and I rode shotgun. We arrived in Green Bay a little after midnight.

As we lined up for the Green Bay Marathon we met Henry plus a few other runners we knew. This race is very close to Henry's home town, so it had special meaning for him to do his 500th here. Andy, Walt, Bob W., and I did the entire race with Henry finishing inside Lambeau Field. We exited Lambeau where Henry's family was waiting for him. They had a small keg of beer, snacks and "cheese curds" waiting for all of us. We dropped off Walt and Andy at the Green Bay airport and Walter, Bob W., and I drove back to Minneapolis and flew out the next day.

Carl's Western States 100 miler

Walter and I flew in a few days early to Sacramento, CA, so we could do some sightseeing before crewing and pacing Carl at Western States. We first went to Yosemite National Park, getting a room in the Park near Yosemite Falls. We went to the Falls, El Capitan, and Glacier Point and hiked around Mariposa Grove. The next day we drove over Tioga Pass, which is extremely scenic and closed because of snow most of the year. Arriving at Tahoe Inn, Tahoe City, we met up with Carl and Andy. We went to Squaw Valley for the race briefing and packet pickup. From there, it was on to Donner Pass Visitor's Center. This is where the Donner party got snowed in and resorted to cannibalism before winter's end.

Race morning was June 23rd, and Carl and Andy were ready to go. At Robinson Flat, about 22 miles into the race, Andy was hurting; he had fallen and injured his back. When I saw Carl at another aid station around 40 miles, he was hurting and taking too long at the station. I decided to start pacing him earlier than planned. At Forest Hills mile 62 I started pacing.

At the next aid station Carl wanted to sit down and eat. "Eat while you are walking. We don't have time to waste," I said. I told Carl I did not come out here again to see him not finish. I said it in a pissed off voice. Carl got a little mad which helped get him going a little harder. We crossed the Rucky Chuck river in waist deep water. Walter was supposed to meet us with dry shoes and clothes. No Walter. We started up the steep hill and met him about 20 minutes later with the supplies. I looked at Carl asking if we really needed to change shoes and we both decided to save time and skip it. Once we crossed No Hands Bridge and made it up the next hill with just a few miles to go I knew we would finish in time. Telling Carl this we slowed our pace and went across the finish line in 29:45, 15 minutes to spare. Carl was pissed at me during the race but told me after he would not have made the cut off if I had not pushed him.

Carl's Vermont 100

On July 21 and 22 I would pace Carl again in the Vermont 100 miler. I started pacing at 10 Bear with 32 miles to go. This time was different from Western States. Carl was way ahead of cut off so there was no need to push. We took our time, joked around, and finished around 28 hours.

Cross Country Trip

Walter and I headed out August 9th on a trip that would last until September 5th. The first race I did was near Danville, Illinois, on August 11th. It was called "Howl at the Moon 8 Hour" trail race. The course was 3.39 mile loops with 80% easy grass and dirt trail and about 20% asphalt with just one sizable hill. One runner had a heart attack just a few miles into the race and died right there. The race continued. I ran some loops with Walt and Gene. It would have been an easy race except for the heat. It was in the 90's and very little shade on the course. I enjoyed the race, great volunteers, food, and all the beer you could drink during and after the race.

The next race was the Grizzly marathon on August 18th near Choteau, MT. This was a loop course with about 6 miles of asphalt and the rest gravel roads. It was moderately hilly. There was a huge 60 square mile forest fire nearby and we were given masks to wear at packet pick up. Fortunately, on race morning the wind was blowing the smoke away from the course. I ran the entire race with Larry Macon and had a good time chatting with him. I did manage to get dehydrated and puked at the end which is nothing new for me.

The "Run with the Horses" marathon was in Green River, WY. This was a point to point race with 23 miles on dirt roads and the rest asphalt. Elevation was between 6,000' and 7,500' with lots of hills. The night before the race they had a "Cajun Shrimp Boil" and pasta dinner plus a microbrew fest going on at Expedition Island where the race ends. This was all excellent. I met Ron and wife DonnaJean there. I did the first few miles with Ron and DJ then ran the rest of the race alone. Some runners saw wild horses but I did not. I had a few beers, jumped in the Green River, and headed for Mississippi the long way.

The Tupelo Marathon was known to be hot and humid and that was why it started at 5:00 am. It was 75 degrees and dark at the start on September 2nd. The course is all asphalt and not that hilly. I ran the entire race with Paula Boone which is always enjoyable. It was in the 90's, humid, and sunny by the time we finished.

I was glad I carried a water bottle because I sweat like crazy and dehydrate easy. This was my 200th marathon and with a lot of 50 Staters we took a group picture. I washed off with a garden hose then Walter and I headed out for our 500 plus mile drive to the next day's marathon in Missouri.

On race morning, I went to the lobby of the hotel at 5:30 am to take the bus to race start of the Heart of America Marathon in Columbia, MO. The bus never showed up and I ended up riding in a van on top of water stop tables. It was about 65 degrees at start. This felt cool compared to Tupelo.

That quickly changed as temperatures went into the 90's on this hilly, shadeless course. I was doing better than expected until around mile 20 when I slowed. I was still passing some runners who looked like they were dead on their feet. There was a large plastic pool at the finish line filled with cold water and I soaked in it for about ten minutes. The official temperature reached 99 degrees, no wonder that pool felt so good.

I have estimated that I have been to a thousand places; here is a partial list for this trip plus some other things we experienced. We traveled through 22 states, one Canadian Province, Alberta. We went to 5 national parks, 4 or more national monuments, several state parks, city parks, and numerous museums. We saw black bears, grizzly bears, mountain goats, mule, and whitetail deer, elk, fox, moose, buffalo, marmots, prairie dogs, wild horses, wild burros, and coyotes. The coldest temperature of the trip was 33 degrees in West Yellowstone, WY, and the hottest 110 in The Badlands, SD.

We went to, in this order: Corn Palace, Wounded Knee, Badlands, and Custer State Park all in South Dakota; Little Big Horn Battlefield, WY, Glacier National Park, Road to the Sun, and hiked Hidden Lake trail in Glacier National Park, MT. Next was Waterton Peace Park, Alberta, Canada, Yellowstone National Park, Beartooth Pass,and Chief Joseph Highway. The Buffalo Bill Museum and Cody Nite Rodeo in Cody, WY, were both awesome. South Pass Ghostown, Wild Horse Loop Road, both in WY, north rim of Grand Canyon, Lake Powell Dam, both in AZ, Monument Valley, AZ (truly spectacular, you have seen parts of it on TV and the movies, but in person it is even more amazing), Four Corners National Monument, AZ, CO, NM, and UT, and the Anazi Heritage Center, CO. We drove the San Juan Highway to Telluride, Silverton, and Durango with many stops including Box Canyon Falls and a tour of the Old 100 Gold Mine.

We stopped at Mesa Verde where we got a private ranger tour of the Spruce Tree House. All of these were in CO. The Tahlonteeske Cherokee Museum Court House, OK, had a display of Chief Sequoyah who wrote the first Cherokee written language. In Tupelo we went to the house where Elvis was born and the hardware store where his mother bought his first guitar.

Walter drove on all these trips and did a pretty good job. He only got the car partly stuck once driving up too close to an oil well. He may have over-reacted to finding his car covered with ashes from a nearby forest fire. Walter goes a little overboard in general with his car. Every time he gases up I have to wash ALL the windows while he fills the tank. He has floor mats on top of floor mats. He does not want one set of floor mats to get dirty I guess.

UltraCentric

Last year I won plane tickets for two plus a hotel for two nights in Grapevine, TX. This worked out perfectly since I was planning on doing the UlraCentic 48 hour race this year anyway. My goal was the same as last year: to run my age in miles on my birthday. Now 62, I had a full 24 hours to run the 62 miles. The race started the day before at 9:00 am and I took it easy just doing 38 miles and getting some sleep before midnight. I figured 38 + 62 = 100 sounded good. I started running at midnight; it was cool and a good night for running. In the morning it got warm then up to 81 degrees for the official temperature. There is no shade on the course and coming from Maine it felt "wicked" hot. Well, I did it again. I weighed myself on a scale provided by the race at the start. At 2:00 pm I checked my weight and was down 12 pounds. I probably sweat 2 or 3 times as much as a normal person and have trouble staying hydrated. I should have carried a water bottle but did not, 5 ounce cups at water stops were not enough for me. Being tired did not help as far as keeping track of liquid intake goes. Will I ever learn?

I sat down and took in about 30 ounces of water, some gel packs, and 3 electrolyte capsules. My back was also hurting big time so it was a struggle getting in the 62 miles but by 9:30 pm I did. Happy freakin' birthday! There were still 11 and a half hours to go in the race. One of the few times I made a smart decision to call it a race. I did 62 miles on my birthday and had 100 miles total so I headed back to the hotel where Denise was already sleeping by the time I got there. Finishing early gave me time the next day to go to Fort Worth, watch the "cattle stampede," and go to the Cow Girl Museum and Billy Bob's Honky Tonk, the biggest Honky Tonk in the world at 100,000 square feet.

ATY 72 hour

It was back to Across the Years 72-hour race; I had the same goal of doing 200 miles. Carl was here again as was Ron Vertrees who never misses a year. I see Carl all the time but Ron just here. I might have said it before but Ron is just the nicest guy and I really enjoy his company. When I started the race, I had a hamstring and hip flexor problem that seemed to get better after 6 hours or so. I got in 80 miles in the first 24 hours. The second day was bad, only 50 miles. By day three all I could do was walk. I was in a good mood though. Carl's wife Fay brought us Starbucks coffee, which Carl is addicted to. I had beer and champaign at midnight on New Year's Eve as the fireworks went off. I finished with 177.7 miles. I took a quick outdoor shower at race site shortly after the 9:00 am race finish and got to the airport in plenty of time for my 1:20 pm flight to Cincinnati where I spent the night because of a snow related fight cancellation. I made it to Portland and home next day, January 3rd.

I felt sick after the race but luckily made it home before diarrhea started. I was also very weak and could hardly walk. I believe I caught something by taking food from bowls that all the runners were sticking their germ covered hands into. I found out later that many of the runners also got sick.

The next year they served more food in individual cups and had hand sanitizer everywhere. I very seldom take food at races that is in bowls; just think of all the sweaty, filthy hands reaching into them! Did some runner just scratch his butt or use the porta potty? Yuck!

2007 Totals:

- Injuries, but none I can't hobble with
- 57 races
- 21 marathons
- 7 ultras

Hawaii HURT 100 miles: Old Mike, Andy V, Bob W, Young Mike

Howl at the Moon: Left to Right:
Carl Hunt, Mike Smith, Me, , Bob Wehr, Andy

Chapter 14:
Plenty of Races in 2008;
I am Diagnosed with
Coronary Artery Disease

A Couple of Trips to Florida

I did the Miami marathon with Ron on January 27th, stayed in Florida for a week with Denise, and had no plans to return to Florida in 2008. A new airline opened up at an old air force base less than 100 miles from my home. I flew them for the Last Chance for Boston marathon in Columbus, Ohio, round trip for $96.30 landing at Columbus airport with Walter on February 15th. About the same time that I booked this flight, I saw a flight for $10.00 each way to Punta Corda, Florida. I saw that the Sarasota marathon was nearby and bought three tickets for $31.80 each roundtrip. The airline would only sell a few tickets at this price. After I got the tickets I called my wife and told her I got tickets for her, friend Nancy, and myself. If someone did not go I was only out a few bucks I figured. Denise and Nancy were delighted and it was back to Florida on February 29th for 5 days and the Sarasota marathon.

Moab 24 Hour

On March 27th Walt and I flew from Portland to Chicago using frequent flyer miles on United Airlines. When we got to our connecting flight gate the plane was still there but they had given our seats away to standby customers. They lied to us about that then booked us on standby putting me as #3 standby and my brother #12 even though they knew we were flying together and have the same last names. We got to Denver late and pissed. The rental vehicle we reserved was supposed to be a compact but when we got to the lot there was a gas guzzling SUV instead. Not wanting to go through the hassle of going back to the counter we took the SUV which turned out to be a very good decision and a lucky one. I was here to do the Moab 24 hour race on March 29th-30th in Moab, Utah.

Having a few extra days we visited Arches National Park, Canyonlands National Park, and took in a few more attractions. The course was a 5.37 mile loop with 400' elevation gain and loss each loop although it seemed like much more than that.

The course consisted of gravel road, slick rock, and loose sand. I had a hard time seeing the course markings on the rock and followed another runner on the first loop and got lost. The downhills across the solid rock were hard on my knees and aching back. When I knew my next lap would be in the dark, I called it a day, figuring I would get lost for sure and my knees would really be pissed at me. I only got in a little over 37 miles.

Our ride on I-70 heading back to Denver changed dramatically as we started up the mountain towards Vail Pass in Colorado at 12,600'. The sign for trucks to put on tire chains was lit up at the base of the mountain. As we started up the mountain we could see why. It was snowing fairly hard and the wind made for near white out conditions. Lucky we had the 4-wheel drive SUV. About a half mile from the top of the mountain all traffic in both directions was stopped.

We were headed east and there was a 70 to 75 vehicle pileup in the westbound lanes. After about an hour we were allowed to continue past the accident which stretched for about a mile. It had started when a tractor trailer jackknifed and an SUV went under it. The guy driving the SUV was killed, his wife seriously injured, and their four children okay. Sadly, they were on their way to Disneyland.

The westbound lanes took 7 and a half hours to clean up and reopen. After all the traffic was cleared from eastbound lanes, they were closed so emergency vehicles and wreckers could get to the scene.

A state trooper with 20 something years experience said he never saw an accident of this magnitude. I do not know how many injuries there were but driving by the accident it looked like there must have been many. We visited Coors brewery and Buffalo Bill's gravesite before flying home the next day.

Hawthorn Half Day Race

Walter, Ron, and I flew into Indianapolis and then met up with Andy and Mike at the hotel we were staying at. Walter and I went to check into our room and it was already occupied. Returning to the front desk I said smiling, "I don't even like sharing a room with my brother, let alone total strangers." We ended up getting one night free. The race we all were here for in Terra Haute, Indiana, was the Hawthorn Half Day on June 14th.

The course was 5k loops on a mix of asphalt and grassy trails with a few hills. It reached 87 degrees and was humid. There was a runner we knew was a cheater. P.P. would cut courses and tell race directors that he mailed in his entry fee but they just haven't received it yet. Another way he would get out of paying an entry is claiming he lost his wallet or he was running for a charity. P.P. did many other despicable things too.

Well, P.P. knew that Mike and I did not like him and knew about his cheating. There were many places you could cut the course in this race but P.P. knew we were keeping track of him so he did not dare. Ron and I ran the entire race together, me calling him Dad at all the aid stations as usual. After this hot, humid race I was really looking forward to a nice cold beer or two, maybe even three. Well as**ole Walter drank all my beer! Boy was I pissed especially because we had to wait for the awards ceremony and I think every-one I knew got an award but me.

On June 21st I did a local race called the Pottle Hill 10k. It is advertised as the toughest 10k in New England because of the hills, especially one big one. I think they exaggerated how hard the course was. I had done this race many times before and knew the last three miles or so are the easiest. I had done a 12 hour race a week earlier but felt fine at the start. About 2 miles into the race and going up a steep hill I had to walk, which I had never done in this race before.

The rest of the race I could only run/walk and my heart rate was 170 which was very high for such a slow pace. When I got done I felt like I was going to pass out and an hour later my heart rate was 110 to 130. My resting heart rate is usually 60. I thought something was wrong so went to my doctor. After some tests he said I had coronary artery disease. The doctor. put me on medications for blood pressure and cholesterol control. On June 28th I ran a 5k and felt fine and my heart rate recovered fast. July 4th was a 10k and same as last weekend I felt good at the end. I ran at least one short race, marathon, or 50k every weekend with mixed results. Heat and pushing hard would cause my heart rate to stay high after a race and I would get dizzy. The strange thing is this was not consistent.

ATY 72-hour race

Guess what? I am back at ATY 72 hour race with a goal of 200 miles. Carl is back also. New to ATY are ultra runners Jeanne Peckinonis and Sara Miller. The four of us will be sharing a "quiet tent." The huge 60' by 100' tent I have always been in is noisy and hard to rest in. The small tent is new this year and was given out on a first ask basis. Jeanne and Sara also did the Hawthorne Half Day and I know Jeanne from New England races. Jeanne's goal was 125 miles so she could outdo her brother's 100 milers. She made a bet with me and all I remember about it is if I did not run 200 miles I would have to wear a pink skirt across the finish line. On the last lap with only 186 miles Jeanne jumped out on the course with the pink skirt. I put it on and crossed the finish line looking pretty sexy I must say except for the hairy legs and three-day beard. When Jeanne got back to Maine she made sure a picture of me in the skirt showed up on a big screen at the Maine Track Club Banquet.

This was the last year I did ATY. The number of ATY runners was limited due to the races being held on a 500 meter course. Each year I would put in to do the race and was picked to do so. There were new race directors for the 2008- 2009 race and I was not picked to run. About a month after the first pick I got an email saying I was in. Well that pissed me off because the RD's knew I had run almost 700 miles on the course and was going for my 1,000-mile jacket goal. They had chosen friends of friends and first timers at this distance ahead of me. They said they wanted to give other runners a chance to do the race. I told them I thought this was unfair, good luck with your race, and I will never do it again. This was one of my favorite races but I now do the Savage 7 marathons the same time of year. Ron Vertrees has passed away and that is one of the things I missed most about doing the race.

In 2008, I was diagnosed with coronary artery disease.

2008 Totals:

- 52 total races
- 20 marathons
- 9 ultras
- total race miles: 1,011

CHAPTER 15:
MY TOUGHEST RACE: SRI CHINMOY SELF TRANSCENDENCE 10 DAY RACE: 2009

This was another fundraiser for Camp Sunshine with a goal of raising $10,000. Mike C.S. came up with the idea, after talking with me, that I should do 500 miles. I thought that was an awful lot for a 63-year-old guy like me. "Damn, that is an average of 50 miles a day." Mike just looked back with that kinda evil grin of his and ensured me I could do it. Well, he talked me into setting 500 as my goal. When Andy found out my goal he told me he would donate $1 per mile for $500, but not a penny if I didn't do 500. Now the pressure is really on me and my old arthritic beat up body. It is going to be a long ten days with no beer and being a vegetarian for this beer drinking, carnivorous old man.

Arriving at the race site the day before, I set up my gear in the big tent and spread my sleeping bag across the wooden planked bed that will be mine for the next ten days. I also put some gear in the dugout area that I was assigned. After shaking hands with some volunteers I knew and the race director, I checked into a nearby hotel in Queens, NYC. I walked around a little and was amazed by all the different ethnic restaurants and people in this crowded borough of NYC.

Day 1: The course this year is roughly the same as when I did the Six Day. A little hill has been added that goes through an asphalt parking lot with a slight pitch. The race started at noon with fewer than 30 runners. There was a slight drizzle that continued off and on to about 10:00 pm. Mark Dorion and Bob Oberhk were back and they are always a pleasure to talk to. You would think the nights would be boring here but this is the city that never sleeps. There are roads you can see from the race course. Every once and awhile you will hear a siren from a police car, ambulance, or fire truck. A motorcycle in the distance got closer and you could hear him shifting gears; when he went by he or she was bent over in an aerodynamic position going well over 100 miles per hour. I have been told the police don't chase them for several reasons.The main one is they probably won't catch them plus they don't want someone killed in the chase. I do 77 miles and feel OK.

Day 2: The weather is okay and I am taking a one hour break every five hours. I am also doing more walking. I've been talking a lot with Luis Rios. Luis lives in Brooklyn, has a rotary phone, never had a driver's license, and uses the subway or buses to get around. Luis has a beard and likes to dress in raggedy clothes. His appearance keeps most people from sitting next to him on the subway. I think that is why he dresses like that. He is a pleasure to talk to and an excellent ultra runner especially for his age of 60 plus. Talking with Luis and the other runners makes the miles go by much faster. He had a bed in the same tent as I did but I never saw him in it but a few times in 10 days. I found out that sometimes he would sleep on the massage table at night which is much more comfortable. I do 55 miles.

Day 3: Just trying to get in 50 miles a day now. My feet are swollen but I do not have any blisters yet. I get in 56 miles, a new personal best for 3 days by 0.3 miles. Not much over my previous personal record, but I will take it. My spirits are high and I am doing the mileage that I wanted to.

Day 4: The temperature gets into the 90's; the sun is out with very little shade on the course. I see some of the women followers of Sri Chinmoy running mile after mile and managing to smile most of the time. The women runners seem to be as tough if not tougher than the men. A woman runner once told me that being able to bear children gives women the ability to endure pain. Followers of the Guru also believe that doing races like this and similar events make you transcend into a better state of mind. I transcended into another state of pain. I have a few blisters now and I am wearing larger size shoes. I do 48 miles.

Day 5: Another day like yesterday, 90's, hot and humid. Brother Walter came down to see me. It was good to see him and shoot the breeze. He came down when I did the Six Day also even though he does not like driving in "The City." Around NYC everybody just calls NYC the city. Ted Corbett visited the runners one day taking pictures and talking to us. Ted Corbett was about 80 at the time. He is one of the best ultra runners who ever lived. Ted Corbett still holds some ultra records. Talking to us he made us feel like we were great runners when none of us will ever be half the runner he was. Ted was a humble man. One of my favorite pictures is Ted Corbett and me with the Ten Day lap board in the back ground. The Six Day runners joined us. It is kind of funny seeing these runners who are "ONLY" doing six days; it's like a half marathoner compared to a marathoner. Most of them started out fast compared to the 10 day runners pace, by night they had slowed. I do 50 miles.

Day 6: Enough is enough! Another day in the 90's, sunny and humid. Records are being set with this heat. This is the northeast in April, not Death Valley in July. I look back fondly at the Six Day race when Sri Chinmoy would hand out ice cream bars to the runners. The Guru has passed away, but his followers still put on sporting events all over the world. The toughest one is the 3,100-mile race around a city block in the summer. I set a six day personal record by 14 miles! Did 50 miles for a six-day total of 334 miles.

Day 7: It is another 90's day, sunny and humid. All the runners are feeling the heat except maybe Pam Reed. She is from Tucson, AZ, and has won Badwater overall. I was surprised to see her here but knowing what a great runner she is I figured she just wanted to try a new challenge. My feet are badly blistered and very swollen. There are three runners over 60 in the race and we are all leaning the same way. I call this "runners' lean." It usually affects older runners when their muscles become fatigued in long races. My theory is the muscles get fatigued unequally, nutrients in your muscles become unbalanced, and/or the course is on a slant as in this case. There was a slant to the pavement in this race and we ran clockwise for all ten days which I believe contributed to our leaning problem. I got in 45 miles between whines and whimpers.

Day 8: Finally, the weather cools after four days of record breaking heat. I am in pretty rough shape. My feet are badly blistered, I have shin splints and achy knees, plus I've gone without beer for seven days and my knuckles are almost dragging on the ground I am bent over so much. I tried to lie on the ground so I could pull my knees up by grabbing my legs with my hands to form a ball; this helps until I start walking again. I have tried massages and a chiropractor at the race but nothing helps my back. I talk to Denise every night which is what I look forward to. She calls Blaine Moore with a report on how I am doing. Blaine puts this online so everyone who is interested can see it. A local newspaper reporter Kathryn Skelton puts it in the paper. Both Blaine and Kathy are enabling me to raise more money. I also get emails from friends that are delivered by the race volunteers every day. I feel like a boy scout getting a letter from home while at summer camp! Happy as happy can be to get emails. Barbara Sorrell, an ultra friend I met at a race, stops by with a check for Camp Sunshine. The amount was odd, I don't remember how much but it was something like $253.27. She told me why it was such an odd amount, it was money she received unexpectedly I believe. For her to come down to the race to see me made my day and the check was a bonus. A painful 42 miles today.

Day 9: Today is pretty much like yesterday, my back my biggest problem by far. There were a few downpours that flooded a small part of the course. Being unable to sleep because I was actually cold has happened the last few days plus being sore all over makes it impossible to get comfortable. All the other runners are in the same boat as me to some extent. Everyone has their own demons. Runners are all very tired and most have blisters. Blisters are considered a minor problem. Shin splints are very common along with very swollen legs and feet. Some runners have cut large sections off the top of their running shoes. Doing this makes room for their swollen feet; others have switched to wearing sandals. I have several different size shoes and put on larger ones as my feet swell. I get 42 miles done and now have 31 miles more to do in 24 hours to reach my goal.

Day 10: I am down in the dumps mentally and physically. I'm struggling to stay on my feet and keep moving. Carl and Fay show up and can't believe how bent over and terrible I look. I have given up on getting to 500 miles. Fay encourages me to keep going and she does a few laps with me. This really helps lift my spirits. It is now taking me 40 to 60 minutes to do one mile! This sounds insane but that is the best I can do. A brisk walk is about 16 to 18 minutes so some people will have a hard time believing such a slow pace. Stopping to bend over every few hundred feet, laying over a hydrant and bench, every lap does not help my pace. I think a tree passed me at 487 miles (smile). The race finishes at noon, we stay for the award ceremony and few handshakes with runners and volunteers, and we head to Carl's.

I am totally wiped out and cannot even drive. With Carl driving my car and Fay driving their car, it's a cold beer and greasy cheeseburger for me. Carl lives in Connecticut and the plan is for me to stay at his home and drive to Maine the next day.

About a quarter mile from Carl's house the car in front of us slows to take a right turn and Carl smashes into it. I saw it coming but did not have time to say anything to Carl. It was a minor accident but my car was not drivable.

As we are waiting for the cops to arrive, Carl's cell phone rings, it is Andy. He asked Carl how I did and then Carl hands me the phone. Andy says, "you know the agreement $500 for Camp Sunshine but only if you did 500 miles?"

I start whining to Andy about my back problems and ask Andy for $491. "I am not giving you $491 (pause); I will give you the whole 500."

Well this made me feel better about the accident. By the time the cop showed up I was sleeping and looked half dead. The cop asked Carl, "what the hell happened to him?" I had no insurance to pay for the damage to my car and Carl insisted on paying to get it fixed.

Once at Carl's they were going out somewhere and asked if I would be okay. I said yes. A little while later I got in the tub and fell asleep. Waking up when the water cooled the only way I could get out of the tub was to crawl out then grab onto the sink to get onto my feet. I think I am getting too old for this Ten Day shit.

The next day Carl gave me a loaner that I drove back to Maine. We agreed that when I came back we would all go into "the City" for some fun. Carl grew up in the Bronx and knows his way around NYC. The girls wanted to go to a play, Carl and I did not. I devised a scheme that worked perfectly. I told Denise that Carl hates plays and I do not want to see him made to go. Carl helped me so much picking me up after the race, fixing the car, blah blah blah. Carl told Fay the same thing about me. It worked; Carl and I went to an Irish pub while the girls enjoyed the play. Leaving our hotel Carl gave us a tour of his old neighborhood.

My $10,000 goal was surpassed by at least $1,000. Local 797 of the Auburn Firefighters' donated $600. A friend of mine Michele Tribou made the best donation. Michele had just recently opened Heidi's Brooklyn Deli. She said money was a little tight with the business just starting and would it be okay to donate $500 at a rate of $50 a month. What a sweetheart, I never got a donation like this before, nice. Michele at one time worked at the YMCA. Her last day of work I brought her some flowers and was giving her a big hug just as my wife walked in. Try to explain that one especially when I don't buy Denise flowers very often! All the donations I got were special to me. You meet the nicest people raising money for children in need.

Big 5 Marathon Entabeni Game Reserve, South Africa, June 20th, 2009

The Big 5 Marathon gets its name from Africa's big 5 animals: lion, elephant, rhino, leopard, and the water buffalo. Walter and I flew to Johannesburg, South Africa from at Atlanta, a 15 hour 8,500 mile flight. The 50 States Club organized a group of us through a travel agent. The package which included almost everything once we got to South Africa. We spent one night in Johannesburg then traveled three hours to Wildside Safari Camp in the Entabeni Game reserve. We stayed in one of 20 or so tents there. All the tents had wooden floors, bathrooms with showers, regular beds with electric blankets and phones. Meals were buffet style in a nice dining area with a bar nearby. The meals and accommodations were excellent. The animals were all around the camp in daylight hours and some wandered in at night. After dark you must be with an armed ranger if you leave your tent.

The most common animals in camp were baboons, monkeys, and impalas. Walt did see a giraffe next to our tent one day. We heard a lion roar close by one night and there were elephant tracks just behind our tent. We went on more game drives than scheduled in the itinerary. The drives were 2 hours or longer and were in the early morning and late afternoon going into darkness. It was winter there and we wore gloves, hats, and a jacket and still felt cold in the open Land Rovers during game drives. The highlights of the game drives were many. Two cheetahs stalking impalas, one making a kill about 100' from us. A mother rhino chasing a male away from her baby. The baby rhino chasing away a jackal that annoyed it once too often. A male lion started roaring about 200' feet from our Land Rover and slowly walked by within a few feet on his way towards a lioness and two cubs. Another time we were looking for elephants for a few hours and saw none.

Heading back to camp we came across a herd of about a dozen. Watching two hippos and a baby munching on water plants was another highlight. We saw zebras, giraffe, wildebeest, warthogs, kudos, and impalas almost every day. The game drives were all great, we saw all this, drove the marathon course, ran the marathon and much more in just a 4 night package in the reserve.

After about a 45 minute drive, we arrived at the marathon start which was at 8:00 am. It was sunny and about 50 degrees as the race started down a hill on a dirt road then we turned onto a steep uphill that is the highest point in the race at 5,200'. The lowest point was 3,600'. The upper part of the course is the easiest with an out and back on a rocky road. Now the fun starts.

While doing the Ten Day race I met a South African who had done the Big 5. Brian told me about a very steep hill on the course and what a killer it was. Having run the Mt. Washington Road Race in NH, the steepest road race in America per mile, I figured this hill would not be so bad ass. We drove up this hill to get to race start and I could see what he was talking about. I have been running with two South Africans almost from the start Paul and Barry. They told me to "skip" down the hill to save my knees from injury.

The three of us walked and skipped down the 1.5 mile hill with an elevation loss of 1,200' with a 40 degree incline some places. This made Mt. Washington look like a gradual upgrade. The hill is the only part of the course that is not gravel or loose sand. It is concrete because it would wash away if not. At the bottom of the hill the course was called Lion Country. Armed rangers try to keep dangerous animals away from the runners. We did not see any dangerous animals during the race.

The course is mostly flat here but is soft beach like sand. After doing this part of the course, we had to go up the steep hill. Paul and Barry are both experienced ultra runners. Paul has done races up to 1,000 KM. Paul had broken his ankle a few months before the race so did not train much for it. We all had a tough time going up the mountain, it's not a hill anymore, I figure, especially Paul. Once on top Paul became very dizzy and felt like he was going to pass out. After a short break he felt better and we continued. It was in the low 70's now with water stops about every 2.5 miles.

My mates and I were going slow walking and running. Paul was still hurting and about 2 miles from the finish we stopped again. We were all out of water and Paul really needed some. A volunteer was sent ahead to bring some back and we waited for Paul. Paul urged me to go ahead, but no way did I want to leave him with just Barry. We got water and slowly finished the race going over the 7 hour cut off time. I think Paul being such a famous and well liked South African ultra runner is why they gave us a finish time anyway. I was 7:20.

The next day we headed back up the mountain to a hotel where the race started. There were African dancers and music to enjoy before a brief awards ceremony. The dinner was excellent with lamb, beef, impala, and plenty of fruits and veggies. Paul and I talked for awhile. Paul told me he designed and manufactured marathon and other medals for a living.

I mentioned I was finishing a marathon in every state for the third time at the Kauai Marathon and he told me he designed that medal. He asked if I told anyone at the race that I was finishing the states and I told him no and that was that, or so I thought.

Paul invited me back and said I could stay at one of his two homes, the one just outside Krueger Park. Hippos and elephants are constantly in his yard along with other wildlife. After exchanging email addresses with Paul it was a hairy after dark ride down the mountain in the Land Rover, probably one of the few vehicles that could make the trip.

A big thanks to Steve and Paula Boone for making all the arrangements. It is always a good time traveling with a bunch of 50 Staters.

Kauai Marathon, Hawaii on September 9th

This is a follow up to the Big 5 Marathon. I met my other brother Paul and his wife Barbra in Kauai and we shared a condo together staying for a week. The race was harder than I expected. It had the dreaded three H's: hot, hilly, and humid. It also rained several times during the race which I liked because it cooled me off.

Approaching the finish line, I could hear them say here comes the guy we have been talking about. Unbeknownst to me, Paul from South Africa had told them I was finishing a marathon in every state for the third time. They called me up on the stage and presented me with a special medal Paul had made. It had my name, 3x50 States plus the regular medal on the ribbon. Both medals look to be gold-plated. You meet the nicest people running marathons.

2009 Totals:

- No Injuries I could not run with
- 48 total races
- 7 marathons
- 9 ultras
- total race miles: 1,285

Day 8 of 10: The Runner's Lean

CHAPTER 16: ANOTHER CROSS COUNTRY TRIP AND TORTURE BY TREADMILL 2010

Brother Walter kept bugging me about taking another long trip out west so I decided to line up as many races as possible in places I had not been to yet. Walter did all the driving and we left his home in Massachusetts on April 6th. We arrived in Abilene, KS, on April 9 after we'd stopped at Jefferson City, MO, to check off another capitol visited and a few other attractions on the way. I ran the Eisenhower marathon on April 10. It was an easy course and I ran it mostly alone. I did see some friends at the pasta dinner the night before but none of them ran my pace. It rose to 80 degrees so it was a little warm for me.

The next day was the Brew To Brew 42 mile ultra. I wanted to do this race because it started at a brewery and ended near a brew pub where I could enjoy a few cold ones after the race. It was also pretty close to the Eisenhower marathon. Brew to Brew starts in Kansas City, MO, and ends in Lawrence, KS. There was an early start for some solo runners and a few relay teams. Most relay teams started at 7. There were only about 50 solo runners and I soon found out the race was designed more for the hundreds of relayers. It was dark at the start and I was concerned about getting lost as runners were going faster than me. There were many turns but early in the race there were volunteers at all of them even the spiral staircase I went up. For the first six miles, the course was on levees next to a river and that made for easy running. After that I was on asphalt roads with some long hills and no shade. I felt pretty good for the first 15 miles or so. After 15, the heat and hills started to get to me. Miles 20 to 23 were steep hills, no shade, and it was hot. I carried a water bottle but would run out between water stops (they were 4-5 miles apart, great for relay runners, not so for solo runners). The course was flat and on gravel roads for about 3 miles.

At mile 29 you take a pontoon boat across a narrow river or you could take a long detour and run to the other side. There was no line for the boat and even if there was I would have taken the pontoon. Miles 30 to 40 were on hilly gravel roads and it was in the 90's. I was just about crawling up a hill thirsty as hell when this bystander asks, "do you want a bottle of water?" I quickly said yes not realizing he was talking to the runner behind me. She declined the water and the nice guy gave it to me saving my dehydrated butt. You meet the nicest bystanders running! There was a water stop at mile 40 where I rested for 5 minutes and took in plenty of liquids. Feeling better I left with a relay runner and we finished the last easy 4 miles along a levee together. After meeting the family of the runner I ran with and getting a hug from her we headed to Topeka, KS, to visit another state capitol. Walter was surprised I did not want to go for a beer. Musta been something wrong with me. The real excitement for the day was when Walter fell asleep driving. I was nodding off and all of a sudden it felt like we were going down a rough road at high speed. Before I could say anything he had the car back on the road. When I asked him what happened Walter calmly said he fell asleep.

With 5 days before my next race, we went to Denver, Garden of the Gods, and Pike's Peak all in Colorado. Garden of the Gods is a must see with its towering rock formations. It has rock climbing and many other attractions you can see from your car or you can hike the many trails. The Garden of the Gods city park is not far from Pikes Peak. From there we went to Cheyenne, WY, and then a long drive to Twin Falls, ID. There we watched people parachute from a bridge over the Snake River not far from where Evil Knievel tried to jump the river on his motorcycle. We arrived in Wenatchee, WA, a day before the race. This is considered "The Apple Capitol of the World" and the apple trees were in full bloom. We drove for miles and saw nothing but huge orchards with various fruit trees covered with blossoms. The Wenatchee Marathon would be the easiest marathon of this trip. The course was two loops on mostly asphalt paths crossing the Columbia River twice each loop. The course was scenic and I saw a few deer while running the race. After a few handshakes and grabbing some food we were off. It was a 200 mile drive to Spokane where I had a 50k trail race scheduled for the next day. I woke up at night shaking, sweating like crazy and feeling cold all at the same time. It turned out be a perfect excuse not to do the 50k and head to Yellowstone National Park instead.

We stopped at Nevada City ghost town and Virginia City's Boot Hill on the way. Six men were hanged in one day by vigilantes and were buried on Boot Hill along with other outlaws. We stayed in West Yellowstone for several days after arriving on April 19th. They had just opened much of the park a few days earlier. It had been closed due to snow. I have visited Yellowstone many times and it is one of my favorite places. The scenery is spectacular and you never know what kind of animals you will see but buffalo and elk are the most common. This trip we saw lots of buffalo and elk, as well as a grizzly fairly close up, bald eagles, and coyotes. One coyote was on the side of the road when he lifted his leg and started peeing on a tree as he looked at us, then just calmly walked away.

As we made our way towards ND we stayed in some interesting small towns and slept in a hotel that was a converted flour mill. We also stopped at the exact center of the nation (including AK and HI) in Belle Fourche, SD, where a few years later I would run a marathon. We slowed down in a small town when we saw a cop car with an occupant behind the wheel. Something didn't look right. Further investigation revealed a manikin dressed in a police uniform. It worked. Once in ND we went to Roosevelt National Park which is in two sections. In the southern park we saw bison, mule deer, prairie dog towns, and at least 50 wild horses. I have seen wild horses before and they would not let you get close to them. Some of these horses would let us walk within 20' of them and their very young foals. In the north section we saw bison, longhorn cattle, and bighorn sheep. Both parks have beautiful scenery and a lot fewer visitors than other parks.

The night before the Tressle marathon, in Minot, ND, I had a temperature of 102 degrees and the chills which was similar to Spokane, WA, the week before. It was about 50 and windy at the start. When I began the race I felt like I could not catch my breath but at least it was not a 50k with a strict cut-off time. There were only 25 runners in the marathon and it got pretty lonely once the half marathoners separated from us. There was one really big hill you did twice. About 19 miles was asphalt and 7 miles on a gravel loop way out in the country. I struggled through the race finishing next to last and was glad I did not have another race next day.

On our way to WI we visited the Great Plains zoo, the Spam museum (the kind you eat, honest), a few state capitols, and some other attractions. We stayed in Milwaukee, toured the Miller Brewery, Milwaukee zoo, and Harley Davidson Museum. Next it was off to Kenosha for the Wisconsin marathon on May 1st. I met Larry and Cheri Gross just before the start with their race packets and numbers I had picked up for them. I felt good at the 7:00 am start. It was sunny, windy, and about 55. It was an easy course with asphalt and some dirt roads with views of Lake Michigan. I caught up with Larry around mile 20. He went out too fast and was paying for it now. You would think after 700 plus marathons he would pace himself better, smile. We stayed together for a while so I could pick on him for crashing then I went ahead to let him suffer alone.

I shook hands with Larry who came in right behind me, grabbed a brat sausage and a cold beer at the finish, and then Walt and I headed west to the

La Crosse, WI, marathon 259 miles away. We went by a bar with a sign that read "lousy beer and ugly waitresses" but we did not have time to stop. Our hotel was overbooked and we ended up in a honeymoon suite. Just where I wanted to be with Walter. He slept on the floor. I felt pretty good, just a little sore from yesterday's race. Around mile 13 I started having stomach problems but felt better by mile 18. I was passing runners the last few miles; they were mostly walking but it still counts, right? A two-day drive and I was at Walter's and then just a short 175 mile ride home the next day.

This to me was another great trip. There were only a few rainy days, no major catastrophes, and we saw a lot of country and some beautiful animals. I made a few new friends and hopefully learned something from the Brew to Brew race. Sometimes I put a little too much on my plate but it always seems to work out. You meet the nicest people traveling in the USA.

Three States in Three Days:
June 11th to 13th, 2010

Walter and I flew into Denver and stayed in Estes Park, Colorado, the first night. The next day we went to Rocky Mountain National Park which borders Estes Park. We did an easy hike to Alberta Falls and then drove the very scenic Trail Ridge road, the highest paved road in the US at 12,183'. There was still plenty of snow on the ground and we saw elk and moose. From there we drove to Laramie, WY. Then it was a very scenic 400 mile drive to Garden City, UT, population a few hundred, the next day. After checking into a condo, we drove the 50 miles or so around Bear Lake. This was the course of the two Bear Lake marathons. There were two hail storms as we drove around, one covering the road with about an inch of hail. It was cloudy and about 45 when I started the race with Lois Berkowitz on Friday June 11th. There were about 75 runners in the race with at least half of them 50 Staters.

Bear Lake straddles the borders of Utah and Idaho. If you do both marathons you can get credit for doing both states towards a goal of finishing a marathon in every state. The 6,000' elevation bothered me the first few miles but I felt better as we continued into Idaho. Miles 20 to 25 were hilly but running the entire race with Lois made the miles go by fast. Walter met me at the finish in this point to point race and squeezed as many runners as possible into the car for the ride back to the start line in Garden City.

Larry Macon won this race one year, really. Of the 6 runners in the race, 4 got lost and the one with the walker was just seconds behind. After a quick shower we drove to the Oregon Trail visitors' center. They have an excellent program explaining the history and difficulties of traveling the Trail.

I also heard about the famous bear Ephraim. He was hunted for years before he was finally caught. Ephraim stood 9'11". There is a monument to pay tribute to this illusive bear. Everyone in the area seems to have heard about this bear. A steak dinner at the Bear Trapper ended the day. The next morning we were shuttled by bus to the second marathon start.

Lois and I would do the entire race together again. It rained and hailed with winds well over 30 mph. It was so windy I kept my head down and would have missed a turn if a friend, Henry Reuden, behind us had not said to turn right down a very muddy road. This was the only section of both marathons that was not asphalt and was about a mile long. The course was similar to yesterday's. I was miserable at times but I felt good at the end. The finisher's medal for those doing both races had two bears back to back on it. After hugs, handshakes, and a few pictures it was off to Estes Park 500 miles away for tomorrow's marathon. It was a hairy ride with rain, very strong winds and icy spots.

I got up at 5:00 am and it was pouring. Henry gave me a ride to the start so Walter could sleep in. Walter does all the driving on our trips so once in a while I have to be nice to him. This would be the most challenging of the three marathons by far. It was raining and 42 degrees at the start which is at 7,600' elevation. I ran the first few miles with Henry. Those miles were fairly easy except for the 7,000' elevation. Then the fun began.

It was 4 miles uphill to 8,150 'in the pouring rain, my head pounding and blood running out of my nose. I kept telling myself "what does not kill you makes you stronger " "pain is weakness leaving your body" and "it will get better". I might have said why the f...k do I do these stupid things. Finally I got to the top of the mountain and it was mostly downhill to Estes Park. Seeing elk and the spectacular scenery made the downhill run a little easier. My problem was I felt so cold.

This continued to about mile 18, then the rain stopped and I started to thaw out. Catching up to Henry and a couple of other friends I started to feel much better and had my fastest miles at the end of the race.

The finish was on a quarter mile track where I waited for Henry and another runner who would get the surprise of her life. Her boyfriend yelled "will you marry me ?!" as she crossed the finish line, and she accepted.

I felt pretty good after the race, just sore and tired. After a hot shower it was off to Estes Brew Pub for a few pints and a huge order of nachos supreme. It was great seeing friends at all the races and running with some of them. As I get older the races seem to get tougher and more challenging but I still enjoy them.

Rio de Janeiro Marathon, Brazil, July 18th, 2010

This was another 50 States Club trip. After checking into our hotel where most of the 50 Staters were staying we went to packet pickup which was mobbed and very confusing. We then ate at a restaurant near the hotel called Giraffes. It was a fast food place that we really liked. We had beans, rice, and pork chops that were very good and easy to order without knowing how to speak Portuguese.

The next day was race morning. We made a good decision and rented a van to get to the start of this point to point race. Fifteen 50 Staters squeezed into the van. We got lost on the way but got there in time for the 7:00 am start. Lois was concerned about making the 6 hour cut off and wanted me to more or less pace her. It was cloudy, humid, and about 70 at the start for the 2,000 runners. Most of the race is fairly flat and runs along beaches. There are some hills that are not bad and a tunnel you run through. Very few spectators watch the race. Along Ipanema and Copacabana beaches people were walking, riding skateboards, and pushing strollers on the roped off marathon course! Two 50 Staters went straight when I told them they should turn. They did finish after 6 hours I believe. It was about 80 and the sun came out by the time we finished. This is winter in Brazil but it sure felt hot to me. Edson Sanches, who grew up in Brazil, helped us get the right bus back to the hotel. Steve Boone waited for a 50 Stater who was getting medical attention. You meet nice guys like Steve when you are a runner. We went as a group to an excellent meal and Samba show that night.

Next day we went for a walk along Copacabana Beach. Denise saw me looking at the girls in thong bathing suits and commented "I don't see what you get out of staring at a girl's butt." Well, let me tell you those thong bathing suits are what they are "cracked" up to be. Later we took a ride on a gondola to the top of Sugarloaf Mountain for an excellent view of Rio. The next day we went to the Christ Statue which is a must if going to Rio. You can drive up most of the way or take a train; we did the latter. The weather was excellent, the crowds minimal, and we had spectacular views. We also walked around an old section of the city. The last day there included a jungle ride which was more like a ride in a large city park. It was worth doing but we saw no wildlife.

This was a good trip but the trips to the Great Wall marathon and Big 5 in South Africa were much better. Rio is a very dangerous city, especially at night. We stayed in a good part of the city but went in groups at night and did not stray very far from our hotel.

Howl at the Moon 8 Hour race on August 14th, 2010

I flew alone into Indianapolis, IN, where Mike picked me up. Both of us would run this race the next day. I mentioned earlier about doing this race but not a lot about what a fun race it is. There was camping on site, which I did not do. They have a beer truck that is at the race site the day before and day of the race. The food at aid stations is excellent as is the food after the race. The volunteers were the best, even dressing up in costumes. This race fills early every year. The course has changed several times but is usually 20% asphalt and 80% grass and gravel trails and roads. I forgot about the hour time change between IN and IL and had to leave the race after I got in the marathon distance which Mike agreed to. It reached 93 and was humid but I felt good after the race because I did not push. Took an outside shower and flew out of Indy at 7:00 pm.

Twelve Hour Torture on the treadmill September 2010

Tish Caldwell asked me if I would do a fundraiser for the Patrick Dempsey Center for Cancer Patients. I told her I only do fundraisers for children. Tish told me she would have all the funds go to the Healing Tree Children's program. This program helps children affected by cancer and is part of the Dempsey Center. Well, that sounded okay but what did she want me to do? Run on a treadmill at the local YMCA for twelve hours. The treadmill was her idea and the 12 hours mine. Since Tish was a good friend and has helped me raise money for Camp Sunshine were two reasons I agreed to do this. The most important reason was to help children, of course.

The only thing that really sucked is I hate to run on a treadmill and had not done so for a few years. As in the past the Auburn firefighters agreed to donate money from their Children's' Fund. They would match whatever I would raise. A children's' group would also match the money raised after the firefighters donation. So every dollar I raised equaled $4! I planned to stay on the treadmill for the 12 hours only taking bathroom breaks; I could also mix running with walking for 40 to 45 miles. I had one of my firefighter's boots for people to put their donations into. I was a long time member of the YMCA and most donations came from people I knew. I have done this fundraiser every year. Now I take breaks going to the gym running and walking with the children from the YMCA day care. Never running on the treadmill except for this fundraiser really does a job on me. I don't remember what year it was but Tish told me she was going to get Patrick Dempsey and bring him back to the gym. I figured this was a big deal him being a movie star so I called my wife and asked her to drop off the camera on her way to work. Tish is in love with the guy and always talking about Mc Dreamy. Denise dropped the camera off and a little while later returned with Patrick. It was a cardboard cutout of him! "What the hell is this, you said you were bringing Patrick Dempsey back?" "Oh, I thought you knew it was a cardboard cutout."

I don't know how much money we have raised but think it is about $2,000 a year. Each year it gets a little harder to motivate myself to do this event but I plan on doing it every September for as long as I can.

St. Patrick's 12 and 24 Hour Trail Race and the Grand Rapids Marathon

Sara Miller, the race director of the St. Pat's races, let me, Ron, and DJ stay at her home. Jeanne Peckinonis from ME was also a friend of Sara's and was there to help her with this inaugural race. There was an excellent pasta dinner at the race site where you could also pick up your race packet. The course was a 3-mile loop on trails with no major hills. There was plenty of ultra food at the one aid station. Ron, DJ, and I were doing the Grand Rapids marathon the next day so we had to leave early after doing little more than a marathon. We ran the entire race together with DJ falling right at the finish line injuring her ankle. Luckily Paula Boone broke her fall to some extent. This was a nice race and I regret not being able to stay for the full 24 hours. The next day my GPS sent me the wrong way to the Grand Rapids race start. I missed the early start but just started running when I got there catching up with Ron and DJ. DJ's ankle was better but still hurting. This was an easy marathon and I finished much faster than I thought I would and felt great. Don Kern was the race director and I like his time limit. You have to finish in a day that ends in Y. The only disappointment was the half marathoners and faster marathoners drank all 12 kegs of beer before I finished! Pissed me off.

2010 Totals:

- No injuries I could not run with
- 67 total races
- 25 marathons
- 6 ultras
- total race miles: 1,027

Chapter 17: More Ultras and My 300th Marathon

Three Days at the Fair (May 2010, 2011 and 2012 in Augusta, New Jersey)

Let me start off by saying that even though these races can be tough if you push yourself, you only have to push if you want to. There is no such thing as a DNF (did not finish) in a race measured in time. I have always pushed myself in a 72-hour race to break the 200-mile mark. I have always fallen short ending up in the 180 plus range. Well, I promised myself this race would be different. My plan was to do what felt comfortable, get some sleep every night, and make sure I had as much "fun" as possible.

I arrived at the race site the day before the race and set up a six-person tent and was prepared with gear for any kind of weather plus a comfortable cot and a lounge chair. Race director, Rick and Jennifer McNulty, were there, so I gave them the assorted 12 pack of microbrews from Maine that I knew they would enjoy. Handing them to Jennifer, I told her she could share with Rick if she wanted. This husband and wife team does an excellent job with the race. It is a family affair for them. Their children and relatives help out and also run in the races in between working the race. Quinn is the youngest at 4 and does laps with his mother Jenn. Next I checked into a motel in Newton, about 10 miles from the race site. An excellent Mexican dinner at nearby Salsa's ended the day.

Three Days at The Fair consists of a 72, 48, 12, and 6-hour race. The location is at a fairground in rural northern NJ. The course was a 0.8578 mile almost flat loop on asphalt and 10% gravel. The races are chip timed with a display that tells you how many laps and miles you have done. Every loop you pass the kitchen where hot food is prepared, sandwiches made, and drinks served.

The start of the 72 hour race at 9:00 am was sunny and in the 60's. My friend Larry and I did the marathon distance together then he took off to go to a meeting in Pennsylvania. It warmed up to 77 degrees, which was too hot for my liking. I was having back problems 12 hours into the race and took a long break and took in lots of electrolytes which really helped get me going again. I sacked out around midnight and rested until 5:00 am. Larry showed up at 9:00 am and we did most of the marathon distance together again. My friend Gene showed up for the 48-hour race so we also did loops together. The weather was great, cloudy, and about 60 degrees. Gene kept telling me he brought a special bottle of beer that I should drink. My stomach had been upset, too many cheeseburgers, bacon, pancakes, etc., so I was holding off on his offer.

Feeling better around 7:00 pm Gene and I sat down for a beer. Gene gave me a 22 oz. bottle of Arrogant Bastard beer that was excellent to say the least. I did not want to drink it all but kind of had to so as not to insult Gene. It was then more laps and a 5 hour break at midnight. Day 3 was more laps with Larry and Gene and I was now joined by my new tent mate Carl. Carl was doing the 24-hour race in the same spirit as me, do some miles but don't kill yourself. It was Gene's 76th birthday and he left early after doing about 35 or 40 miles total. Larry did the marathon distance for the third day in a row and headed for the Delaware marathon which he did the next day. I also did some laps with Max McNulty. Max is ten and told me his goal was 100 miles in the 48-hour race. "One hundred miles is a lot, Maxwell, do you think you can do it?" I asked. "Well, I did this race last year and did 13 miles," he said with confidence in his voice.

Lots of Mexican food, cloudy weather, and good friends made the first half of day 3 go by fast. It was off to bed at midnight just as the rain started. I got up at 4:30 am. It had stopped raining and with just over 4 hours left in the race I was feeling good except for swollen feet and sore knees. By now all the 24 hour and up racers were hurting to some degree. After a few loops it started pouring but it was a warm rain and it did not bother me a bit because I was in such a good mood. I told race director Rick the puddles cooled off my burning feet and the rain washed all the pollen out of the air, what more could you want? At the end of the race there was a pancake breakfast and awards ceremony. Everything was over within an hour. All runners who did 100 miles or more got a medal. You can accumulate miles over the years and the medals for 250, 500 and so forth keep getting bigger and better. I packed up my tent, took a nice long hot shower, and headed home with a nap on the way.

I did a little over 150 miles; if I had pushed for 200, I never would have made it and would not have been able to drive so quickly after the race. There was plenty of room to camp right next to the course, a very large bathroom, with showers on course and the food is excellent. There is a walk-in refrigerator at your disposal and the volunteers will cook up what you want, if possible. All the volunteers act like one big family and doing laps you get to know the runners. This was my second year here. Last year was a disaster. I signed up for the 24-hour race but had both stomach issues and severe back problems. I was planning on leaving the race early and head to the Delaware marathon. Feeling so bad, I left earlier than planned doing just 39.5 miles. I did recover and felt good at the Delaware marathon. In 2012, Ron who also lives in Maine drove down with me to the Three Days at the Fair race. The big tent worked great for us. There was plenty of room for cots and that's a lot better than sleeping on the ground for this arthritic body of mine. Since this was my third year here, I knew many of the runners from previous years. On a loop ultra course you see the same runners all the time. Ron and I enjoyed the 72-hour race, the runners, food, and relaxed atmosphere of this family run race.

Hilo to Volcano 50k and Maui Marathon (January 22 and 23, 2011)

To start this trip Denise and I purposely got bumped off our Delta flight out of Portland. We ended up with a free cab ride to Boston, breakfast and lunch vouchers, plus a $400.00 voucher each and we arrived in Honolulu just an hour later than planned. Not bad considering we were flying on frequent flyer miles to start with. We got to the Hilton Hawaiian Village Resort around midnight their time. Next day was spent relaxing on Waikiki Beach. The Hilton is right on the beach, has 2,800 rooms, about ten restaurants, and if you do the Honolulu marathon, it is within walking distance to the start. We liked to eat at Wailona Coffee Shop across the street from the hotel. They have good food and reasonable prices; it is where the locals eat.

We took an early flight into Hilo, Hawaii. After checking into Naniola Volcano Resort we took in a couple of local attractions, drove the race course, picked up my race packet, and ate at Ken's, another favorite of ours. The Hilo to Volcano 50k is mostly a relay race but this year had 28 solo runners. If you are running solo you can start when you want and tell the officials at the finish line your time. Three of my friends, Jim, Larry, and Walt, and I decided to start at 3:00 am so we would have plenty of time to catch our flights for the next day's Maui marathon. I thought the race started on Coconut Island, but it actually starts in the parking lot for the island on the other side of the bridge to the island. My friends hollered and screamed out my name, but I never heard them. They waited a few minutes, then started without me. I waited for them about ten minutes then started. Outside a bar there were a bunch of drunks getting ready to fight, one had a knife; this quickened my pace for a short distance. Catching my friends a few miles later made me feel a little better knowing I would have some company in the race. There are no aid stations on the course, so Denise drove the course supplying us with what we needed. She did an excellent job meeting us every 2 to 4 miles. It is nice to have a wife who not only tolerates my running trips but also helps when needed. The course starts at sea level, stays flat for about 4 miles, then it is almost all uphill to over 3,500' at mile 27. The last 4 miles are rolling hills. Miles 1 to 27 are on a highway that is not very scenic.

It stayed dark until 6:30 am, the clouds kept the temperature in the 60's, and at times there was a light drizzle. Once it got light I noticed that Walt, a very experienced ultra runner, had new shoes. They were on sale for $40.00, big mistake. As we continued towards the volcano, Walt's feet started to blister badly. The last 4 miles is when the sun came out, it was in the 80's, and Walt was doing a painful run/walk routine. After crossing the finish line, we told the race director our times and thanked him for putting on a race for 30 bucks, which included a long sleeve tech shirt, finisher's medal, and lei. There was plenty of food at the finish which we took advantage of. Everyone thanked Denise for her help, it was then a shower and off to the airport for our flight back to Honolulu for a connecting flight to the island of Maui.

On the way to the car rental Denise told me she had had a little accident with the car. She pulled down a side road and had to pee really bad. Jumping out of the car quickly she forgot to put it in park and the car rolled down the hill hitting a guard rail and damaging the front grill. Well pee happens. When we returned the car we gave the attendants all the food, water, and sports drink we had left over from the race. The two girls thanked us, walked around the car, and said aloha not mentioning the moderate damage to the grill. Yippee. We missed our Maui flight but still made it there just a little bit late. It was about a 45-minute ride to our excellent hotel in Lahaina. The Lahaina Beach Resort, I think, is the place to stay in Lahaina. It has an ocean beach, pool, mountain views, and is walking distance to everything in Lahaina including the race finish.

On race morning I walked from the hotel to where the bus would pick us up to drop us off at the early 4:30 am start. The bus got us there late and the race had already started. After a few miles and some turns Walt and I were still on course when we reached the main highway that we would stay on to within a mile of the finish. The road is narrow in places and we had to watch out for traffic and potholes. Once sunrise arrived, we were treated to ocean views for 20 miles and saw whales in the distance several times. There are some hills on this course, but it was much easier than the 50k. The nice breeze helped when it got in the 80's along with the many aid stations. We were also treated to ice cold rum a spectator was serving to runners. You meet the nicest spectators running. Walt wore sandals in this race because his feet were so blistered; I'll bet he does not wear new shoes in a 50k again. I ran the entire race with Walt. Jim and Larry also did the double. There was a bunch of picture taking as about 10-50 Staters celebrated Terry from Canada finishing a marathon in every state here. After saying our goodbyes it was a short walk back to the hotel where I had a chance to look over the finisher's medal. It is a beautiful medal on both sides and I could tell just from looking at it my running friend Paul from South Africa designed it. The back of the medal has a raised view of Maui and a line showing the marathon course. This is my favorite race in the Hawaiian Islands.

It was now time to relax. The next three days were spent lounging around the pool, snorkeling, and whale watching. The Pacific Whale Foundation has some nice boat trips from 2 to 7 hours long. The 7-hour trip brings you to 2 different islands for snorkeling and we must have seen at least 20 different humpback whales. On this trip they feed you a light breakfast and BBQ style lunch. Once the snorkeling is over, it is an open bar for the rest of the trip. It was a long trip home. We left Wednesday at 11:30 pm and got to Portland around 11:30 pm Thursday.

In conclusion, let me say that I think most runners would like the Maui marathon. They also have a half marathon and a 5k. It is a very scenic course, lots of aid stations, and just a few steep hills. On the downside, it will probably be hot and all the races are expensive. The Hilo to Volcano 50k is not scenic, has 4,000' of elevation gain, no aid stations or spectators. On the upside it's only 30 bucks, you can start whenever you want, and it is one of the easier ultras in the Hawaiian Islands.

My 300th Marathon
(Hyannis, MA marathon Feb. 27, 2011)

This is not my favorite marathon, not even close. Just about every year I do it the weather is terrible. I have done it in snow and rain with the wind from a Northeaster howling. The worse year was when I had the flu and Walt Prescott had some broken ribs. It had snowed a few days before and a lot of the catch basins were covered with snow. The day of the race it rained so hard the streets were covered up to our knees with ice cold water in places. This is a two loop course so what really sucked is you knew you had to go through the water twice. This year it was snowing lightly and I just had a bad attitude and was not enjoying the race. I caught up to a 19-year-old college student who had never attempted the marathon distance before. He was with friends who were all ahead of him. He wanted to quit because the race was taking a toll on him. This was around mile 18. I told him if he quit he would remember it the rest of his life. I told him no matter what I would stay with him to the finish where he would feel great once he crossed that line and got his medal. Having no injuries, I knew he could do it if I got those demons out of his head. He wanted to quit at the next aid station still. I knew now his parents were waiting for him at the finish so I used this to my advantage. I got all over him about how he was not injured; just tired, which was no excuse for quitting. "You said your parents are going to be at the finish. How are you going to feel getting out of a sag wagon instead of finishing the race?" I am an old man, my back and knees are killing me, and I am tired too, but I will finish. Long story short, I finished the race and met his parents and friends. Everyone congratulated him and I knew I did the right thing by busting his butt. This changed my race also. I was so happy he made it that my spirits were high and I would put this particular race day as a good one for sure.

Land Between the Lakes 60k Trail Run (Grand Rivers, Kentucky, March 12, 2011)

I flew from Portland to Memphis, TN, with brother Walter two days before the race. Nashville is actually closer, but the tickets were more expensive and I like Memphis. We checked into the downtown Quality Inn, top floor, excellent view of the Mississippi and more. If you do the Memphis marathon, they have a good prerace breakfast and it is walking distance to start. We went to the Flying Saucer for dinner and had a few pints from their huge beer selection. If you drink 80 pints of different beer they put your name on a plate and mount it on the wall or ceiling. I guess that is how they got the name Flying Saucer. No, I don't have a plate on the wall, yet.

We had a continental breakfast at the hotel and then it was a 3-hour drive to Grand Rivers, Kentucky. This is a very small town in the western part of the state. We checked out part of the course to see how muddy it would be, then picked up my race packet along with two more for friends who we would meet later in the day. Patti's Inn and Suites is where we stayed. Excellent motel, reasonably priced, and they even started breakfast at 4:30 am for the runners.

The Land Between the Lakes has four different distances; you can run 23k, a marathon, 60k, or 50 miles. If you do the 50 mile or 60k you get a beautiful finisher's belt buckle. My friends and I all wanted the belt buckle, so we opted for the 60k. Our biggest concern was making the time cutoffs. This can be a difficult course when it's muddy or snow covered. Fortunately, we picked a year when there was very little mud on the course. I left the motel with friends Kendel and Walt Prescott, so brother Walter could sleep in. I promised Lois I would run the entire race with her and asked friend Frank to run with us. Frank has run the race four times, twice finishing the 60k distance and twice dropping back to the marathon because of trail conditions. It was perfect weather at the 6:00 am start, sun coming up, and about 50 degrees. All the races start at the same time and go out on a paved road for the first 1.7 miles then onto a single track trail loop 11.3 miles long in the Land Between the Lakes National Recreation Area. The 23k is one loop and back 1.7, the 60k is three 11.3 mile loops and back. The 50 miler is four loops and an out and back thrown in. The second half of the loop contains most of the hills. The 60k has little over 3000' of elevation change. It seemed hillier than that to me. This is a scenic course with views of the lakes and hills. There were aid stations every 3 or 4 miles with a good assortment of food. The hot egg sandwich was my favorite.

Everything was going well until we hit the hills around mile 30. It was in the 70's now. We were an hour ahead of the cutoff time and I knew we would make it. Going up a steep hill Frank was having problems catching his breath and was also cramping up. After a mile or so of stop and go I told Lois to take off and that I would stay with Frank. I had a water bottle and Frank was not carrying one. I figured he was dehydrated and shared my water with him. We took a short break at the last aid station then walked every step of the last two miles. Frank could not even run the last few feet at the finish line. We made the cutoff with time to spare even after all that walking.

At the finish area a few running friends got Frank something to drink and sat him in a chair. I told him I was headed to get some food at the Community Center. I was sitting there eating my chili and next thing I know some runner comes in screaming "is there a doctor in house?!" Frank was cramping up badly. Long story short, I left him my room key so he would have a place to shower and I took off with brother Walt. Frank, Kendel, Walt, Walter, and I all went out to dinner after Frank recovered enough. This is one of the best trail races I have ever done. Two friends, not counting Frank, did get hurt. One broke her finger and made a splint with a plastic spoon and duct tape. The other young lady broke her nose and you could see blood on the trail where she did her face plant. They both finished the race. Did I mention there are rocks and roots on the course? It was fairly difficult but no technical trail stuff and there is a chance to get a belt buckle and not have to run a 100 miler for it. Hear that Phil, Jeanne? Don't want that belt buckle, do the 23k or marathon and enjoy the run and scenery. Flying into Nashville is about a 2-hour drive and there is a lot to do in Memphis or the Nashville areas. We spent the night in Grand Rivers and flew home the next day without a hitch.

Madison Marathon (Montana July 24, 2011)

Walter and I flew into Salt Lake City. The Bozeman airport is closer but the tickets more expensive and driving from SLC you go by Yellowstone where we spent a day. This was one of the most scenic marathons I have ever run. It was a small marathon located in the Gravely Mountain Range. The closest town to the race is Ennis, MT, where we stayed. We drove the marathon course the day before the race. It was spectacular. The course is between 8,500' and 9,600' making it the highest road marathon in the country. This was late July and there were still snow drifts on the side of the road. Where there was no snow, there were many types of beautiful wildflowers covering the ground. Visibility was over 100 miles with mountains off in the distance.

The race is on a dirt road and is 13.1 miles to where the half marathon ends and full marathoners continue 6.55 miles and turn around and come back the same way. Two weeks before the race the director was worried about the snow melting enough to hold the races. This is federal land and a permit was needed for the race which was limited to 200 runners. To get an idea of how remote it is we drove through a private ranch for 7 miles. Cattle on the road slowed us down and pronghorn antelopes were common sights. There are sheep, elk, bear, deer, coyote, and an occasional wolf in the area. Stay away from the sheep because Great Pyrenees guard dogs protect the sheep and might not like you around.

We visited nearby Virginia City, Nevada City and Boot Hill where we had been before. Back in Ennis we went to an excellent pasta dinner where we saw a bunch of running friends. Larry did not have any money so I had to lend him some for the pasta dinner. I thought lawyers made good money? A bunch of 50 Staters took an early start. Cowboy Jeff Bishton rented a van and drove us to the start from the finish area. This was necessary because there was no bus available for early starters. We all chipped in for the van but Jeff was not taking the early start, he simply got the van to help us out. Nice guy, that Jeff. The race started at 9,200 ' near Black Butte Mountain which is in view for most of the first part of the race. A short steep climb left me gasping for air. The course is a real roller coaster. It seems like you are always going up or down a hill. Mile 6 was the highest elevation at 9,600'. If you do this race bring a camera because the views are truly spectacular. By now I had adjusted somewhat to the elevation. I can almost breathe. It was in the 50's, sunny with very low humidity. Stopping frequently to take pictures and enjoy the scenery was making this an enjoyable race.

I had been running close to Larry but he slowed down with terrible back pain. When I reached him he was bent over in pain and determined to continue. At 13.1 miles the 70 or so marathoners continued and the elevation was a mere 8,550' now. By now, it had warmed up to 70 or so and huge biting flies came out to attack the runners. I never saw flies this big, they were about the size of hummingbirds and had vampire like teeth, honest. Give me Maine horse and deer flies any day. By mile 16 just about everyone is feeling the effects of this tough course and the ups and downs were not getting easier. Reaching the turnaround at 19.55 miles it felt good to be heading towards the finish line. Several of my friends were behind me and this gave me a chance to see them. Larry was hurting so badly I tried to get him to quit. Larry would have nothing to do with it and ended up finishing the race. The water stops on the course were every 3 to 4 miles and some were unmanned. When I got to the mile 23 water stop there was no one there and no water. My water bottle was empty but I had no problem with just 3 miles to go.

After I crossed the finish line I told the race director the situation and he got water out there right away. I felt very good and finished faster than I thought I would on such a tough course and having done a 50k 8 days earlier. Driving out we saw Henry with a white shirt covered with horse flies, Larry making slow progress, and Sharon Kerson not far behind. I think this was the first time they held the race and they only had a few glitches. This is definitely a race I want to do again.

24 Hours the Hard Way (Bluff Creek Park Oklahoma City, OK October 23 -24 , 2011)

I flew into Oklahoma City the day before the race and went to packet pickup at the race site where I also enjoyed an excellent pasta dinner. The course was about a one-mile loop, all asphalt, a wide path with no hills to speak of. It was in the 50's at the start. I ran with a runner I had just met named Ed for a few laps. When it warmed up John tucked his hat in the back of his shorts. A little while later he went into the porta pottie to take a dump. Forgetting about his hat when he pulled down his shorts the hat went into the toilet. By this time I knew the race director, Chisolm, a little. I started talking to him about how he really caters to the runners. Next I said you would do just about anything to help them during the race? Chisolm said. "yes, I would." Explaining about the hat in the toilet I asked him if he would reach down and get it. Well Chisolm can take a joke, but he still would not fetch the hat.

I also ran and walked with a runner who had had his esophagus and part of his stomach removed due to cancer. John had to eat through a tube yet he was out here doing the best he could in a 24-hour race. You meet some awfully tough and inspiring individuals. We had a severe storm with heavy rain and lightning which stopped the race for an hour so it was decided this would be a 23-hour race. I was happy to just get in 74 miles and this was my 4th time finishing all the States and DC. The first time 24 hour runners got a very nice ring.

The next day I went to the huge and very nice Cowboy Museum. The day I arrived I went to the OKC bombing site and museum. This is a very emotional place and if I could do just one thing in OKC I would go here.

2011 Totals:

- no serious injuries
- 68 total races
- 21 marathons
- 9 ultras
- total race miles: 1,189

Chapter 18: Ironhorse and Other Races: 2012-2013

Ironhorse 100k (Florahome, FL, February 2012) – I had a DNS (did not start) but I had a good excuse

Denise bought me a large shadowbox for my birthday in 2011 with the shelves made for belt buckles. I had some belt buckles from races but not enough to fill the cabinet. The buckle for doing the Ironhorse 100k is awesome. It has an ironhorse locomotive on it. I talked to several friends and we agreed to do it.

The Saturday before the race, February 12th, I promised my granddaughter I would bring her to a father-daughter dance that she looks forward to every year. I was feeling lousy big time but did not want to disappoint McKenzie so we went to the dance anyway. McKenzie loves to dance so we were on the dance floor all night.

The next day I felt about the same, not good. I went to the hospital the next morning and they operated on me for a ruptured appendix. The appendix probably ruptured a day or two earlier and spread through me. I spent 7 days in the hospital sucking on ice chips. They told me I could have died.

Well I will tell you what almost killed me is when the doctor nonchalantly said she was going to remove the tube from my groin area. She was an excellent surgeon with an accent that made her sound like Arnold Schwarzenegger. She yanked on the tube and it felt like someone kicked me in the nuts as hard as they could.

With her deep voice she asked if that hurt. I answered yes, she laughed and said she did it once and the person yelled so loudly people ran in the room from the hallway. Now prepared, she pulled the rest of the tube out without a problem. I was discharged from the hospital and still felt lousy for another week. I was still in the hospital when my friends ran Ironhorse. Three weeks from the day of the dance I ran a 5k and it was a challenge; I felt so weak for having done nothing. I missed the Hyannis Marathon I was signed up for and heard the weather was great for a change.

Columbia SC Marathon (March 10, 2012)

This was my comeback marathon four weeks after my surgery. The time limit was 6 hours and I was told that it was strictly enforced. Did you know Columbia is a hilly city? I pushed as hard as I could and finished in 5:56:38. A few days later I checked the results and they had 18 runners finish over 6 hours. I think they had to tell me it was a strict cut off because that is what the city wanted. The next weekend I ran the Georgia marathon and felt much better.

2012 Totals:

- 75 total races
- 24 marathons
- 8 ultras
- Appendix only thing that kept me from running

Chapter 19: I Make it to Ironhorse 100k and Several Other Races (2013)

Ironhorse 100 Mile, 100k, and 50 Mile (Florahome, FL, February 9-10, 2013)

My wife Denise and I flew to Jacksonville, Florida, on February 1st. I did the Melbourne Marathon on the 3rd with Ron Paquette and we planned to also run the Ironhorse 100k together. I was supposed to do Ironhorse in 2012, but I was in the hospital instead sucking on ice chips, no food, for 7 days. Arriving at our motel, we met up with good friends Ron, Carl Hunt, and Andy Velazco. Both of them had no plans of what distance they would run for sure.

It was near perfect weather at the 7:00 am race start, 50's and only warmed up to about 70 degrees during the day and back in the 50's at night. The 100k is two 25 mile loops and 12 miles mostly out and back at the end. The loops are about 13.5 miles of forest service roads, mostly beach-like sand and gravel, 2 miles of old railroad bed with sharp rocks, and the remainder of the course is asphalt on an old railroad bed. Aid stations were about 5 miles apart with water, ultima, and a few had some food. The water tasted like it came from a nearby swamp, but the volunteers were super. The first loop seemed easy to Ron and me. Andy injured his ankle at about 12 miles and Carl stayed with him. I tried to get Andy to call it a day when his ankle got sore, but he insisted on finishing the loop. They both called it a day at mile 25. They did not plan on doing much more, so it was not really a DNF.

I had a few miles early in loop 2 where I felt terrible but recovered to my regular slow pace. Ron had injured his shin area in the third marathon of the Savage 7 on December 28th. He finished the marathon but was hurting big time. Ron had to do some painting in Melbourne the next day and by this time his leg was reportedly several different colors of the rainbow and it was not because he spilled some paint on it. Interestingly, about 16 runners signed up for all 7 marathons at the Savage 7, but only 10 of us finished them all.

Janice Gagnier of the Maine Track Club was one of them. At least four suffered some type of leg injury. Ron's injury started to bother him in loop 2. Both of us found loop 2 to be much tougher than the first time we did the loop. The rocks seemed sharper, the beach-like sand deeper, and the miles longer. I tripped over a rock that was so small we had a hard time finding it after I got up from my face-plant fall.

Figuring I was not going to set a course record, I had covered myself with suntan lotion thinking at least I would get a tan. Between the lotion and my sweat the sand stuck to me to make an awful mess. I felt and looked like a giant cinnamon doughnut.

About 15 miles into the loop it got dark and started to feel cold to us two old guys. We could have dropped back to do the 50 miler and get credit for it but you get a nice belt buckle for the 100k and that is the race we signed up for. It was awful tempting to just do the 50 miler when people started cheering us at the 50 mile finish line, congratulating us. We told them we were doing the 100k so "don't cheer for us, we ain't done yet."

As in most ultras, the last miles are the toughest. In this race it seemed especially true. Ron is 71 and I am 67, maybe this is why these races seem to get tougher every year? Going over the rocky section of the course for the last time a 100-mile runner came up from behind us and said " you have the midnight wobbles; you guys are zig-zagging all over the place."

Boy, was he right. By mile 55 we were hurting big time especially Ron with his shin. Getting through the sharp rock section felt great, less than 3 miles on asphalt to go and no rocks or roots to trip over! At the finish line we were greeted with cheers and that "we did it feeling." It would have been so easy to drop to the 50 miler, but I would rather be "Dead Firetruck Last" in the 100k than drop to the 50 miler. BTW "Dead Firetruck Last" is much better than "DNF" (did not finish) in my humble opinion.

A few handshakes and a Budlight, crummy beer, but it was free, and we left for a hot shower and a good night's sleep. We all met in the morning for breakfast then went our separate ways. Andy and his wife Kathy flew their plane back to Atlanta; I think they flipped a coin to see who would be the pilot. Ron headed south to Melbourne to meet up with wife DJ.

Denise and I drove Carl to the Jacksonville airport. We then checked into a nearby motel to stay another day. It was great seeing old friends once again and finishing yet another race with Ron. BTW, I tell people I meet that I am Ron's adopted son. He adopted me when I was 14 so he could work me hard on his farm up in Maine. Whenever we go through an aid station I always refer to him as "Dad." If I go back to this race, I will do the 50 miler. I've done the 100k, so why not the 50 miler?

Bataan Death March and The Dustbowl (March 17 to the 22nd, 2013)

I flew out of Boston with my brother Walter to Amarillo, TX. We arrived at 4:15 pm and drove 380 miles to Las Cruces, NM, late that Friday night. The next day was a little sightseeing and to White Sands Missile Base for packet pickup and to hear the history of the Bataan Death March which took place during WWII in the Philippines. I also met some of the survivors of the Death March. They are truly remarkable veterans who went through a living hell on earth. If you do this race you should take the time to look up the history of the March, it is amazing how some survived.

I left the hotel early for the 7:05 am start because we needed to be on base by 5:00 am. Runners lined up in corrals, Wounded Warriors first, then military with weighted back packs, light military, and light civilian, then just plain old runners like me. It took me about 30 minutes after the gun went off to get to the start line where I shook hands with a couple of survivors. It was about 50 degrees at the start but was 81 degrees by the time I finished. Low humidity and strong winds made it feel more comfortable. Most of the course is on sandy trails that are dusty from mile 2 to 7. Then it is a long uphill climb on asphalt roads from 3 to about 13. After that I was on a trail that was mostly downhill for about 20 miles with the last few miles on the asphalt road I ran up on. Then it was back on sandy trails to the finish. At about mile 22 I hit what they call the sand pit. The sand here was like beach sand that you sink into and it made for slow going.

This is one of my favorite races because of the survivors there, plus all the military doing the race. Can you imagine doing this race with a 35 pound back pack and combat boots? How about a wounded warrior with one leg? The cutoff time is 13 hours; would you want to be on this course that long?

There was plenty of food at the finish and then I was off to the "Dust Bowl Races." Walter drove 380 miles and through a small dust storm to Dalhart, TX, for my next race. The Dust Bowl series was new this year. It consists of five marathons in five days in five different states: Texas, Oklahoma, Kansas, Colorado, and New Mexico. Of the six races I did in six days, Dalhart was the one that was toughest on me. My knee hurt from the start, I was tired from Bataan, and the 6.5-hour drive exhausted me. The course was not that tough. It was four loops around a scenic lake Rita Blanca on a gravel trail with a few hills and some loose sand here and there. There were thousands of ducks and geese on the lake and a few hawks in the area. You could see the remains of birds that the hawks were feeding on, a wing here, a wing there. The weather was good for running, 35 degrees at the start, sunny, and about 55 degrees at the finish. An easy 72-mile drive after the race, and we were in Guyman, OK, for the next day's race.

This race was in Thompson Park on a one mile concrete trail around Sunset Lake. The weather again was nice, sunny, and cool. With just two small hills on the course the concrete did not seem that bad. We had plenty of geese and ducks here also. I felt better today after the race than yesterday. A two hour ride and we were in Ulysses, Kansas, for the third Dust Bowl race. The Chamber of Commerce treated us to a free pasta dinner at their museum location which also gave us a chance to learn about the Dust storms that devastated the area in the 1930's.

Dust Bowl #3 was at the Brentwood Golf Course. No hills, mostly asphalt, and a 1.14 mile loop made this the easiest race yet. Again, the weather was just about perfect, sunny and cool. As in the other Dust Bowl races, I did laps chatting with friends and took my time to enjoy and save a little energy for the next race. After some food at the finish line, it was the same routine again, a two-hour drive to Lamar, Colorado.

Dust Bowl #4 was in Willow Creek Park. The course was mostly gravel with a little asphalt and one short steep hill in the 3.16-mile loop. Great weather again, feeling good, seeing a few deer, and talking to new and old friends made for a fun race. Clayton, New Mexico, was where we would be staying for #5. A 140 mile easy, scenic drive and we were there. The race was actually about 25 miles away from where our hotel was.

Dust Bowl #5 was in a state park and was the toughest of the five races with a mix of gravel trails and a short asphalt road. It was a double out and back with some steep hills and loose rock. You ran on top of a dam in one section. You repeated this course 8 and a half times. I felt great at the end of the race. This was also another nice weather day. I said goodbye to my friends, thanked the race director and volunteers, and headed for Amarillo, TX. A big steak dinner Texas style ended the day.

All the Dust Bowl races were very well organized, they had plenty of food at aid stations that were run by great volunteers and it was easy driving distances to each race. The race director and his friends were great. He did an exceptionally good job considering these were all new races.

I have to thank my brother for all the driving he did and only being stopped once for speeding. He has a streak going now. Three trips in a row he has been stopped that resulted in three warnings! I think the cops feel sorry for the old guy. A nice flight out of Amarillo ended another great trip.

Bay of Fundy Marathon (June 23, 2013)

The Bay of Fundy is an International marathon starting in the small Maine town of Lubec, crossing into Canada onto the island of Campabello, then returning to Lubec, Maine. This was the first year they had the marathon. Ron, DJ, and I decided to do it since it was a Maine race and sounded like a good one. The first six miles or so of the race were easy but once we crossed into Canada the course became very hilly. The Canadian part of the race was an out and back totaling about 20 miles.

The weather was good for running most of the race. It was a little warm for a few miles, then clouded up with very light rain and cooled off. I had been running with Donna Jean and Ron from the start.

The last four miles I started having chest pains and was pushing hard to keep up with them. At mile 24 I told them to go ahead and reluctantly they did. I still went as hard as I could thinking the pain was indigestion or a stomach problem.

After finishing I felt like I was going to pass out, and asked Denise to drive the car, which was about a half mile away or closer. Once in the car my jaw started hurting. I told Denise about the chest and jaw pain and she said I could be having a heart attack. We drove to the motel, I took a shower, and I felt much better. I had an appointment the next day for my yearly physical. The doctor said I did not have a heart attack but he scheduled me for a stress test.

Gorham 4 miler (June 27)

This was a flat course and it was about 60 degrees at the 6:45 pm start. I felt the worst at the beginning of race then it became easier to breathe. I felt good at the end, no problems.

Ed Sheperd 5k (June 30)

Flat course, but it was hot. Started easy and picked up pace, again no problems.

L. L. Bean 10k (July 4th)

This race has the same conditions every year it seems, hot and humid. It's a hilly course but I felt pretty good until about mile 5. I was pushing and these 10k's lately seem to be awful tough for me. Unlike a marathon or ultra I keep my heart rate near its maximum beats per minute. When I finished the race I felt like I was going to pass out when standing still so I walked slowly towards the massage tent. Standing in line for a massage I got very dizzy and had to sit in a chair with my head lowered. I stayed there for about ten minutes, got a massage, and drove home with the air conditioner on high. A few hours later I had chest pains which I now believe was angina. I also believe I was dehydrated.

Moxie 5k (July 13)

This was a hilly course, sunny and 65 degrees. I did not push hard until last half mile downhill. Felt good at end.

Old Port Half Marathon (July 14)

Hot, humid, and hilly describes this race. It was about 80 degrees at the start and I would guess in the 90's in the sun. I felt okay until about mile 9 then started walking more. I felt some tightness in my chest so I took some crushed aspirin and then from 11 on I walked almost all the way to the finish. There was a medical tent right at the finish line. My blood pressure was 78/50. I was dehydrated, got an IV, and they put ice packs under my arms and groin area. I felt better in a matter of minutes. The doctor said I had a cardiovascular problem and it was probably angina.

Fletcher 5k (July 21)

It was sunny about 65 degrees, fairly hilly course. I did not push because of chest pain history. Felt excellent at end.

Stress Test and Echo cardiogram (July 25)

These tests showed that my coronary artery disease was worse and I had a problem with my bicuspid aortic valve. I was told my heart was not getting enough blood when I was running. The cardiologist also said I should not run or "I MIGHT drop dead like Jim Fixx." I was devastated. I tried to get him to say I could run if I took it easy and he still said no. I told him I respected what he said but I love running too much and will keep running. Might as well drop dead doing something I love, right?

Great Cranberry Island 50k (July 27)

This race was two days after I was told never to run again. Was I going to drop dead on an island off the coast of Maine? I must say I was concerned and decided to wear a heart rate monitor and not push hard. This is the 50k Ron and I do almost every year and we know most of the runners and race directors very well. The island has an asphalt road 2 miles long with a hill on each end and this is the course. It was sunny and warm with a slight breeze, better than usual. I took it easy and kept my heart rate below 145 most of the race. I'm alive! I'm alive! I said to myself after finishing. I did have some tightness in my chest during the race. I now carry nitro with me at all times.

A Procedure in August

A catheterization procedure revealed 50% blockage in my right coronary artery. I went for a second opinion and the cardiologist said the same thing as the other doctor. I asked about a stent and he said the blockage would have to be at least 70% before they would put one in. I am being treated with blood pressure medication, beta blockers, and the maximum dose of statins. Denise works with my family doctor and he met with both of us. He said I should not run "do you want to leave her a widow?" etc. My response was "do you want me to sit home, drink twice as much beer, gain 50 pounds, and drive Denise crazy?" I look at the positive side of things, the doctor said I could drop dead not that I would. I know other runners with heart problems and they are still running. Doctors tend to be on the conservative side. They are not going to tell me to run and worry my wife is going to sue them if something happens. Both my parents died of cancer and I do not want to go that way.

I did the Maine Marathon one year and Howard Spear the race director called me to the side immediately after I had finished. He told me Julius Mazul was doing the half and dropped dead from a heart attack about 100' before the finish line. Julius was a good friend of mine whom I admired for many reasons especially his toughness. He usually finished last in most races dragging his 77-year-old bow-legged body across the finish line. His favorite saying was "everyone who finishes is a winner." After his funeral the finish line was set up and his ashes run across the finish line. His wife received a finisher's medal, Julius went out a winner. I know Howie very well and always get a hug from him when I finish the race. If I drop dead at his race I hope he does the same for me.

Center of the Nation Marathons Series (September 16th to 20th)

This is a series of marathons and half marathons in five states on five consecutive days. You do not have to do all of them and there are no time limits or awards except a caboose for those who finish last and first timers get something. The races were in the following states in this order: North Dakota, South Dakota, Wyoming, Montana, and Nebraska.

Brother Walter and I flew into Rapid City four days before the races started. We used this time for sightseeing. In South Dakota we went to Custer State Park which is very scenic and has lots of wildlife, buffalo, whitetail deer, bighorn sheep, mountain goats, and wild donkeys. The buffalo sometimes wandered outside the park and onto the highways nearby. We also went to Mt. Rushmore, drove the Needles Highway, and went to the Badlands where we saw some bighorn sheep. The first night we stayed in the small town of Custer where I ran the Leanhorse 100 mile race a few years ago. At night I could see dozens of deer all around me there. Custer is called "The Whitetail Capital of the World." I walked the same Michelson Trail where Leanhorse was run on and sure enough there were plenty of deer to see at night.

Next stop was Sturgis, SD, where over 100,000 bikers have a rally every year, then up to ND. We stayed in the small town of Medora just outside Roosevelt National Park South. The Cowboy Hall of Fame there is excellent as was the elkburger I had at the Little Missouri Saloon and Dining. Wild horses in Roosevelt National Park South are usually easy to spot and get close to. In Roosevelt North we saw buffalo and bighorn sheep. There are plenty of gas and oil wells in this part of ND and the highway was full of trucks hauling oil-related products.

To keep this as short as possible I did all the races with friends. We ran, walked, and talked together a good portion of each race. All the races had excellent food on the courses and were very well organized. Most people do not do all the races and if you want you can switch from the marathon to the half marathon. My brother Walt drove all the time as he always does. His driving really helps especially when I have long distances between races. The most runners in any race was less than 200 combined total for full and half. The race director puts on these five states series in many different sections of the country. For more information go to www.mainlymarathons.com. To check out runner opinions on these races go to www.marathonguide.com. In the following chapter, Race Director Clint Burleson describes the origins and development of the Mainly Marathons concept.

The first race was in Bowman, ND, about 15 miles from our motel. It was about 50 degrees and very windy at the 6:30 am start. The course was a 1 mile plus out and back on asphalt with one hill beside a lake. It got to about 75 degrees but a 20 mph wind kept it from getting too warm. Then a 110 mile ride and we were in Belle Fourche, SD where I ran the second race. This course was mostly on a concrete path 1.9 miles long in a park just a mile from our motel. This was the worst of all the races, 50 degrees at the start and 90 degrees by the finish and no shade on concrete makes you happy to get 'er done.

We stayed in Belle Fourche for the next 2 races because there are no towns near the other two locations. Race #3 was in Colony, WY, on a dirt road in the middle of nowhere. We used longitude and latitude on our GPS to locate the start as we did for race #4. This was about a 45 minute ride from our motel on a nice 2.18 mile hard pack dirt road with no rocks and a couple of hills. I do not remember seeing but one or two vehicles go by during the entire race. I finished just in time as we hit a thunder and lightning storm that left hail covering the road about an inch thick. It was about 50 degrees at the start and in the 80's when I finished the race. We took a ride to Devils Tower before returning to the motel. About 45 minutes each way it was well worth the ride. The prairie dog town there is always fun to watch.

Race #4 was the most isolated. The only building in Albion, WY, is an abandon school house. The last person living here left in 1964. Yesterday's storms brought in some cooler and wild weather. After an hour drive to the start, we were greeted with a temperature of 40 degrees and winds of 30 to 40 mph. The course was on a 2 plus mile dirt road with lots of rocks and hills. Being on the open prairie there was no protection from the wind. The wind was at your back on the way out but when you turned to come back it was right in your face. Runners were bundled up with some only having a small portion of their face not covered. By the end of the race my eyes were hurting from the wind even though I had my glasses on. I am glad I am from Maine as the cold weather affected some of the other runners more than me.

After the race it was a scenic 200 mile ride to Chadron, Nebraska. A 15-minute ride from our motel and we were at a tree covered state park. I mention the trees because being out on the prairie for a few days makes you appreciate them a little more. This course was a 2.18-mile asphalt loop with about a 0.25-mile single track dirt trail and a few big hills. The scenery was excellent as was the weather, 50's, sunny and no wind. After a few pictures with friends, volunteers, and the race director's family it was a 1.5 hr. drive to Rapid City and an early flight home next day. I have already signed up for the

Riverboat Series in the southeast. I really enjoy these series and hope to keep doing at least one a year.

Lake Tahoe Triple (September 2013)

My wife Denise and I flew out of Portland to Sacramento on Wednesday so we would have some time for sightseeing before the first marathon. We stayed in south Lake Tahoe right on the border with Stateline, Nevada. The Lake Tahoe area has plenty of things to see and do. The Lake is in both California and Nevada and surrounded by a forest of huge trees, ski areas, and a very scenic highway. Reno, Carson, and Virginia City are a short drive away. Reno has another good-sized close by airport. Squaw Valley is where the Western States 100-mile race starts and is just a few miles from the Lake. If you come here, plan on at least a few extra days to enjoy one of the most beautiful places in the west.

The Lake Tahoe Triple is three marathons in three days which takes you completely around the lake. Each day has a different start. The roads and bike trails you cover during the races around Lake Tahoe are about about 72 miles so the last six miles of the last marathon are an approximate repeat of the first six miles of the first day's marathon. All three races are extremely scenic traveling close to the shore in many places. The Lake is at about 6,200' altitude and there are plenty of hills, the highest about 7,000'. The Cal-Neva day 2 marathon is the easiest of the three.

The first marathon, Emerald Bay, began on Friday at 7:00 am. It was about 35 degrees, at 6,800' with the first 2 miles downhill. The first 13 miles were the easiest, mostly flat after the downhill then the last 13 are really hilly with a long climb to the finish at 7,000'. The start was in California and we finished in Nevada. It had warmed up to the 50's and was a nice sunny day. The scenery was spectacular.

Saturday's Cal-Neva Marathon started at yesterday's finish. It was sunny and about 30 degrees at the 7:45 am start. My hip and knees were sore so it took a few miles to loosen up. The first 11 miles or so were mostly downhill. After the half marathon finish the hilliest parts of the course start. There is a hill at about mile 22 that I found to be a "killer hill." I had run these three marathons 10 years ago and still remember this hill from then. The last four miles I enjoyed with my new friend Nick. It was in the 50's and sunny when we finished in Tahoe City, CA. There are buses that take you to the start of all three marathons, but Denise would pick me up at the finishes. Nick hitched a ride with us as far as Stateline, NV.

Sunday's Lake Tahoe marathon is the biggest of the three races and it starts at yesterday's finish area. I took the early start for slower marathoners at 6:30 am. It was 40 degrees when Nick and I started off together. The first 15 miles or so were on a mix of roads and a bike path with very few hills. Mile 15 is where the "Hill from Hell" starts at 6,200' and climbs to 7,000' over more than a mile. It was then about a three quarter mile downhill to Emerald Bay then a mile climb up to Inspiration Point at 6,800'. Spectacular scenery helped make this part of the course along with the next two miles downhill a little easier. Inspiration Point is where the first marathon started and is about mile 20. The next 6 miles is pretty much a repeat of the first marathon, the 2 mile downhill then about 4 miles of flat, paved bike trail. About 60 and sunny at the finish made for a perfect end for the Tahoe Trip

Each race had a nice finisher's medal and if you did all three you got a special large medal with a stand. There are also three half marathons, kayak, swimming and bike races. The first two half marathons are easy. Both start between 6,800' and 7,000' and finish at 6,200' with no hills to speak of. The only hard part is the altitude. Day three is a tough half with lots of climbs including the infamous "Hill from Hell." These are just a few of the events put on over the three days. There is also a 72 mile run, 10k, 5k and other distances. There is also a sunset pasta cruise Saturday night that was excellent.

The same race director puts on the Maui marathon that I thought was excellent. It is in January. More information can be found at www.laketahoe-marathon.com.

We flew back Monday and agreed this is a place we want to visit again. I hope to be able to do the Triple again. BTW Denise spent a lot of time in the casinos giving a boost to the Nevada economy.

Rhode Island Ultra (November 10th) and Myles Standish Marathon (November 17) #400

Three weeks before the Myles Standish race that would be on my 67th birthday it dawned on me that if I did another marathon or ultra my birthday race would also be my 400th marathon/ultra. The closest race would be the Rhode Island 6 hour ultra in Warwick, RI. The race was November 10th on an asphalt loop path 2.7 miles long. I had run this race before and knew it was an easy course except for all the turns which adds a little distance. The weather was good and I pushed a little at the beginning to make sure I would finish at least a marathon under the 6 hour time limit. I did 27 miles in 5:45 and felt good at the end of the race.

The Myles Standish marathon was in Plymouth, MA, about 20 minutes from my brother Walter's home where I had stayed for the RI race and now this one. Walter isn't much of a cook but does a really good job heating up a frozen chicken pot pie for my pre-race dinner. It was about 36 degrees at the early start of this point to point hilly marathon on mostly asphalt roads. The first 16 miles or so were in a forested state park with several lakes for scenery. From there it was on to paved roads with a few miles of flat gravel road. Most of the race was hilly so the flat gravel road was a nice break. When I realized this would be my 400th marathon on my birthday I emailed the race director telling him this and asked for race number 400. I got that number and as I approached the finish line they announced my name and that it was my 400th. A few runners actually wanted a picture with me. Can you believe that! Cowboy Jeff Bishton waited at the finish line to congratulate me - I appreciated that.

BTW Jeff is from Florida and got his nickname when he started wearing cowboy hats in races. I don't think he has ever been on a horse. I felt good after the race with just a few sore muscles from a race I liked and will do every year I can.

2013 Totals:

- No injuries or diseases I could not run with (my opinion)
- 73 total races
- 40 marathons
- 4 ultras
- total race miles: 1,378

CHAPTER 20:
CLINT BURLESON AND
MAINLY MARATHONS

One of the best ways for 50 Staters to collect states and for Marathon Maniacs to increase their marathon statistics is to register for one or more of the Mainly Marathon series of races. Clint Burleson is the mastermind behind these race series and here he relates the background and development of this popular concept of multiple races on multiple days.

How it All Began – Prologue

While a sophomore and junior in high school, I ran cross-country. It wasn't a glamour sport, anyone could make the team, and I was proof of that. Slow and undedicated, the distance was two miles, so it was all about speed.

The highlight of those unmemorable years was a runner from the neighboring rural community, Garry Bjorklund. To see him run was beauty, and he had no competition in the area. Garry went on to participate in the 1976 Olympics and to win the first Grandma's Marathon in Duluth, MN for 1977 and Grandma's half-marathon is now named for him.

Before my senior year the cross-country distance was increased to three miles. "Forget it", I thought, "three miles is way too far to run. I quit!"

The Very Ancient History

April 15, 1982: In spite of my previous teenage running attitudes, I decided I wanted to run a marathon. My father said to me, "Be careful, son, you are not a spring chicken anymore." I was 28.

I wasn't running, but had two months to get ready for Grandma's, our hometown marathon. The two months and the eventual 26 mile struggle taught me much about myself, about training, determination, running and marathoning. And how long distances are conquered more by the mind than by the body. During the race there was no food on the course, just water and Gatorade every three miles. Luckily a spectating friend who was meeting me occasionally on the course stopped and brought me a hamburger. Bless him! The cut-off time for Grandma's back then was 4:30, after that the clock was still running, but no medals. I missed it by 20 minutes, so no bling!

June 16, 1987: Out to do my third marathon (the second was mostly a long training run) and I had trained tremendously for this. I was now living in southern New Mexico and studied running and ran long, studied more and ran fast and on race day (back to Grandma's again) couldn't run as fast or as far as I wanted. It was my PR and I would never surpass it, but it was 5 minutes short of my goal and I learned about The Wall. That Grandma's also included my brother, Jeff, running his first. He has run every Grandma's since.

While living in New Mexico, I would frequently drive back to Minnesota to visit family and enjoyed the part of U.S. Highway 54 that left NM, cut across the panhandles of TX and OK and entered KS in less than 150 miles (this isn't just a random fact, it is important to later developments, stay tuned).

June 1988: Scott, my sister Vicki's son runs his first marathon, Grandma's, of course. He has only missed one since (family wedding).

The Middle Ages

January 8, 1991: I decide that I want to direct a race, and it had to be a marathon with all of the trimmings, Half, 5K, 1 Mile, relays. It was a point to point from White Sands National Monument to downtown Alamogordo, NM, involving bussing, major traffic control, 15 aid stations and over 200 volunteers. Each year's event after that first one took 14 months of planning and work. At that time the only other marathon in southern NM and west TX was in Roswell, NM, the long running Turtle Marathon. Not even El Paso had a 26.2-mile race. We held The White Sands-Alamogordo Marathon on the first Saturday in December and it continued for six years. The second year we received a blizzard the night before, seven inches of snow shut down the highway from the Monument to Alamogordo and the race had to be cancelled. By 1996 I had moved to Las Cruces, 60 miles west, and no one could be found to take over the event.

June 19, 1991: Jane, Jeff's wife, runs her first marathon, at Grandma's.

June 21, 1994: Jeff and Jane's daughter, Jill, runs her marathon, yup, at Grandma's.

I had continued to run about one marathon a year, getting back to Grandma's usually once in every five.

The Renaissance

December 15, 1999: Hannelore Grunenberg asks me out on a date.

March 1, 2000: We have our first date! (I am slow at more than just running)

2002: I was slowly increasing my number of marathons each year from four to six, seven, eight, ran my tenth state in 2004 and joined The Club! (50 States Marathon Club), did my first 50k in 2003. This long distance running was beginning to become an addiction. In 2005 I was able to meet up twice with Jeff and Jane to do marathons/ 50ks in OK and TX. I wasn't the only one starting a new bad habit, and we have continued this tradition of meeting around the country for marathons.

October 2003: Hanne and I start a business dealing in antiques toys, especially toy trains with those cute little cabooses! But this turns out to be one way to work very hard while earning very little. It is quite difficult to compete with eBay.

March 2005: I asked, she said, "Yes", so on June 25, we did.

May 6, 2006: Shiprock Marathon in NM, I met Paula Boone and Larry Macon. I have had the good fortune over the years since to run at a pace close to Larry's (especially on a Sunday when he has already run at least one marathon that weekend) and to pick many of the same races. The numerous running conversations with Larry greatly influenced what was to happen later.

But the discussion that took place during that Shiprock run was the one that started it all. Paula and Steve Boone are the driving forces behind the 50 States Marathon Club, a group that has inspired thousands of runners to get out and run more and to do so while seeing much of this country. Paula and Steve are also successful race directors in the Houston area and had tried to organize a four-day, four-state series of marathons in the Four Corners area where AZ, NM, CO and UT all meet. But the land in this region is all reservation and permissions could not be obtained. In addition, the largest town in the area, Shiprock, does not even have a motel. As Paula was telling Larry and me about this my mind flashed and I thought, "There are way better places in the country to do a multi-state series and if I were to try it, I know just the area to do first."

December 31, 2008: I retire from teaching at a community college. But trouble is brewing, no work obligations, finally some time to spare, so I hit the road running marathons.

June 17, 2009: Maggie (my great-niece, Scott's daughter, Vicki's grand-daughter) runs her first marathon at the age of 13. Grandma's!

Faster forward, 50+ slow marathons later and dozens of conversations with Larry, Jeff and others about marathons, marathoners and multi-day series.

The Modern Age

May 20, 2012: Hanne, who had no sympathy for people running 26 miles (then), said "If you really think that there would be as many as 20 runners who would do five days in a row, then start this business and I will help." We figured at 20 runners a day, if we kept the expenses low, that we could break even. Of course, at that, all of our time would be for free.

But by that afternoon we had a domain name, a website, and I was having conversations with five towns across the Dust Bowl region of TX, OK, KS, CO and NM for a series to be held the following March. Mainly Marathons had begun! We also began work on a four-day series for our hometown in Las Cruces, NM for the upcoming fall. This was going to be our "trial run".

The next day I began listing the events on calendars and sending emails too many of the more "Maniacal" marathoners announcing a new type of running company. 5-Days, 5-Marathons, 5-States! No time limits, no awards for speed, quantities of good food and drinks, races for those who just want to have some fun during their efforts.

Within a couple of weeks it was obvious that there were many more than 20 who would participate each day. I started calling five more states: ND, SD, WY, MT and NE, The Center of the Nations Series was now underway.

June 16, 2012: Back at Grandma's, Jeff and I did our 100th marathon, Jane, a tad behind, at 96.

October 29, 2012: We held the first annual Day of the Dead Series at La Llorona Park in Las Cruces, NM, runners and walkers using three miles of the bike path that went south from the park. Participants came from all over the country, and a few from abroad, to see what this new running company was about. That first year we attracted the top endurance marathoners in the country to Las Cruces, the top male and female world record holders for most marathons run in a year, along with Jim Simpson who had the most life-time marathons. Notables at our first event included Yolanda Holder, Larry Macon, Steve Hughes, Vincent Ma, David Johnson and Parvaneh Moayedi, all of whom had done or went on to top 100 marathons in a year. Parvaneh missed the first day and arrived on Day 2 with her arm in a cast. She had fallen three days before during a 100 mile race and broke her arm. The up side was that she fell at mile 12 instead of mile 96 and that she still went on to do three days of our Dead Series. During those four days Larry broke his world record for most marathons run in a year, Yolanda used the four marathons to go on and break her world record, and Jim Simpson topped the North American record of most lifetime marathons by running his 966th. The serious endurance marathoners were taking us seriously. Our local newspapers, on the other hand, did not. When I sent them a press release covering the runners and the accomplishments happening in a little town park, they thought that it must be a joke and did not print or follow up. The next year was a "different story", though.

The crew for the Original Dead Series included my sister, Vicki, doing the timing, Hanne with food preparation, a local woman, Beth, at the far aid station and me, just hanging around until Day 4 when I ran with Jeff and Jane as she did her 100th marathon.

2012 Mainly Marathons Statistics: 4 races, 1 state

2013!

March 18, Dalhart, TX, and we began the first ever 5-Day, 5-State Series, The Dust Bowl Series. With about 100 runners and walkers each day, including many notables, and the star of this book, Mike Brooks!

Day 1 included my great-niece Jackie Shirley, Vicki's granddaughter from the Kansas branch of the family, running her first half-marathon. She went on to do two more half-marathons over the next two days.

Articles of clothing are found every day at a race and one morning's announcements included, "Mike Brooks, my sister has your pants", to the embarrassment of those mentioned.

Assisting Vicki with the timing on this series was Cathy Duesterhoeft so that her husband Norm could run for free. Norm, seeing we were short-handed, began helping on the second day with setup in the mornings and packing up in the afternoons, running a marathon in between. Cathy and Norm have been with us ever since and are now part of our permanent crew. Also running that week was George Rose who went on to write a book about that first 5-Day, 5 State series, We're All in This Together. George and his wife Kate joined us as crewmembers during the summer of 2014.

The week was exhausting for Hanne and I and the crew and, of course, most of the runners. We had brought our two dogs and worked out of a pick-up truck and a small, but classic travel trailer which proved way too small to carry all of the supplies needed while we attempted to live in it.

With Dust behind we began to focus on the Center of the Nation Series (CON) coming up in September. We bought a new travel trailer with a "garage" in back for carrying supplies, and then had to buy a bigger pickup truck to pull it. This was our big gamble, but with 225 runners signed for each day at CON we had to expand. All went pretty well at this series, but behind the scenes it was chaos. We were terribly understaffed to handle a crowd of this size and we all worked until we were dead tired, then had to drive to the next race location. My brother Jeff and his wife, Jane, came and ran their first series, as did our nephew Scott. And with Vicki there it was an odd sort of a family reunion. Weather was a challenge, in South Dakota we had 91 degrees, two days later in Montana it was 45 degrees, overcast and strong winds. The Wyoming and Montana races were held in ghost towns, Colony, WY and Albion, MT, probably the most excitement those towns had seen in years!

We finished the year with our Day of the Dead Series, this time spread over three locations, El Paso, TX, Willcox, AZ and Las Cruces, NM.

2013 Mainly Marathons Statistics: 14 races, 11 states

2014

We were now planning four new series for 2014, Riverboat, New Mexico State Parks, Heartland and Appalachian, along with keeping our original three as annual events. The Dead Series was lengthened to seven days, but all in Las Cruces. 2014 was going to be a busy year! Hanne had cut back to half-time at her job with the German Air Force, working the other half for Mainly Marathons. And my retirement was a thing of the past; I was as busy as I had ever been.

We experienced some exciting notoriety in 2014, The Wall Street Journal did an article on CON and we were written up at a number of newspapers, Rapid City, Casper WY, Amarillo and a number of smaller papers. Our big thrill was when we won two places in the Marathon & Beyond Top 25 medal competition, taking numbers 10 and 13 for our Dead and Dust medals of 2013. And our last place caboose awards got mentioned in a separate article in that same magazine. Norm became our "Marathon Chef" late in the year providing the runners with a variety of health-conscious endurance foods.

2014 Mainly Marathons Statistics: 36 races, 25 states

The Present Time:

We returned two days ago from Dust 2015, I got to run them all, and we leave in five days for the Riverboat and Independence Series. We are hauling boxes of Dust paraphernalia out of the trailer while loading supplies for the next series. Hanne has been working 12 hour days to get caught up with entries and computer work. Norm and Cathy are handling repairs, stuffing packets, buying food and prepping t-shirts. What had begun as a rather crazy idea grew into a hectic business. One where we have met hundreds of wonderful folks (runners and walkers are a pretty good group) and made dozens of friends all across this country and even a few from overseas.

This year we will be doing nine series:

- New Mexico State Parks
- Dust Bowl
- Riverboat
- Independence
- Heartland
- New England
- Center of the Nation
- Appalachian
- Day of the Dead

2015 Mainly Marathons Statistics: 55 races, 40 states

If you see us on the road, stop by and say "Hi", we enjoy making new friends and reconnecting with the old ones and if, on a race course, you say, "Looking Good!" I won't believe a word of it.

CHAPTER 21:
MY FAVORITE MARATHONS BUT
MORE BAD NEWS: 2014

Ron's Bucket List Ultra 50k Skydive
(February 1 – Clewiston, FL)

I mentioned to Ron Paquette that I was thinking of doing a 50k that included a skydive. Ron said skydiving had always been on his "bucket list" so we decided to go ahead and do it. Last year I did a 100k with Ron that was on my bucket list because the previous year I was in the hospital and missed the race. The race director gave me a "ruptured appendix" discount because I paid for it the year before.

My wife Denise and I flew into Orlando the day before the race and drove for about 3 hours to get to Clewiston where we met up with Ron. We checked into a nearby motel and then picked up our race packets and a five page release form for the race and jump. We were told to be at the airport race site by 7:00 am.

The next day it was about a 15-minute drive to the race start. Last year was the first time they had the race and only about 20 people did it with just half of that number doing the jump. This year there were over 100 runners and 55 jumpers. Besides the 50k there was also a 100 miler, 50 miler, marathon, half marathon, and 10k. The race director was not prepared for 55 runners to skydive, 5 at a time, so to put it as kindly as I can the organization was a little messed up. At 8:30 am the race director let Ron and me start one of the 8 mile loops which consisted of just about equal parts grass, paved, and rough dirt roads. The clumps of grass twisted your feet and were the worst part of the course. No hills and no scenery help describe a boring course. Hot, humid, and lots of little bugs after dark plus not well marked at night gave me something to whine about. We were taken off the course to do our tandem jump around 10:30 am but did not get to jump until 1:30 pm which really sucked.

Now for the best part of the day: we finally got to jump! After about 5 minutes of instructions and suiting up we were ready. The plane would take five runners at a time plus their tandem instructors along with a few solo jumpers who had nothing to do with the race. I was a little worried I would screw something up but there really wasn't much to remember. The most important thing was to keep your legs up when landing so the instructor would land his body first. I jumped solo once and had to take a class that lasted about 4 hours, tandem you don't have control like solo so there is not so much to know. We climbed to about 14,000' and free fell to about 4 or 5,000' at about 120 miles per hour, according to the instructor. What a rush; it was awesome, fastest 2 miles I ever did in a race. One runner shattered his ankle on landing. Gotta keep your feet up! I heard another one puked during the jump and another passed out. I spoke to some very experienced jumpers and they claim this is a very safe sport. I believe as long as you don't panic if there is a problem, that is probably true. Watch out for the trees and power lines though.

Ron and I both really enjoyed the jump. Ron got to cross that off his bucket list but now we still had three 8 mile loops to go. Both of us were just wanting to get it over with now after all the time we wasted waiting around. We could have dropped down to the marathon distance but then it would not have been a "skydive ultra." I figured once it got dark it would cool off, but not so. The wind stopped, it seemed to get more humid, and then little bugs started biting and buzzing me. Ron smelled so bad they wouldn't go near him. Since we hadn't planned on finishing in the dark, we only had tiny flashlights, one with a dying battery and the other you had to keep your finger on the button so it would work. We finished around 8:30 at night and then took off in opposite directions for three hour drives.

The race director knows he had a lot of problems and plans to fix them. The skydive was great and the course was easy, but I did not like it. There are plenty of distances to choose from and you do not have to do the skydive if you don't want to.

The next weekend I did a scenic, flat 50k trail race in Florida. Ron and wife DJ did a 12 hour race in South Carolina that I heard was a little muddy. BTW the nice 50k I did was near Sarasota and it is called the MTC 50k short for Manasota Track Club. There was also a 25k. I would highly recommend this race if you like easy and low key.

Irish Rover 5k (March 2) but More Bad News

It was a perfect mild winter day in Maine to run, in the 40's and sunny. I felt sluggish from the start. I had a hard time breathing going up a long hill and runners I usually finish ahead of beat me by minutes. I even had a hard time drinking a Guinness after the race. I told Denise this and also mentioned a little discomfort on my right side. I decided to be proactive and go to the doctor the next day. Well it took four days, 5 blood draws, a CO2 test, x ray, and finally a CAT scan to figure out I had blood clots in my lung. The doctor does not know what caused the clots and put me on blood thinners for the rest of my life. I was also told I could have died for the third year in 3 years. Gonna change doctors. I did a 5k the next weekend and felt fine.

Riverboat Marathon Series (April 12-16)

Walter and I flew out of Portland to Memphis two days before the first marathon so we could go to Mammoth Cave National Park. From there it was off to my first of five marathons in five states in five days. Belmont State Park in Columbus, KY, was a very scenic location overlooking the Mississippi River. The course was hilly, about half asphalt bike path and half dirt trail. It was a 2.184-mile figure 8 that you repeated until 26.2 miles was done. I did most of the race with Frank and Chuck. Another friend, Norm, came upon a large snake on the dirt trail and badly twisted his ankle trying to get away from it. He is a big, tough retired Army guy who is very afraid of big, bad snakes.

As soon as I finished, it was off to Millington, TN, about 130 mile drive and close to Shelby State Park. This race was a 2.184 out and back on asphalt bike trails. It was about 80 degrees but a lot of the course was shaded by big trees. Yesterday felt hotter, with less shade, and high 80's. I did the entire race with Frank. These courses give you a chance to see the other runners often and to me are more fun and give you a good chance to meet other runners. Some runners will do all five marathons or half marathons; others might do just one or two. Norm hobbled through the marathon but was having a tough time with his ankle.

A 200 mile drive brought us to the small town of Lake Village, AR. A 10 mile drive the next morning and we were at Lake Chicot State Park for race #3. This was a 1.31 mile out and back on asphalt road with no traffic. About 10 minutes into the race thunderstorms rolled in. Lightning flashes, pouring rain, and loud thunder continued off and on during the entire race. Some runners jumped into their cars, some dropped from the marathon to the half, and a few quit. I was running with Sabra, Clint pulled up on his bike and asked her if she wanted to get out of the rain and lightning but he looked over at me and said "keep running." The course was flooded in many places but some runners had a" singing in the rain" attitude and made the best of it. No sense bitching about something you can't change. Norm fell spraining his ankle worse than before. He had to drop to the half.

A short 40 mile drive and we were at our motel in Greenville, Mississippi. Race #4 was about a 30 mile drive from motel to Hollandale, MS, at Leroy Percy State Park. This was another 1.31 out and back on paved roads with no traffic. What a difference a day makes! Sunny, windy, and cool made for perfect running weather on this flat, scenic course.

By now most runners knew each other or were at least saying something to you when they saw you on the course. All these races had roughly 100 to 130 runners in them and about 20 doing all 5. To keep track of your laps you would get a rubber band each time you completed a lap plus volunteers would check your lap off. The volunteers were great and so were race director Clint, his wife Hanne, and sister Vicki.

I left the race in a hurry and forgot my wind pants and water bottle which plays into tomorrow's race. It was a 120 mile drive to Winnsboro, Louisiana, and our motel 100 yards from race start. This would be the shortest course. Arriving at the race start, I asked if anyone had my pants. Vicki had them and everyone wanted to know how Vicky got my pants. I just said that we were staying at the same motel and figure it out for yourselves. The race was in Civitan City Park on paved bike trails with the course shaped like a lollypop. It took 22 laps to do 26.2, that is a lot of rubber bands. This was a scenic course with one hill and lots of old magnificent trees.

I enjoyed watching the squirrels, ducks, and turtles each lap. Everyone was in a great mood for #5 except one friend who could not finish the race due to fatigue and an injury. She was in her 60's with a few health problems. She told me sadly how slow she has become and I responded with "how many women in their 60's with your problems can do 4 marathons in 4 days?" I saw her in May when she did all 4 marathons in the New Mexico State Park series. They don't make them gutsier than her. Taking pictures with my running friends and volunteers it was back to Memphis to catch our flight the next day. Walt had gone to the Vicksburg National Park Battlefield and was happy to check off two National Parks on this trip.

New Mexico State Park Series (May 8-11)

I had some frequent flyer miles that were expiring so Walter and I used them on this trip. The closest airport to the race where I could use them was El Paso, TX. It was about a 450 mile drive to our first race but Walter had never been to Mexico so this worked out. El Paso borders Mexico. The first race was at Sugarite State Park near Raton, NM. It actually started in Colorado and finished in New Mexico. The start and finish were within a few hundred yards of each other. The course was 1.66 miles out and back on a paved road and dirt trail along Lake Maloya with some small hills and about 7,500' elevation. The elevation made it hard for me but the temperature was good, about 30 degrees at the start and it never got hot. There was also a half marathon and 5k with many more runners than just the four in the marathon. This was a scenic course.

It was a very scenic 65 mile ride to Eagles Nest State Park where we checked out the start area. The entire area is beautiful with high mountains still covered with snow and a lake. Our motel was just a few miles from the start. We ate at Calamity Jane's and watched the snow falling during our meal; luckily it did not accumulate much. It was about 30 degrees at the 6:00 am start. This was a lollipop shaped course that you did twenty times on mostly asphalt and a few hundred yards on a gravel road. The 8,200' was a killer for this flatlander; other than that it was an easy course with just a couple of small hills. This was pretty much like yesterday as far as the number of runners go. There were four marathoners and more half and 10k runners. Hanne, Clint's wife, slid a garter belt up my leg about half way through the race and that is where it stayed until the finish. I was hoping it would fill with $5 and $10 bills, but I only got a buck. I battled it out with friend Parvanah and came in last getting a nice award for doing so. Another friend, Pam Penfield, got it the day before. It was another scenic ride, about 200 miles, to Tucumari where we would stay for the night.

We drove to the wrong entrance to Ute State Park and ended up getting to the fourth race late and missed the start. This was all my fault; I should have read directions better. I started about ten minutes late. The course was between 3,800' and 4,500' elevation, 6.55 miles out and the same course back times two. It was about equal parts dirt trail and paved roads. You went downhill to the base of a dam, then mostly uphill to the turnaround. It got to 88 degrees on this shadeless course, but three waterstops and low humidity helped, and I carried a water bottle. The last lap there were cold towels on the course. This was the toughest of the four races for me. I did have jaw pain which can be a sign of cardiac problems. There were eight finishers.

NM park rangers were at all these races. One ranger heard me ask for a sandwich, told me to go ahead, and he delivered it to me on an ATV, napkins and all. You meet some nice park rangers running. Hanne usually has hummus for me at these races, but it spoiled this time and there was none. The same park ranger who delivered my sandwich heard this. His wife made hummus and it was at the race the following day and it was gooood. Park rangers have the nicest wives.

We stayed at the same hotel for the 35 mile drive to Cochas Lake State Park. It was about 65 degrees at the start. The course was 6.55 miles out and the same back, just like yesterday, except a much easier course. About 90% was asphalt road with a stretch of out and back at a turnaround on gravel road where the steepest hill was. This was not a hilly course and it was very scenic crossing a dam, with the lake in view most of the time. A four or five foot rattlesnake slithered across the road in front of me. It was the biggest snake I ever saw in the wild and the fastest moving one. The state park rangers and Army Corps of Engineers manned the aid stations as well as cheered the runners on. I was having a little chest pain so took it slow. To me this was the nicest of the races, it never got real hot, and was an easy scenic course. There were nine finishers. Clint has always had more finishers in his other state series and I am sure these races will grow. Saying my goodbyes a few hugs and handshakes and we were headed for Juarez, Mexico.

I had been to Juarez before and there is nothing there I wanted to see or do. The only good part about visiting it is you leave appreciating what a great country we live in. This was something Walter wanted to do so we walked across the bridge into Mexico, looked around for a few hours, and left. Walter now feels the same way as I do about Juarez.

Three days at the Fair Quadzilla 50k (May 15-18)

The course and the variety of races available have changed. The course this year was a one-mile lollipop shape on 95% asphalt and 5% gravel roads with virtually no traffic or hills. It is mostly a loop with a short out and back. There was a 72, 48, 12, and I think 6 hour race. You could also do a mix of four marathons or 50k's or do four of either one. Frank pitched his tent next to mine and we did some laps together. Gene Bruckert who was celebrating his 79th birthday wanted to do 79 miles. I would be sitting on a bench drinking a cold beer and try to get Gene to join me. Gene likes his beer but wanted to get in 79 miles so he would not stop no matter how much I told him the beer was sooo good. Gene set a new goal the third day and he exceeded it by a mile.

With one knee bone on bone, and the other not much better, Gene got in 101 miles. Good thing he did not stop for a beer or two. I did the four 50k's at a relaxed pace. The last time I was here Rick asked me what my goal was and I told him to be in bed by ten. I had the same attitude this year. Four 50k's in three days might sound like a lot but that is 72 hours. Some runners ran over 200 miles in the same time period. Another good year here and more friends and memories made.

Pineland Farms 50k
(New Gloucester, Maine - May 25)

This is the 9th year in a row I have done this 50k, every year since its inception. This is a hilly figure 8 course on a mix of gravel roads, trails, and fields where they have mowed a path for runners. You do the course twice for the 50k. There is also a 50 miler and 25k. The day before, they have a 5k, barefoot 10k, and a 5k that you run with your dog. I live about ten miles from the race, so I usually have a runner or two sleep over. Gene and Ron are regulars. Some runners have stopped by for my excellent chicken parmesan with pasta dinner. The reason they like it so much is they have a few beers first and I wait until they are starving. Beer and being very hungry makes my cooking taste good. Lois and Cheryl have also stayed over together. One of them was snoring so loudly Denise and I could hardly get any sleep and that was with the doors closed!

Ron and I usually do either part or the whole race together. It is getting tougher as we get older and we almost always say we will do the 25k next year but never do. One year Ron, Gene, and I were still out on the course when the kegs went empty. Eric, the race director, sent someone to a bar to pick up a keg or two of beer. Pabst was all that was available. The story I heard is Eric knew how much Ron, Gene, and I look forward to a cold beer so he sent for the kegs. After the race there is also a barbeque. You can also camp near the race site. This is by far the biggest ultra in Maine. Between the shorter races and ultras there must have been 800-1,000 runners. Eric does an excellent job with these races.

Self Transcendence Marathon
(Rockland State Park, Congers, NY - August 25)

This race is put on every year close to the Guru Sri Chinmoy's birthday. Followers come from all over the world to celebrate, and the race is part of the celebration. The Sri Chinmoy Marathon Team puts on this race as they do many other events including the 6 and 10 day races. Ron and I do this race every year and a big part of why we like it so much is the presence of Sri Chinmoy's followers. We also see friends there every year. The course is about a 3 mile loop on a wide asphalt path with very little elevation change. It's a scenic course where followers of the guru volunteer at all the aid stations. They also sing, play musical instruments, chant, and read poetry along the course. They serve up small cups of seaweed at one aid station. It is usually hot and humid. I had a hard time keeping up with Ron, so I told him to go ahead about half way through the race. I slowed down just a little and felt much better. They had excellent food at the finish line, all vegetarian. The thing that sucks is all the traffic we hit driving home to Maine every year. Next time we might stay the night of the race to miss the rush hour traffic.

Kansas City, MO and Des Moines, IA Marathons (October 18-19) 5 x 50 State Finish

I never thought when I started running marathons in all the States that I would do them more than once. Walter and I flew into Des Moines, Iowa, then drove the 200 miles or so to KC, MO, for the first of the two marathons I needed to finish the States for the 5th time. It was cold, perfect running weather for me at the start. The first half of the race was hilly. Larry and Mike from Dallas and I ran together for most of the last half of the race which was a lot less hilly than the first half. I felt good at the finish, no chest pain, just the normal soreness as I jumped into the car for a three hour drive to packet pickup for the second race.

Race morning was the same as yesterday, nice and cold. I ran the first three or four miles alone then caught up with Mike, whom I met yesterday. He was with a runner that was already hurting so we stayed together for a few miles and then I went on ahead. After a few miles, I met up with a first time marathoner who went out too fast. She was hurting physically and mentally saying she did not know if she could finish the race. I stayed with her for a while meeting her husband along the course. I talked to her about the race being mostly about staying strong mentally, attitude, and that she was just tired, not injured. I also gave her the speech about if you quit you will remember it the rest of your life, blah, blah, blah. She had plenty of time to finish because there was a 7 hour cut off. She promised me she would be okay so I went ahead. I met her husband again and told him to keep encouraging her to finish every time he saw her. I said the same to her mother.

Mike caught up to me and said the runner he was with dropped out. We ran several miles of the most scenic part of the course together, me holding him back. We ended up crossing the finish line with another 50 Stater. Mike was a lot of fun to run with and we had a good time. Walter took a few pictures of us together, and as I was walking away the mother of the first time marathoner called me over. She thanked me for encouraging her daughter who was only a mile or two away from finishing. Her daughter said she was going to quit until I talked to her. The mother and husband kept following her during the race telling her she could do it. This made finishing the States a 5th time all the more special. They had a special medal for all the runners who did KC and Des Moines. This was called the I-35 Challenge named after the road between the two cities. Chris Burch did an excellent job as race director of the Des Moines races except for running out of beer by the time this old guy finished. He did offer to buy me a beer at the after race party though. I said five was definitely enough when I finished these two races. Stupid me is now thinking of trying for six.

The Savage 7 Races (always held the day after Christmas through New Year's Day)

First a little background on the Savage 7 race directors; I consider all of them good friends.

Bettie Wales finished her first marathon in 1993, her 100th in 2011, 200th in 2014 and 102 marathons in 2015 for a total of over 300. Bettie is one of only 5 women in the world to have run 100 or more in a calendar year. At 70 years old she is probably the oldest also. As I write this she has probably finished running a marathon in every state for the second time and accomplished her goal of running a 50 miler in 2015.

Chuck Savage has run well over 300 marathons and ultras and has done so in all 50 States. Chuck started the Ocala marathon, the New England Challenge Marathon series, and the Savage 7. At the age of 75 in 2015, he is still an amazing marathon runner and shows no signs of slowing down.

Cheryl Murdock is the baby of the bunch at 63 or so. She has completed over 300 marathons/ultras, all the states and also shows no signs of slowing down. Cheryl loves to run but has given up the chance to do so in order to be race director of the Savage 7 series twice.

Thanks to all of you for putting the time and effort in to make these races the best possible.

Now for the story behind the race series:

Chuck Savage who lives in Ocala, FL, got the idea of the Savage 7 in 2010. Chuck is an architect and December 26 through January 1 was always a slow time of year for him. Frank thought up the name for the races. Chuck started the Ocala marathon and had been race director for many years so he had what it would take to put on 7 marathons in 7 days. Chuck is also the race director for the New England Challenge, 5 marathons in 5 States on 5 consecutive days.

The first year the Savage 7 races took place on a quarter mile track in Ocala, FL. The next year 2011-2012 it was held on a quarter mile track in Pensacola, FL by never before race director Cheryl Murdock. The third year it was held in a school parking lot in Winter Park, FL. The course was 50 loops on mostly asphalt. Bettie Wales had never been a race director before and did an excellent job with the races, as did Chuck and Cheryl previously. Bettie found it rewarding to see the satisfaction on people's faces as they completed races each consecutive day. Chuck and Cheryl must have found it rewarding also as they both have directed the Savage 7 a second time.

In 2013, the race went back to Ocala, but to a different location with Chuck as director. I have done all the Savage 7 races except for the first year and think this course is by far the best. The course is mostly in a park and is basically five loops, all on asphalt and no traffic, but watch out for bikes.

The course has two aid stations, some small hills, and is partly shaded. Quoting the website: "The Savage Seven is the perfect place for first timers to earn the rank of 'marathoner.' Or maybe you are up to the challenge of completing a marathon on several days. We offer a generous 8 hour cut-off time, lots of food, fun, and friends".

There are usually fewer than 50 runners, the laps are counted manually, and there are no cheering crowds, just friendly volunteers encouraging you all the time. If you like a low key race that is not overpriced and want to make some friends this might be the race (or races) for you. I meet friends here every year and also make new ones.

All finishers get a medal for each race plus a special award if doing all seven. The host hotel has been the Days Inn with a very good rate and just 5 miles from the race start. These are definitely some of my favorite races. With an 8 hour cut-off I hope to be doing these races for many years to come. Chuck Savage will be the race director in 2015-2016 and it will stay in the same location.

Ron came down the second year and we stayed together. Race morning we left the motel, with him driving and me as navigator. When the GPS said take next left I told Ron to turn left and he went right over the highway divider. I guess I should have said next left. Well, within a minute or two, we were pulled over and surrounded by seven cop cars. Ron's son was following us in a fancy sports car. The cops thought we went over the highway divider to get away from him and this might be a drug deal or something similar gone bad. Ron very politely explained the situation and they let us go. They probably thought another two old dumb bastards from Maine.

That same year there was a girl there with a beautiful, long, blonde ponytail and I told her I wanted to buy it to pin on the back of a baseball hat and wear it. No way did she want to do that. Each day I offered her more money, I even offered to put it on EBay and outbid everyone.

Still she would not part with her ponytail. Well I told her the hell with you I will grow my own ponytail. My hair was about a quarter inch long when I told Liz this back in 2011. Well I have not cut my hair since then. I see Liz at different races and always compare ponytails with her. I also grew a beard to go with it.

Some people who have not seen me for a while do not recognize me. My license has the old shaved head, no beard picture on it and the TSA always does a double take. Denise says I look like a homeless person with my worn jeans and t-shirts. I like the worn look something like Luis Rios. I have been thinking of holding up a sign at a busy intersection. The sign would read "Veteran who wants beer money." I am a vet and want beer money, no lies there.

That same year I was running with this lady I know and she was telling me how poor she was growing up. Then she started telling me how she did not like her piano lesson teacher! I don't think there was a piano in the whole city of Somerville where I grew up. Well, I explained to her what poor was. "When I was a kid if I did not wake up with an erection Christmas morning I had nothing to play with!" Well I don't think she stopped laughing for 5 or 6 laps.

October Coastal Marathons

I try to do all three of these races every year. The first two are in Maine and the third in Massachusetts. All are very good destination marathons with things to do in the area, especially sightseeing. The Maine Marathon is the easiest to get to if you fly into Portland. All three races have sold out in the past. I have done almost all the marathons in New England and these are my favorites. I have done Boston but having done almost every big city marathon in the country I prefer the smaller marathons now. Also I could not qualify for Boston again.

Maine Marathon

The Maine marathon is held the first Sunday in October. This is my hometown marathon because I live 30 miles north of Portland where the race takes place. I was on the race committee for years and had the pleasure of working with race directors Howard Spear and Bob Aube along with other committee members. This race is also supported by the Maine Track Club which I have been a member of almost since I started running. Serving different positions on the Maine Track Club such as vice president and member-at-large, I got to know how much work this all volunteer club and the marathon committee does for this race. Howard takes great pride in the fact that nobody is paid on the committee and all the money the marathon makes goes to non-profits.

There is also a half marathon and relay with the marathon. The races sell out every year and are capped at 3,500 runners total. This is a scenic race which starts and finishes in Portland. There is an early start for slower runners. Many 50 State runners do the New Hampshire marathon the day before. It is roughly an out and back where you make a circle near half way for a few miles. You get to enjoy ocean views and New England fall foliage on this sometimes hilly course with the first and last few miles almost flat. If you fly into Portland you are just a few miles from the start. There is much to see in the Greater Portland area. The shore is dotted with lighthouses and old forts. L.L.Bean flagship store is not far and Portland is famous for its many fine restaurants.

Mount Desert Island Marathon

The MDI marathon is one of my favorite marathons, and Ron agrees. It is held every year around the third Sunday in October. Mount Desert Island is home to Acadia National Park which I think is the most scenic area on the east coast. The race does not go into the park but is very scenic with many mountain and ocean views. There is also a relay and half marathon. The race starts in Bar Harbor and ends in Southwest Harbor. It is a hilly course that most runners would pick because of the scenery and challenge it offers. They would not be looking to set a personal record. The race does have a cap, so you might want to sign up early. There are many attractions in the area, the biggest being Acadia National Park, Bar Harbor shopping, and the many fine seafood restaurants with Maine lobster and fish. The closest large airport is Bangor International a little over an hour away. Next closest would be Portland, a 3.5 hour ride. It is a longer ride from Portland taking route 1 but it is very scenic traveling along the coastline and through many small towns.

Even though race director, Gary, is a very fast runner he still caters to us slower ones by having an early start at the Mount Desert Island marathon and waits for the last runner to finish. Mary Ropp helps Gary with all or most of the races that the Crows put on. The Crow Athletic Club is headed by Gary and is based on MDI but has members all over the USA and Canada. Mary also manages the Crow website and does an excellent job with everything she is involved with including designing some excellent finishers' medals.

Cape Cod Marathon and Clam Chowdah Challenge

This is a race I have done almost every year since I started doing marathons. Cape Cod, Massachusetts, is a beautiful place, but in the summertime it is crowded and the traffic is terrible. This marathon is held the last weekend in October and alleviates that problem. In the last few years, they have added a half marathon which is run on Saturday and the marathon Sunday. You can sign up for both and do what is called the Clam Chowdah Challenge. Both races are held in Falmouth and like the Maine and MDI marathons are very scenic. The half is a very scenic out and back with most of the course along the shoreline with just one small hill. This is the most scenic and easy half marathon I have ever run. The first ten miles of the marathon is mostly flat on this loop type course. After mile ten, it is a hilly course in the country and along the shore where it flattens out about mile 22 to the finish. The marathon has an early start. There is an excellent free clam chowder lunch after the race which also serves pasta, rolls and other treats.

In 2015 I did the usual, lots of slow marathons and ultras. My cardiologist found another bad valve in my heart, the mitral. When I asked if it had to be replaced he said, " If you live long enough'" I have a lot of issues with my heart but none that needs surgery right away. My knee is now "bone on bone" according to my sports medicine doctor but I can deal with the pain with the help of Orthovisc shots in the knee, but it will eventually need replacement.

In 2015 my youngest brother died unexpectedly in his sleep. This was devastating to the entire family. Paul was enjoying his retirement to the max, especially his grandchildren. I always thought Walter or I would die long before Paul. He seemed by far the healthiest of the three Brooks brothers. Shortly after Paul's passing one of my best friends, Harry Schepers, died from cancer. I did get a chance to see him several times while he could still communicate well. We talked about old times at the fire department, our many

150 mile bike rides for multiple sclerosis, and our fishing trips. Both Paul and Harry are sadly missed by many friends and family.

I turned 70 in 2015 and planned on doing a big fundraiser in 2016 hoping to raise $14,000 for Camp Sunshine. My plan was to run 7 marathons in 7 different states on 7 consecutive days. Finish Line Sports Stores Youth Foundation pledged $7,000 which I tried to match through other donations. This goal was fulfilled.

What follows is a report I wrote for a local running club publication about this challenge:

Camp Sunshine Fundraiser:
7 Marathons in 7 States in 7 Days @ Age 70

Hello from the back of the pack. This is a race report but more importantly it is a report about a very successful fundraiser. My plan was to run/walk 70 miles for Camp Sunshine on my 70th birthday, 11/17/2015, in a Lewiston, Maine, park. After talking to Mike Smith at Camp Sunshine we decided that doing 7 individual marathons would draw more attention to Camp Sunshine and raise more money.

In preparation for the races I got a cortisone shot in my bone-on-bone knee and another one in my spine. I have a herniated disc that was pushing against a nerve causing pain down my left side. These two shots minimized the pain I would have in all 7 races. Glad there was no drug testing (smile).

The races are popularly known as the Mainly Marathons Riverboat series and the marathons take place in LA, AR, MS, TN, KY, MO, and IL, in that order. In addition to marathons, the organization also offers 5ks and half marathons. My brother Walter and I flew into Memphis and took in a few sights before driving south to the first race in Louisiana, stopping at the Vicksburg Battlefield in Mississippi. There is no time limit on any of the races and the only awards are for first time marathoners and whoever finishes last. The goal of most runners is to just finish. Some runners do all 7 but most do just one or several. If someone is trying to do races in all 50 states, this is an easy and economical way to do it. One plane ticket, fewer motel stays and rental cars, etc. As slow as I am no time limit really helped me.

The first race was in a city park on an out and back course with only one hill that. It took 22 laps to complete 26.2 miles. All these laps might seem boring but there were turtles to watch (one passed me on lap 19), ducks, a very large snake on the side of the trail, and always someone to cheer on or talk to. After completing each lap I picked up an elastic band to keep track of my mileage. There were lap counters also and a camera at the turnaround to keep everybody honest.

In a previous race, Hanna, the R.D.'s wife, had put a garter belt on my leg and added a dollar bill on one of my laps. That gave me the idea to wear a garter belt in all 7 races to raise more money. With the garter belt on my left leg I started out on my first race after Clint, the RD announced why I was wearing the garter belt. The girls put the money into the garter belt while the guys would hand me the money. In all these races, I did laps with friends, talking as we ran and walked. I have done hundreds of marathons with these friends and we still find plenty of things to talk about. On each lap you pass by the well-stocked aid station. Norm is the cook who travels with his wife Kathy to all the races. He cooks burritos, beans and rice, soups, and many other delicious dishes. Be careful or you could gain weight doing these races! When it is hot Norm hands out freeze pops. His wife counts laps, helps with registration, and does several other jobs like reminding me to pick up my gear at the end of each race. I stopped during the race to do a TV interview that lasted about 20 minutes. My only goal in these races is to get the word out about Camp Sunshine, raise money, and finish. The race went well, it was sunny, in the high 70's, and I had fun.

After finishing this first race, we were off for a 100-mile ride to our next motel. Brother Walter does all the driving, packs up the car, and keeps the beer cold. As we drove, we passed by a lot of very modest homes and I wondered if there is some poor kid suffering from a serious illness inside. What a blessing it would be for that child and his family to spend a week at Camp Sunshine. My main goal is to let people in the southeast know that Camp Sunshine is available to them for free.

Race #2 was in an Arkansas state park on a very flat out-and-back 1.31-mile course, paved with some crushed gravel. It took 20 laps to finish the marathon on this scenic tree-lined course. The last time I did this race it poured rain with thunder and lightning. I was running with Sabra when Clint told her "go jump in your car, Mike keep on running." This year it was sunny and in the 70's. I chatted with old friends and met new ones. On these out-and-back courses you see all the runners every lap which really makes for a very social event.

Race #3 was in another state park, this time in Mississippi. The course was much like yesterday's, 1.31 miles out-and-back, scenic, flat, and on paved roads. We were lucky that none of the courses were flooded. The south had had record breaking rain weeks before we arrived and the water had receded only recently from some of the courses; you could still see some minor flooding in places. More good weather, more money in the garter belt. As we drove the 175 miles to our next location I did a phone interview with a newspaper reporter. Camp Sunshine had hired a media company to publicize the races. A Poland TV station even picked it up!

Race #4 was about 30 miles north of Memphis in Meeman-Shelby State Park, Tennessee. This was a 2.184 mile out-and-back paved and rather flat course. It was well-shaded by large trees and temps were in the 70's with off and on showers. Norm the cook and I decided to have a contest to see who could raise the most money wearing a garter belt. Norm bribed runners from his position as cook. When I finished the race we counted the money, Norm $172, me $166. Norm should become a politician the way he talked runners into donating to Camp Sunshine. A 125-mile drive and two phone interviews later and we were at our motel for the next Riverboat series marathon.

Race # 5 was on a two loop course. The south loop was paved and had two hills, one very steep but short. This loop had excellent views of the Mississippi River with the constant movement of barges. The second loop was on a grass trail through Civil War Earthworks. This was by far the toughest course but also the most scenic. The marathon required 18 loops. It poured on our way to the race but it turned out to be a hot humid sunny day. I was still feeling good and having fun each day. An easy 60-mile drive and we were at our motel just two miles from the next day's race site.

Race #6 was in a city park in Cape Girardeau, Missouri. The course was a 2.62 mile out-and-back partially shaded paved trail with easy hills. It was sunny and warm. I should mention that all the courses were open to the public and I did get some strange looks for wearing a garter belt. What did they think, I wondered? We had to stay about 30 miles north of the next race but it was an easy two-hour drive, including checking out the race site. Most of the meals we ate during the series were fast food. This was partly necessary because of limited time and my brother not liking to try new food. Well, this night brother Walter had a craving for Kentucky Fried Chicken. Did I mention he has Crohn's disease? KFC had a buffet and Walter really loaded up on the fried chicken. Big, big mistake. He was sick all night and part of the next day and blamed it all on the Colonel. He swears he will never do that again!

Race # 7 was the easiest course. Tunnel Hill State Park in Vienna, Illinois, was the location of this 2.184 mile out-and-back course on a gravel rail trail. Mike Smith from Camp Sunshine came down with his son Caleb to do the marathon with me. Mike had never done a marathon and I was hoping to get a little revenge. In 2009 I told Mike I was planning on doing the Ten Day race in New York City as a fundraiser for Camp Sunshine. Mike came up with the idea that I should run 500 miles! I told Mike" that is 50 miles a day, I am 64 and think that goal is a little much." Well, Mike talked me into trying for 500. I did fine the first 6 days with 330 plus miles despite record breaking heat. I had severe back pain the last 4 days but just needed 31 miles the last day. I could only go a few hundred feet and would have to stop, stretch, and sometimes roll on the ground. Unfortunately I came up short, with only 491 miles but I did manage to raise $11,000 for Camp Sunshine, $1,000 more than my goal. That was the most painful race I have ever done and the 500 mile goal was the reason. This is why I wanted to see Mike suffer a little in this marathon (smile). He started the race, developed a hot spot/blister on his heel and was having back pain. After a few more miles he felt better and finished the marathon in good shape, bummer. I did a 30-minute TV interview during the race which included running back and forth in front of the camera. Guess what? the mic was not on so I had to do about 15 minutes of it over again. Mike finished before me and I was presented a beautiful stained glass award for my fund-raising efforts.

We next drove to Memphis and spent the next day touring that neat city . We had a 6:00 am flight the next morning and it turned into the trip from hell. Our flight left late so we missed our connection in DC. Our standby flight was overbooked. We finally got on a plane only to wait almost 2 hours on the ground because our flight plan somehow got lost. Going up and down stairs to shuttle buses with my luggage caused my knee lots of pain. I am just glad this happened after the races. I also just found out I am going to have open heart surgery in July and hope to have my knee replaced in January. I was told over 2 years ago not to run because of my heart so I am looking forward to getting this valve and knee replaced. Hopefully, I will come out better. Lucky me that everything held together during the races.

The fundraiser was a huge success. So far we have raised $17,700, enough to send 7 families to Camp Sunshine. I like all the 7's: 7 marathons in 7 states in 7 days at 70 and 7 families going to Camp Sunshine. Thanks to Walter for all the driving and keeping the beer cold. Thanks to Mike Smith for all your help with the fundraiser. I would not have raised half as much without your help. A special thanks to everyone who donated. Because of your dona-tions, 7 families will be spending a week at Camp Sunshine where they can relax, meet other families with the same problems, get counseling, and just enjoy a week in Maine.

Donations can still be made at www.crowdrise.com. Just enter Mike Brooks or mail checks to Camp Sunshine, 35 Acadia RD, Casco, ME 04015.

Mike, Nellie, Bettie, Jim S, Chuck S, Frank Bartocci at Savage 7

Savage 7 L TO R:
Bettie Wailes (race director), , Eddie Vega, Jan Gagnier,
Cowboy Jeff Bishton, Ponytail Lizz,
Cheryl Murdock (race director other years)

THE FUTURE

My next goal is to do my 500th marathon at the Maine marathon. I managed to complete 6 marathons and two 50k's between May 12th - May 30th, bringing me to 499 marathon/ultras. This would allow me plenty of time to get my knee replaced before my 500th with no extra races needed or so I thought. However, when I arrived home the day after marathon #499 there was a voicemail from my doctor that said "don't do anything strenuous and call the office." After several tests it was determined that I need to replace my aortic heart valve which had worsened since my last exam. It made sense to get the valve job right away and do the knee joint later. The result - I had open heart surgery on July 22, 2016, and now have a cow valve as part of my heart. I think it was from a bull since I seem to be attracted to big udders on milk cows (smile). I feel confident I will do the Maine Marathon on Oct. 2. Odds are I will get my knee replacement in January.

When I was younger I always drove my cars to a point where the only place they belonged was the junk yard. I am starting to feel a little like one of those cars now but I'm not quite ready for the junk yard yet. I have two bad valves in my motor (heart), blockage in my fuel line (coronary artery disease with 50% blockage in the right coronary artery), out of alignment (bad knee makes me favor one side), bald tires (big toe does not bend, both feet screwed up), and frame is rusted (degeneration in the spine and arthritis). According to the doctors I would not pass for an inspection sticker either. I could pretty much tell when a car was getting close to going to the junk yard. I feel I pretty much know the same about myself. Checking everything over I think I still have lots of miles left. Those miles will not be in the passing lane, they will be close to the minimum speed allowed but I will putter along for years to come, I hope.

The body is only one part of what you need to run. The body will hurt at times so you have to love what you are doing to continue, especially as you age and it becomes harder to do. "Pain is weakness leaving your body." "What does not kill you makes you stronger." "It will get better; this is just a bad spot." I try to remember these three things. The first two may not be true but it helps to think they are. So a big part of my still running will be that I love to do races, visit places, and meet new and old faces.

2015 Totals:

- 35 marathons
- 4 ultras
- 65 races total

THE FUTURE: AN UPDATE

This book has taken me longer to get published than I thought it would. I am not going to update everything but will add some here.

After I had my heart valve replacement I had a reaction to a medication that led to a series of problems which led to 2 infections from 3 different organisms. This caused me to be re-hospitalized for another 7 days and to undergo additional surgeries. I was discharged on August 11, 2016 on IV antibiotics (at one point there were 6 different infusions a day). What I didn't realize is that the antibiotic plus other medications I was on were affecting how my kidneys were functioning.

After I ran a 5K On August 28th I learned that my kidneys were only functioning at about 25%, this was a result of the medications and the fact that I was dehydrated going into the race. Boy, did I get my butt chewed out by my doctor!

Thankfully this was reversible and in 3 weeks my kidneys were back to normal. On October 2, 2016 I ran my 500th marathon as planned at the Maine Marathon in Portland. I never make a big deal out of different milestones in my running but really wanted to do my 500th at the Maine Marathon for many reasons including it being my hometown Marathon. I was concerned about being able to finish the 26.2 miles in a decent time until I talked to my friend and race director Howard Spear.

He said, "I don't care how long it takes, we will wait for you" (at the finish line). That was all I needed to hear for it to be a green light to do it. My close friend Ron Paquette agreed to stay with me the entire race. I could only run a few steps at a time so I mostly walked this one.

When we got to about mile 11, my wife Denise and daughter Heidi were waiting for me as planned. I was surprised to see that my niece Kristie, her husband Jim, and their children Jo Jo and Maggie were also there wearing T-shirts which read "Team Mike Marathon #500!!"

I had no idea they were coming up from Massachusetts as I was trying to keep my 500th a little quiet in case I dropped dead or did not finish. Denise had the t-shirts made up unbeknownst to me.

I was hurting physically but could not have been stronger mentally now. We met them again at about mile 15. Donna Jean joined hubby and I for a mile or so then went and got me some Tylenol while I sat for a few minutes with Denise and Heidi.

Totally exhausted, but not hurting too badly, Ron and I walked the last 4 or 5 miles with our friends Dave Goodrich and Larry Macon. Crossing the finish line, we were greeted by many friends and a big cheer as they announced my name.

Brother Walter, daughter Katie and her two daughters Maddie and McKenzie, sister-in-law Barb, niece Kerri, her husband Erik and their kids Nathaniel and Alex, were all there sporting "Mike's 500th" t-shirts. This is one of my greatest memories, having friends and family supporting me while I was able to "get 'er done" so soon after my medical problems, even though my time was 8:29:39.

I did three marathons, Oct. 13, 14 and 15th. Frank Bartucci stayed with me all the time at South Carolina race and Henry Rueden did the same in Georgia. The last race in Alabama I finished last and got a nice caboose for doing so. Next was a few short races and the Savage 7 marathons. I was hoping to do all 7 of the Savage 7 marathons, having completed 35 of them in the last 5 years.

Well, my bone on bone knee and pain shooting down that same leg kept me to just finishing three. Good friend Marsha White walked the last 5-mile loop in marathon 3 with me which helped take my mind off the pain. I finished last by about 40 minutes. By the way, Marsha did a lot of work on this book and did it on time and superbly. Her poor husband Darcy had to read it several times to pick up any errors.

The knee I was supposed to have replaced in January cannot be done until September at the earliest. The surgeon wants to wait at least a year from date of infection for fear infection might still be in my body.

Updated totals as of December 31, 2016:

- 100 ultra-marathons
- 406 26.2 marathons
- 1163 total races

When I was younger I always drove my cars to a point where the only place they belonged was the junk yard. I am starting to feel a little like one of those cars now, but I'm not quite ready for the junk yard yet.

I have two bad valves in my motor (heart), blockage in my fuel line (coronary artery disease with 50% blockage in the right coronary artery), am out of alignment (bad knee makes me favor one side), bald tires (big toe does not bend, both feet screwed up), and my frame is rusted (degeneration in the spine and arthritis).

According to the doctors I would not pass for an inspection sticker either. I could pretty much tell when a car was getting close to going to the junk yard. I feel I pretty much now the same about myself.

Checking everything over, I think I still have lots of miles left. Those miles will not be in the passing lane, they will be close to the minimum speed allowed, but I will putter along for years to come, I hope.

The body is only one part of what you need to run. The body will hurt at times, so you have to love what you are doing to continue, especially as you age and it becomes harder to do.

"Pain is weakness leaving your body."
"What does not kill you makes you stronger."
"It will get better; this is just a bad spot."

I try to remember these three things. The first two may not be true, but it helps to think they are. So a big part of my still running will be that I love to do races, visit places, and meet new and old faces.

Mike with Clyde and Kelly Shank, 2 weeks after 500th marathon

**500th marathon: Katie, Madison, Barb, Mike, Denise, Heidi,
Walter, Kerri, Eric, Nathaniel, Alex, McKenzie and Nellie the dog**

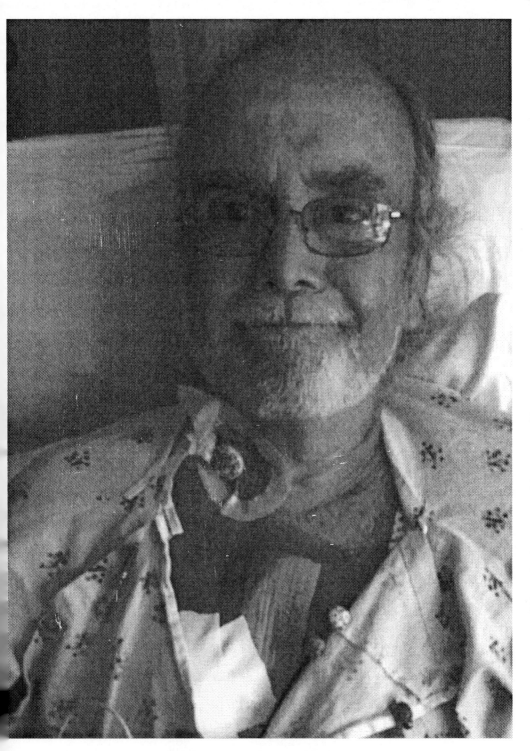

2nd day post op open heart surgery

RUNNING CLUBS I BELONG TO:

50 States Club:

History: The 50 States Marathon Club was incorporated in the state of Illinois in March 2001. About 130 people had already completed marathons in 50 states before this time. There was an informal group that many of those finishers belonged to. It was felt that a formal organization with a set of rules and a board of directors would be in order.

Bob Lehew was our first president, with Rick Worley as vice president, Tom Adair as secretary, Steve Boone as treasurer, Layne Reibel as membership director, Lois Berkowitz as newsletter editor and Victor Bhatt as reunion coordinator.

The club is a non-profit membership organization dedicated to the promotion of health and fitness through running marathons. We are all bound by a common love of running, a common desire to see the vast areas of our country, and the common affection of meeting and sharing our experiences with other runners.

Steve and Paula Boone along with all the board members donate many, many hours of their time to this nonprofit Club.

50 States and DC Marathon Group:

The group shares a goal of finishing a marathon in every State and DC. The Group was the forerunner of the 50 States Club and many runners belong to both organizations.

Marathon Mainiacs:

This is the fastest growing and largest of the marathon clubs. Their goals are many but basically to do lots of marathons. It is also the easiest club to join.

100 Marathon Club:

The Club, I believe, was started by Bob and Lenore Dolphin. In order to be a member you must have run 100 marathons and/or ultra marathons. Bob is in his 80's and still running marathons. I once did the Yakima River Marathon in Washington State just because Lenore promised me a hug at the finish line. She is a sweetheart. Bob and Lenore are the race directors of this scenic marathon.

Megamarathon Club:

This is a truly international club that has more members in other countries than the USA. To be a member you must have run 300 marathons/ultras or more. There are no dues and the USA records are updated every 6 months by Walt Prescott.

Maine Track Club:

This is a local club that I have been most active in. I have been vice president, member-at-large, and on several committees in the past. I should volunteer more than I do at MTC races but like to run them too much. I usually write an article for the club newsletter. The club has about 600 members.

Central Maine Striders:

This running group puts on races 30 miles plus north of where I live. I travel to these races when I can for several reasons. Ron, Donna Jean and several other friends are usually at these races. The races are well organized and very reasonably priced.

Crow Athletics Club:

This club is headquartered 130 miles, as the crow flies, north of my home. I try to do the club's marathon every year and used to do their 50k before it was discontinued. My main reason for being in the club is the friendships I have made with their members. *Caw! Caw!*

ACKNOWLEDGEMENTS

This book never would have made it to print without the help of my daughter Heidi, who spent many hours editing the book. Since I am not a writer and never will be, our collaboration worked out nicely since we got to spend some valuable time together.

I am very thankful for all the contributions made by many of my running friends and race directors who wrote about our experiences together. Many of them are pretty good writers and added a great deal of humor to these stories.

My brother Walter drove me all over the country several times and has been my chauffeur on countless trips. Sometimes he drove 500 miles between back to back races.

My thanks to the thousand plus people I met while traveling and running who gave me something to write about as well as many fond memories.

Fellow runner and friend Marsha White also helped edit and proofread the book for me. Another friend and runner, Blaine Moore, got the book published. Thanks to both of you.

Last but definitely not least is my wife Denise. Whenever I asked her if it was okay with her if I took a certain trip, she would always say "do it while you can." Never once did she complain about all the money I spent on these trips. Denise also came with me on many of my trips, especially if it was to a warm place like Hawaii or Florida or where she could find a casino. We never chose a vacation where I didn't do at least one marathon. Thanks, Denise, for your continued support, love you.

MIKE'S MARATHONS

1	10-15-1995	3:38:15	Bay State Marathon (Lowell, MA)
2	11-12-1995	4:00:18	New York City Marathon (New York, NY)
3	04-15-1996	4:16:18	Boston Marathon (Boston, MA)
4	06-09-1996	4:04:22	Sugarloaf Marathon (Carrabassett Valley, ME)
5	08-18-1996	3:57:24	Festival by the Sea Marathon (St. John, NB, Canada)
6	01-05-1997	4:30:09	Walt Disney World Marathon (Lake Buena Vista, FL)
7	05-25-1997	3:56:07	Vermont City Marathon (Burlington, VT)
8	09-28-1997	4:05:48	Clarence DeMar Marathon (Keene, NH)
9	11-02-1997	4:06:55	New York City Marathon (New York, NY)
10	11-29-1997	3:52:28	North Central Trail Marathon (Sparks, MD)
11	02-01-1998	4:00:15	Las Vegas Marathon (Las Vegas, NV)
12	03-07-1998	3:57:02	Nantucket Marathon (Nantucket, MA)
13	04-26-1998	3:53:23	Jersey Shore Marathon (Long Branch, NJ)
14	05-24-1998	3:58:48	Vermont City Marathon (Burlington, VT)
15	08-16-1998	4:18:39	Festival by the Sea Marathon (St. John, NB, Canada)
16	10-03-1998	4:19:12	New Hampshire Marathon (Gilsum, NH)
17	10-17-1998	8:58:52*	Maine Track Club 50 Miler (Brunswick, ME)
18	11-08-1998	4:01:34	Ocean State Marathon (Narragansett, RI)
19	11-21-1998	10:24:15*	JFK 50 Miler (Hagerstown, MD)
20	12-06-1998	4:34:37	PMRI Delaware Marathon (Middleton, DE)
21	01-10-1999	4:19:23	Walt Disney World Marathon (Lake Buena Vista, FL)
22	01-17-1999	4:52:17	Houston Marathon (Houston, TX)
23	02-28-1999	4:28:00	Cape Cod Times Marathon (Hyannis, MA)
24	03-20-1999	4:55:15	Virginia Beach Marathon (Virginia Beach, VA)
25	04-18-1999	4:26:57	Fred's Marathon (Worcester, MA)
26	05-30-1999	4:26:01	Vermont City Marathon (Burlington, VT)
27	08-06-1999	98.9 miles*	Run Around the Lake 24 Hour (Wakefield, MA)
28	09-19-1999	8:02:45*	Pisgah Mountain Trail 50k (Chesterfield, NH)
29	10-09-1999	4:07:51	Hartford Marathon (Hartford, CT)
30	10-24-1999	4:17:53	Marine Corps Marathon (Washington, DC)
31	11-21-1999	4:18:00	Philadelphia Marathon (Philadelphia, PA)
32	02-06-2000	4:18:00	Mardi Gras Marathon (New Orleans, LA)
33	02-19-2000	4:22:52	Myrtle Beach Marathon (Myrtle Beach, SC)
34	04-08-2000	4:20:53	Camp Lejeune Marathon (Camp Lejeune, NC)
35	04-29-2000	4:23:59	Country Music Marathon (Nashville, TN)
36	05-28-2000	4:36:56	Vermont City Marathon (Burlington, VT)
37	08-20-2000	4:55:34	Marathon by the Sea (St. John, NB, Canada)

38	09-16-2000	103 miles* USATF 24 Hour Race (Oleander Park, OH)
39	10-01-2000	4:37:37 Maine Marathon (Portland, ME)
40	10-22-2000	4:28:08 LaSalle Bank Chicago Marathon (Chicago, IL)
41	11-18-2000	4:11:49 Midsouth Marathon (Wynne, AR)
42	12-09-2000	4:24:35 Rocket City Marathon (Huntsville, AL)
43	01-13-2001	4:35:06 Mississippi Marathon (Clinton, MS)
44	02-18-2001	4:32:40 Desert Classic Marathon (Scottsdale, AZ)
45	03-04-2001	4:26:05 Los Angeles Marathon (Los Angeles, CA)
46	03-18-2001	4:36:59 Maui Marathon (Maui, HI)
47	04-29-2001	4:53:17 Oklahoma City Marathon (Oklahoma City, OK)
48	05-27-2001	12:26:17* Rocky Mountain Double Marathon (Laramie, WY)
49	06-02-2001	4:46:02 Governor's Cup Marathon (Helena, MT)
50	06-09-2001	4:56:00 Marathon to Marathon (Marathon, IO)
51	07-27-2001	27:31:54* Vermont 100 (Woodstock, VT)
52	08-26-2001	4:22:16 Omaha Arts Marathon (Omaha, NE)
53	09-08-2001	4:20:44 YMCA Marathon (Bismarck, ND)
54	09-30-2001	4:53:11 Duke City Marathon (Albuquerque, NM)
55	10-07-2001	4:35:50 Maine Marathon (Portland, ME)
56	10-14-2001	4:43:34 Lakefront Marathon (Milwaukee, WI)
57	10-20-2001	4:50:41 Indianapolis Marathon (Springfield, IN)
58	10-21-2001	4:40:02 Louisville Marathon (Louisville, KY)
59	10-28-2001	4:29:43 Mystic Places Marathon (Mystic, CT)
60	11-17-2001	4:38:10 Oklahoma Marathon (Tulsa, OK)
61	11-18-2001	4:47:00 Gobbler Grind Marathon (Kansas City, KS)
62	11-25-2001	4:34:02 Seattle Marathon (Seattle, WA)
63	12-01-2001	4:20:04 Springfield Marathon (Springfield, MO)
64	02-02-2002	4:39:51 Tybee Island Marathon (Tybee Island, GA)
65	02-03-2002	4:53:08 Ocala Marathon (Ocala, FL)
66	02-24-2002	4:22:53 Sheraton Hyannis Marathon (Hyannis, MA)
67	03-23-2002	4:53:33 Martian Marathon (Northville, MI)
68	04-06-2002	23:50:15* Umstead 100 Endurance Run (Raleigh, NC)
69	05-04-2002	4:18:42 Ogden Marathon (Ogden, UT)
70	05-19-2002	4:27:30 Sugarloaf Marathon (Carrabassett, ME)
71	05-26-2002	4:21:55 Coeur d'Alene Marathon (Coeur d'Alene, ID)
72	06-01-2002	4:13:39 Newport Marathon (Newport, OR)
73	06-08-2002	4:21:23 Hatfield McCoy Marathon (South Williamson, KY)
74	07-20-2002	28:26:47* Vermont 100 (Burlington, VT)
75	09-18-2002	8:39:27 Pikes Peak Marathon (Manitou Springs, CO)
76	09-14-2002	100.6 miles* USATF 24 Hour (Sylvania, OH)
77	09-29-2002	4:26:54 Twin Cities Marathon (Minneapolis, MN)
78	10-06-2002	4:27:55 Maine Marathon (Portland, ME)
79	10-13-2002	4:22:10 Mt. Rushmore International Marathon (Rapid City, SD)
80	10-20-2002	4:31:38 Mt. Desert Island Marathon (Bar Harbor, ME)
81	10-27-2002	4:28:58 Compass Bank Cape Cod Marathon (Hyannis, MA)
82	11-09-2002	5:22:30 Stone Cat Trail Marathon (Ipswich, MA)
83	11-17-2002	5:17:49* Nifty Fifty 50k (location? RI)
	(personal record)	
84	12-14-2002	11:04:44* Sunmart 50 Miler (Huntsville, TX)
85	01-05-2003	4:49:09 Hops Marathon (Tampa, FL)
86	01-12-2003	4:44:12 Walt Disney World Marathon (Lake Buena Vista, FL)
87	02-16-2003	4:59:44 Gulf Beaches Marathon (Clearwater, FL)
88	02-23-2003	5:30:23 Sheraton Hyannis Marathon (Hyannis, MA)
89	03-29-2003	5:23:35 Ellerbee Springs Marathon (Ellerbee, NC)
90	03-30-2003	5:16:16 Virginia Creeper Marathon (Abington, VA)

91	04-05-2003	28:02:43* Umstead 100 Mile Endurance Run (Raleigh, NC)
92	04-26-2003	6:22:00 Delaware Triple Crown Trail Marathon (Newark, DE)
93	04-27-2003	5:27:30 New Jersey Shore Marathon (Long Branch, NJ)
94	05-04-2003	4:41:06 Flying Pig Marathon (Cincinnati, OH)
95	05-18-2003	4:21:34 Sugarloaf Marathon (Carrabassett, ME)
96	05-25-2003	4:37:12 Buffalo Nissan Marathon (Buffalo, NY)
97	06-21-2003	4:18:31 Mayor's Marathon (Anchorage, AK)
		(completed 50 States and DC)
98	07-12-2003	104.1 miles* Mt. Desert Island 24 Hour Run (Bar Harbor, ME)
		(personal record)
99	08-17-2003	8:48:33 Pike's Peak Marathon (Manitou Springs, CO)
100	09-20-2003	4:38:47 US Air Force Marathon (Dayton, OH)
101	09-21-2003	4:35:35 Lewis & Clark Marathon (St. Charles, MS)
102	09-28-2003	4:36:56 Adirondack Marathon (Schroon Lake, NY)
103	10-05-2003	4:33:06 Maine Sportshoe Marathon (Portland, ME)
104	10-09-2003	5:25:06 Lake Tahoe Triple Marathon (Inspiration Point, CA)
105	10-10-2003	5:06:10 Lake Tahoe Triple Marathon (Jct. Rte. 58 & 50, Nevada)
106	10-11-2003	5:09:56 Lake Tahoe Triple Marathon (Tahoe City, CA)
107	10-18-2003	5:55:55* Maine Track Club 50k (Brunswick, ME)
108	10-19-2003	4:58:18 Mt. Desert Island Marathon (Bar Harbor, ME)
109	10-26-2003	4:47:29 Cape Cod Marathon (Falmouth, MA)
110	11-08-2003	4:32:10 Chickamauga Battlefield Marathon (Ft. Oglethorpe, GA)
111	11-09-2003	5:54:52* Peachtree City 50k (Peachtree City, GA)
112	11-15-2003	4:25:04 Suntrust Richmond Marathon (Richmond, VA)
113	12-13-2003	6:17:42* Sunmart 50k Trail Run (Huntsville, TX)
114	12-14-2003	4:48:53 Dallas White Rock Marathon (Dallas, TX)
115	12-30-2003	152.86 miles* Across the Years 48 Hour (Phoenix, AZ)
116	01-25-2004	5:17:31 Hops Marathon (Tampa, FL)
117	02-01-2004	4:55:58 Miami Tropical Marathon (Miami, FL)
118	02-28-2004	4:47:14 Blue Angel Marathon (Pensacola, FL)
119	02-29-2004	5:26:03 Mardi Gras Marathon (New Orleans, LA)
120	03-21-2004	5:24:12 Bataan Death March Marathon (White Sands, NM)
121	04-03-2004	4:55:40 Yakima River Canyon Marathon (Ellensburg, WA)
122	04-04-2004	5:22:53 Whidbey Island Marathon (Whidbey Island, WA)
123	04-17-2004	4:49:44 Charlottesville Marathon (Charlottesville, VA)
124	05-02-2004	4:46:09 Lincoln Marathon (Lincoln, NE)
125	05-15-2004	4:51:16 Brookings Marathon (Brookings, SD)
126	05-16-2004	6:19:46* TIMTAM 50k (Ames, IA)
127	05-30-2004	13:39:43* Wyoming Double Marathon (Cheyenne, WY)
128	07-12-2004	46:17:10* Badwater 135 Ultramarathon (Death Valley, CA)
129	08-14-2004	83.1 miles* Around the Lake 24 Hour Run (Wakefield, MA)
130	08-21-2004	5:27:23 Grizzly Marathon (Choteau, MT)
131	08-28-2004	4:56:03 Mesa Falls Marathon (Ashton, ID)
132	09-11-2004	4:51:37 YMCA Marathon (Bismarck, ND)
133	10-03-2004	5:10:44 Maine Sports Shoe Center Marathon (Portland, ME)
134	10-10-2004	4:43:23 Steamtown Marathon (Scranton, PA)
135	10-16-2004	5:16:58 Green Mountain Marathon (South Hero, VT)
136	10-24-2004	4:53:35 Detroit Free Press Marathon (Detroit, MI)
137	10-31-2004	4:51:58 Cape Cod Marathon (Falmouth, MA)
138	11-14-2004	5:05:30 Healthy Huntington Marathon (Huntington, WV)
139	12-04-2004	5:55:34 Tecumseh Trail Marathon (Bloomington, IN)
140	12-29-2004	180.5 miles* Across the Years 72 Hour (Phoenix, AZ)
141	01-09-2005	5:41:58 Walt Disney Marathon (Lake Buena Vista, FL)
142	01-30-2005	5:22:04 Ocala Longhorn Marathon (Ocala, FL)

143	02-13-2005	5:09:42 Mercedes Marathon (Birmingham, AL)
144	03-12-2005	11:51:59* Carl Touchstone 50 Mile Trail (Laurel, MS)
145	03-20-2005	5:15:52 Hilo International Marathon (Hilo, HI)
146	04-24-2005	6:38:00* Jack Bristol Lake Waramaug 50k (New Preston, CT)
147	04-29-2005	5:08:09 Country Music Marathon (Nashville, TN)
148	05-15-2005	4:56:57 Sugarloaf Marathon (Kingfield, ME)
149	05-22-2005	4:58:30 Green Bay Marathon (Green Bay, WI)
150	06-04-2005	74.38 miles* FANS 24 Hour Race (Minneapolis, MN)
151	07-29-2005	50.56 miles* Around the Lake 24 Hour Race (Wakefield, MA)
152	08-13-2005	5:47:44 Crater Lake Marathon (Crater Lake, OR)
153	08-14-2005	6:46:11 Haulin' Aspen Trail Marathon (Bend, OR)
154	09-17-2005	4:53:34 Top of Utah Marathon (Logan, UT)
155	09-25-2005	5:23:03 Quad Cities Marathon (Moline, IL)
156	10-08-2005	28:03:50* Heartland Spirit of the Prairie 100 Miler (Cassoday, KS)
157	10-22-2005	4:46:25 Old Mulkey Marathon (Tompkinsville, KY)
158	10-29-2005	4:57:04 Marine Corps Marathon (Washington, DC)
159	12-12-2005	4:37:34 Mountain Home Marathon (Mountain Home, TN)
160	12-10-2005	4:36:11 Kiawah Island Marathon (Kiawah Island, SC)
161	01-08-2006	5:31:03 Walt Disney World Marathon (Lake Buena Vista, FL)
162	02-18-2006	5:10:48 Clermont Marathon (Clermont, FL)
163	02-19-2006	5:06:41 Five Points of Life Marathon (Gainesville, FL)
164	02-26-2006	5:14:25 Hyannis Marathon (Hyannis, MA)
165	03-05-2006	4:47:42 Sarasota Marathon (Sarasota, FL)
166	03-25-2006	4:55:23 National Marathon (Washington, DC)
167	03-26-2006	5:23:09 Cape May Marathon (Cape May, NJ)
168	04-08-2006	28:41:29* Umstead 100 Mile Endurance Run (Raleigh, NC)
169	04-30-2006	320 miles* Self-Transcendence 6 Day Run (New York, NY)
170	05-20-2006	7:44:56 Great Wall of China Marathon (Tianjin Province, China)
171	05-27-2006	8:37:31* Pineland Farms 50k (New Gloucester, ME)
172	06-10-2006	5:27:51 Teton Dam Marathon (Rexburg, ID)
173	07-01-2006	8:49:02 Leadville Trail Marathon (Leadville, CO)
174	08-26-2006	29:34:10* Leanhorse 100 Mile Trail Run (Hot Springs, SD)
175	09-16-2006	6:45:06 Equinox Trail Marathon (Fairbanks, AK)
176	09-24-2006	5:22:49 Boulder Backgrounds Marathon (Boulder, CO)
177	10-01-2006	5:11:41 Maine Sportshoe Center Marathon (Portland, ME)
178	10-15-2006	5:11:58 Mt. Desert Island Marathon (Bar Harbor, ME)
179	10-21-2006	5:54:08 Breakers Marathon (Newport, RI)
180	10-22-2006	4:58:13 Mystic Country Marathon (East Lyme, CT)
181	10-29-2006	4:54:07 Cape Cod Marathon (Falmouth, MA)
182	11-17-2006	131.52 miles* UltraCentric 48 Hour Race (Grapevine, TX)
183	12-10-2006	7:33:39 Otter Creek Trail Marathon (Brandenburg, KY)
184	12-16-2006	5:18:00 Coast to Coast Marathon (Narragansett, RI)
185	02-02-2007	5:20:30 Mardi Gras Marathon (New Orleans, LA)
186	03-31-2007	5:27:59 Olathe Marathon (Olathe, KS)
187	04-01-2007	5:25:12 Hogeye Marathon (Fayetteville, AR)
188	04-07-2007	5:25:02 Ocean City Marathon (Ocean City, MD)
189	04-29-2007	6:25:07* Jack Bristol Lake Waramaug 50k (New Preston, CT)
190	05-06-2007	5:13:40 Race of Champions Marathon (Holyoke, MA)
191	05-19-2007	5:14:49 Fargo Marathon (Fargo, ND)
192	05-20-2007	6:09:37 Green Bay Marathon (Green Bay, WI)
193	05-26-2007	6:35:25* Pineland Farms Trail Challenge 50k (New Gloucester, ME)
194	06-02-2007	5:33:25 Ridge Runner Marathon (Cairo, WV)
195	07-08-2007	6:23:38 Maine Woods Trail Marathon (Weld, ME)
196	07-28-2007	6:13:26* Great Cranberry Island 50k (Great Cranberry Island, ME)

197	08-11-2007	31.11 miles* Howl at the Moon 8 Hour Trail Race (Danville, IL)
198	08-18-2007	6:19:57 Grizzly Marathon (Choteau, MT)
199	08-25-2007	5:40:12 Run with the Horses Marathon (Green River, WY)
200	09-02-2007	5:55:12 Tupelo Marathon (Tupelo, MS)
201	09-03-2007	5:23:58 Heart of America Marathon (Columbia, MO)
202	09-29-2007	5:26:32 New Hampshire Marathon (Bristol, NH)
203	09-30-2007	5:37:11 Clarence DeMar Marathon (Keene, NH)
204	10-07-2007	5:52:46 Maine Marathon (Portland, ME)
205	10-14-2007	5:02:02 Mount Desert Island Marathon (Bar Harbor, ME)
206	10-20-2007	6:23:18* MTC 50k (Brunswick, ME)
207	10-27-2007	4:29:26 Ridge to Bridge Marathon (Morganton, NC)
208	10-28-2007	5:42:45 Palmetto Marathon (Greenville, SC)
209	11-04-2007	4:49:52 Manchester Marathon (Manchester, NH)
210	11-16-2007	100 miles* UltraCentric 48 Hour Race (Grapevine, TX)
211	12-02-2007	5:17:38 St. Jude Marathon (Memphis, TN)
212	12-29-2007	177.712 miles* Across The Years 72 Hour Race (Buckeye, AZ)
213	01-27-2008	5:49:36 Miami Marathon (Miami, FL)
214	02-17-2008	5:42:35 Last Chance for Boston (Dublin, Ohio)
215	03-02-2008	5:35:40 Sarasota Marathon (Sarasota, FL)
216	03-29-2008	37.59 miles* Moab 24 Hour Race (Moab, Utah)
217	04-20-2008	6:51:23* Jack Bristol Lake Waramaug 50k (New Preston, CT)
218	05-05-2008	5:41:23 Cox Marathon (Providence, RI)
219	05-10-2008	5:33:38 Lake Wobegon Trail Marathon (St. Joseph, MN)
220	05-11-2008	6:49:17 Central States Mothers Marathon (Ames, IA)
221	05-18-2008	5:49:22 Delaware Marathon (Wilmington, DE)
222	05-25-2008	8:16:20* Pineland Farms Trail Challenge 50k (New Gloucester, ME)
223	06-01-2008	7:30:54 Nipmuck Trail Marathon (Ashford, CT)
224	06-14-2008	45.4 miles* Hawthorn Half-Day Race (Terra Haute, IN)
225	07-19-2008	6:55:12* Great Cranberry Island 50k (Great Cranberry Island , ME)
226	08-02-2008	5:48:09 Frank Maier Marathon (Juneau, AK)
227	08-31-2008	5:32:54 New Mexico Marathon (Albuquerque, NM)
228	09-01-2008	6:14:47 Turtle Marathon (Roswell, NM)
229	09-14-2008	5:53:50 Erie Marathon (Erie, PA)
230	09-20-2008	7:25:36* Bohemian Alps 50k (Brainard, NE)
231	10-05-2008	4:52:05 Maine Marathon (Portland, ME)
232	10-18-2008	5:05:23 Indianapolis Marathon (Indianapolis, IN)
233	10-19-2008	5:18:57 Grand Rapids Marathon (Grand Rapids MI)
234	10-26-2008	5:41:34 Cape Cod Marathon (Falmouth, MA)
235	11-02-2008	5:08:43 Manchester Marathon (Manchester, NH)
236	11-09-2008	5:13:43 Harrisburg Marathon (Harrisburg, PA)
237	11-16-2008	5:16:36 Tulsa Marathon (Tulsa, OK)
238	12-06-2008	5:25:01 Baton Rouge Marathon (Baton Rouge, LA)
239	12-29-2008	186.7 miles* Across The Years 72 Hour Race (Buckeye, AZ)
240	01-24-2009	5:48:42 Diamond Valley Lake Marathon (Hemet, CA)
241	01-25-2009	5:36:34 Carlsbad Marathon (Carlsbad, CA)
242	02-22-2009	5:28:41 Hyannis Marathon (Hyannis, MA)
243	03-01-2009	5:36:22 Bank of America Marathon (Tampa, FL)
244	03-14-2009	51.0 miles* Delano Park 12 Hour Race (Decatur, AL)
245	04-04-2009	5:42:00 Yakima Marathon (Yakima, WA)
246	04-22-2009	491 miles* Sri Chinmoy 10 Day Race (Queens, NY)
247	05-24-2009	8:09:59 Pineland Farms 50k (New Gloucester, ME)
248	06-20-2009	7:20:00 Big 5 Marathon (Entebeni, South Africa)
249	06-27-2009	6:48:00* Kennebec River Trails 30 Miler (Augusta, ME)
250	07-18-2009	6:56:09* Great Cranberry Island 50k (Great Cranberry Island, ME)

251	08-08-2009	31.6 miles* Howl at the Moon 8 Hour Run (Danville, IL)
252	09-06-2009	6:15:34 Kauai Marathon (Kauai, HI)
253	09-19-2009	53.2 miles* Hinson Lake 24 Hour Race (Rockingham, NC)
254	10-04-2009	5:40:07 Maine Marathon (Portland, ME)
255	10-10-2009	5:50:48 Baltimore Marathon (Baltimore, MD)
256	10-11-2009	5:42:13 Steamtown Marathon (Scranton, PA)
257	10-18-2009	5:35:28 Mount Desert Island Marathon (Bar Harbor, ME)
258	10-25-2009	5:45:25 Cape Cod Marathon (Falmouth, MA)
259	11-01-2009	5:26:57 Manchester City Marathon (Manchester, NH)
260	11-15-2009	28.9 miles* Rhode Island 6 Hour Race (Warwick, RI)
261	11-22-2009	5:43:48 Harpeth Hills Flying Monkey Marathon (Nashville, TN)
262	11-29-2009	5:26:13 Space Coast Marathon (Cocoa Beach, FL)
263	12-06-2009	5:31:40 Marathon of the Palms (West Palm Beach, FL)
264	12-12-2009	6:11:45 Ed Sandler Roxbury Marathon (Roxbury, CT)
265	01-01-2010	6:01:11 Texas Marathon (Kingwood, TX)
266	01-31-2010	5:53:28 Callaway Gardens Marathon (Pine Mountain, GA)
267	02-28-2010	5:47:10 Gasparilla Marathon (Tampa, FL)
268	03-06-2010	8:25:19* Carl Touchstone Trail 50k (Laurel, MS)
269	03-07-2010	6:14:23 Little Rock Marathon (Little Rock, AR)
270	03-13-2010	33 miles* Delano Park 12 Hour Race (Decatur, AL)
271	03-20-2010	5:34:57 National Marathon (Washington, DC)
272	04-10-2010	5:50:56 Eisenhower Marathon (Abilene, KS)
273	04-11-2010	44 miles* Brew to Brew Ultra (Kansas City, MO to Lawrence, KS)
274	04-17-2010	6:15:53 Wenatchee Marathon (Wenatchee, WA)
275	04-24-2010	5:53:52 Tressle Marathon (Minot, ND)
276	05-01-2010	5:58:45 Wisconsin Marathon (Kenosha, WI)
277	05-02-2010	6:04:42 LaCrosse Marathon (LaCrosse, WI)
278	05-14-2010	39.5 miles* Three Days at the Fair (Augusta, NJ)
279	05-16-2010	5:46:30 Delaware Marathon (Wilmington, DE)
280	05-30-2010	8:27:12* Pineland 50k (New Gloucester, ME)
281	06-11-2010	6:13:30 Bear Lake Marathon (Utah to Idaho)
282	06-12-2010	6:18:28 Bear Lake Marathon (Idaho to Utah)
283	06-13-2010	6:17:02 Estes Park Marathon (Estes Park, CO)
284	07-18-2010	5:49:08 Rio de Janeiro Marathon (Rio de Janeiro, Brazil)
285	08-14-2010	26.3 miles* Howl at the Moon 8 Hour Ultra (Danville, IL)
286	08-24-2010	6:06:26 Self-Transcendence Marathon (Nyack, NY)
287	09-12-2010	6:06:46 Sioux Falls Marathon (Sioux Falls, SD)
288	10-03-2010	5:25:00 Maine Marathon (Portland, ME)
289	10-16-2010	27 miles* Saint Pat's 12 Hour Ultra (South Bend, IN)
290	10-17-2010	5:27:25 Grand Rapids Marathon, (Grand Rapids, MI)
291	10-23-2010	5:37:03 Columbia Power Marathon, (Umatilla, OR)
292	10-24-2010	5:47:57 Columbia River Marathon, (Hood River, OR)
293	10-31-2010	5:47:10 Cape Cod Marathon, (Falmouth, MA)
294	11-07-2010	5:24:54 Manchester Marathon, (Manchester, NH)
295	11-20-2010	5:25:44 Mesquite Marathon, (Mesquite, NV)
296	11-11-2010	6:06:35 Kiawah Island Marathon (Kiawah Island, SC)
297	01-22-2011	8:41:14* Hilo to Volcano 50k (Hilo, HI)
298	01-23-2011	5:33:40 Maui Marathon (Maui, HI)
299	02-20-2011	5:38:36 A1A Marathon (Ft. Lauderdale, FL)
300	02-27-2011	5:43:50 Hyannis Marathon (Hyannis, MA)
301	03-12-2011	10:29:23* Land Between the Lakes 60k (Grand Rivers, KY)
302	04-13-2011	7:55:00* Jack Bristol Lake Waramaug 50k (New Preston, CT)
303	04-30-2011	6:30:00* Cornbelt 24 Hour Ultra (Eldridge, IA)
304	05-01-2011	5:31:10 Lincoln Marathon (Lincoln, NE)

305	05-12-2011	151.83 miles* Three Days at the Fair (Augusta, NJ)
306	05-29-2011	8:08:57 Pineland Farms 50k (New Gloucester, ME)
307	06-06-2011	5:47:12 Wyoming Marathon (Casper, WY)
308	06-11-2011	5:53:54 Hatfield-McCoy Marathon (Williamson, WV)
309	07-16-2011	7:33:06* Great Cranberry Island 50k (Great Cranberry Island, ME)
310	07-24-2011	6:35:27 Madison Marathon (Ennis, MT)
311	08-21-2011	5:49:37 Moose Tooth Marathon (Anchorage, AK)
312	08-25-2011	5:42:58 Self-Transcendence Marathon (Nyack, NY)
313	09-17-2011	6:11:09 Walker North Country Marathon (Walker, MN)
314	10-02-2011	5:49:05 Maine Marathon (Portland, ME)
315	10-16-2011	5:57:03 Mt. Desert Island Marathon (Bar Harbor, ME)
316	10-22-2011	71.82 miles* 24 the Hard Way (Oklahoma City, OK)
	(4th Finish of States)	
317	10-20-2011	5:56:21 Cape Cod Marathon (Falmouth, MA)
318	11-06-2011	5:55:28 Manchester Marathon (Manchester, NH)
319	12-10-2011	5:56:47 Rehoboth Beach Seashore Marathon (Rehoboth Beach, DE)
320	12-26-2011	6:50:03 Savage 7 Marathon #1 (Pensacola, FL)
321	12-27-2011	6:37:43 Savage 7 Marathon #2 (Pensacola, FL)
322	12-28-2011	6:40:55 Savage 7 Marathon #3 (Pensacola, FL)
323	12-29-2011	6:14:30 Savage 7 Marathon #4 (Pensacola, FL)
324	12-30-2011	6:34:02 Savage 7 Marathon #5 (Pensacola, FL)
325	12-31-2011	5:46:01 Savage 7 Marathon #6 (Pensacola, FL)
326	01-01-2012	6:15:22 Savage 7 Marathon #7 (Pensacola, FL)
327	01-06-2012	5:42:37 Walt Disney World Marathon (Lake Buena Vista, FL)
328	03-10-2012	5:56:38 Columbia Marathon (Columbia, SC)
329	03-18-2012	6:27:38 Publix Georgia Marathon (Atlanta, GA)
330	04-29-2012	8:08:40* Lake Waramaug 50k (New Preston, CT)
331	05-10-2012	127.8 miles* Three Days at the Fair #1 (Augusta, NJ)
332	05-11-2012	90.7 miles* Three Days at the Fair #2 (Augusta, NJ)
333	05-12-2012	37.7 miles* Three Days at the Fair #3 (Augusta, NJ)
334	05-20-2012	5:35:52 Sugarloaf Marathon (Kingfield, ME)
335	05-27-2012	8:07:36* Pineland 50k (New Gloucester, ME)
336	06-08-2012	5:51:12 Bear Lake Marathon (Fish Haven, ID)
337	06-09-2012	6:10:52 Bear Lake Marathon (Garden City, UT)
338	07-07-2012	6:43:00 Joseph Smith Marathon (Sharon, VT)
339	07-08-2012	6:31:18 Mad Marathon (Waitsfield, VT)
340	07-21-2012	7:30:15* Great Cranberry Island 50k (Great Cranberry Island, ME)
341	08-24-2012	5:56:17 Self-Transcendence Marathon (Nyack, NY)
342	09-09-2012	5:57:15 Sioux Falls Marathon (Sioux Falls, SD)
343	09-11-2012	31 miles* Patriots 9/11 Ultra (Olathe, KS)
344	09-30-2012	5:53:25 Maine Marathon (Portland, ME)
345	10-01-2012	7:37:10 Bug Light Fat Ass Marathon (South Portland, ME)
346	10-02-2012	7:25:55 Back Cove Fat Ass Marathon (Portland, ME)
347	10-07-2012	5:41:06 Valley Harvest Marathon (Wolfville, NS, Canada)
348	10-14-2012	5:46:12 Mount Desert Island Marathon (Bar Harbor, ME)
349	10-21-2012	5:57:16 Seven Bridges Marathon (Chattanooga, TN)
350	10-28-2012	6:13:24 Cape Cod Marathon (Falmouth, MA)
351	11-02-2012	27.5 miles* Nashua 8 Hour Ultra (Nashua, NH)
352	11-03-2012	27.0 miles* Granite State 8 Hour Ultra (Nashua, NH)
353	11-04-2012	5:45:21 Manchester City Marathon (Manchester, NH)
354	11-17-2012	5:53:48 White River Marathon (Cotter, AR)
355	11-18-2012	6:08:34 Route 66 Marathon + .3 Miles (Tulsa, OK)
356	12-26-2012	6:40:05 Savage 7 Marathon #1 (Winter Park, FL)
357	12-27-2012	6:26:59 Savage 7 Marathon #2 (Winter Park, FL)

358	12-28-2012	6:52:25	Savage 7 Marathon #3 (Winter Park, FL)
359	12-29-2012	6:39:35	Savage 7 Marathon #4 (Winter Park, FL)
360	12-30-2012	6:34:34	Savage 7 Marathon #5 (Winter Park, FL)
361	12-31-2012	6:34:21	Savage 7 Marathon #6 (Winter Park, FL)
362	01-01-2013	6:45:55	Savage 7 Marathon #7 (Winter Park, FL)
363	01-05-2013	6:24:06	Mississippi Blues Marathon (Jackson, MS)
364	01-13-2013	6:33:23	First Light Marathon (Mobile, AL)
365	02-03-2013	5:53:27	Melbourne Marathon (Melbourne, FL)
366	02-09-2013	17:51:49*	Ironhorse 100k (Florahome, FL)
367	02-24-2013	6:06:17	Hyannis Marathon (Hyannis, MA)
368	03-10-2013	5:49:27	Lower Potomac Marathon (Piney Point, MD)
369	03-17-2013	6:33:20	Bataan Death March Marathon (White Sands, NM)
370	03-18-2013	7:34:49	Dust Bowl Marathon #1 (Dalhart, TX)
371	03-19-2013	7:04:14	Dust Bowl Marathon #2 (Guymon, OK)
372	03-20-2013	6:41:48	Dust Bowl Marathon #3 (Ulysses, KS)
373	03-21-2013	6:52:51	Dust Bowl Marathon #4 (Lamar, CO)
374	03-22-2013	7:15:23	Dust Bowl Marathon #5 (Clayton, NM)
375	04-21-2013	9:16:54*	Lake Waramaug 50k (Preston, CT)
376	05-04-2013	5:52:32	Wisconsin Marathon (Kenosha, WI)
377	05-05-2013	6:19:52	Borgess Kalamazoo Marathon (Kalamazoo, MI)
378	05-11-2013	5:48:37	Lake Wobegon Marathon (St. Joesph, MN)
379	05-19-2013	5:50:33	Sugarloaf Marathon (Kingfield, ME)
380	05-23-2013	6:47:10	Red Island Marathon (Warwick, RI)
381	05-26-2013	8:58:24*	Pineland Farms 50k (New Gloucester, ME)
382	06-08-2013	6:05:48	Hatfield-McCoy Marathon (Williamson, WV)
383	06-23-2013	5:57:40	Bay Of Fundy Marathon (Lubec, ME)
384	07-27-2013	8:06:50*	Great Cranberry Island 50k (Great Cranberry Island, ME)
385	08-23-2013	6:42:17	Self-Transcendence Marathon (Nyack, NY)
386	09-16-2013	6:53:00	Center of the Nation Marathon #1 (Bowman, ND)
387	09-17-2013	7:31:00	Center of the Nation Marathon #2 (Belle Fourche, SD)
388	09-18-2013	7:29:00	Center of the Nation Marathon #3 (Colony, WY)
389	09-19-2013	7:03:00	Center of the Nation Marathon #4 (Albion, MT)
390	09-20-2013	7:22:00	Center of the Nation Marathon #5 (Chadron, NE)
391	09-27-2013	6:26:13	Emerald Bay Marathon (Lake Tahoe, NV)
392	09-29-2013	6:37:22	Lake Tahoe Marathon (Lake Tahoe, CA)
393	09-28-2013	6:31:22	CAL/NV Marathon (Lake Tahoe, NV)
394	10-06-2013	6:28:08	Maine Marathon (Portland, ME)
395	10-12-2013	5:54:45	Freedom's Run Marathon (Shepherdstown, WV)
396	10-20-2013	6:06:42	Mount Desert Island Marathon (Bar Harbor, ME)
397	10-27-2013	6:13:23	Cape Cod Marathon (Falmouth, MA)
398	11-03-2013	5:45:15	Manchester City Marathon (Manchester, NH)
399	11-10-2013	27.01 miles*	Rhode Island 6 Hour Ultra (Warwick, RI)
400	11-17-2013	5:49:49	Myles Standish Marathon (Plymouth, MA)
401	12-26-2013	6:55:38	Savage 7 Marathon #1 (Ocala, FL)
402	12-27-2013	6:48:12	Savage 7 Marathon #2 (Ocala, FL)
403	12-28-2013	6:50:01	Savage 7 Marathon #3 (Ocala, FL)
404	12-29-2013	6:35:26	Savage 7 Marathon #4 (Ocala, FL)
405	12-30-2013	6:36:33	Savage 7 Marathon #5 (Ocala, FL)
406	12-31-2013	6:25:54	Savage 7 Marathon #6 (Ocala, FL)
407	01-01-2014	6:29:47	Savage 7 Marathon #7 (Ocala, FL)
408	02-01-2014	11:52:05*	Sky Dive 50k Ultra (Clewiston, FL)
409	02-08-2014	7:54:49*	MTC 50k (Osprey, FL)
410	02-23-2014	6:17:19	Hyannis Marathon (Hyannis, MA)
411	04-12-2014	7:47:05	Columbus Belmont State Park Marathon (Columbus, KY)

412	04-13-2014	7:29:34	Meeman-Shelby State Park Marathon (Millington, TN)
413	04-14-2014	7:29:24	Lake Chicot State Park Marathon (Lake Village, AR)
414	04-15-2014	7:04:46	Leroy Percy State Park Marathon (Hollandale, MS)
415	04-16-2014	6:37:18	Civiton Park Marathon (Winnsboro, LA)
416	04-27-2014	7:55:15*	Lake Waramaug 50k (New Preston, CT)
417	05-08-2014	6:52:28	Sugarite State Park Marathon (Raton, NM)
418	05-09-2014	6:58:13	Eagle Nest State Park Marathon (Eagle Nest, NM)
419	05-10-2014	7:57:06	Ute Lake State Park Logan Marathon (Logan, NM)
420	05-11-2014	7:30:09	Conchas Lake State Park Marathon (Conchas, NM)
421	05-15-2014	9:05:27*	Three Days at the Fair Quadzilla 50k #1 (Augusta, NJ)
422	05-16-2014	17:29:07*	Three Days at the Fair Quadzilla 50k #2 (Augusta, NJ)
423	05-17-2014	22:53:47*	Three Days at the Fair Quadzilla 50k #3 (Augusta, NJ)
424	05-18-2014	10:54:22*	Three Days at the Fair Quadzilla 50k #4 (Augusta, NJ)
425	05-25-2014	8:46:41*	Pineland Farms 50k (New Gloucester, ME)
426	06-15-2014	6:26:13	Bay Of Fundy Marathon (Lubec, ME)
427	07-26-2014	42 miles*	24 Hours Around The Lake (Wakefield, MA)
428	08-17-2014	7:19:27*	United Physical Therapy 49k (Anchorage, AK)
429	08-25-2014	6:34:09	Self-Transcendence Marathon (Congers, NY)
430	10-05-2014	6:48:37	Maine Marathon (Portland, ME)
431	10-18-2014	6:12:09	Kansas City Marathon (Kansas City, MO)
432	10-19-2014	6:35:49	Des Moines Marathon (Des Moines, IO)
433	10-26-2014	6:26:48	Cape Cod Marathon (Falmouth, MA)
434	11-02-2014	6:27:14	Manchester City Marathon (Manchester, NH)
435	11-16-2014	6:19:47	Myles Standish Marathon (Plymouth, MA)
436	12-26-2014	7:09:13	Savage 7 Marathon #1 (Ocala, FL)
437	12-27-2014	7:49:33	Savage 7 Marathon #2 (Ocala, FL)
438	12-28-2014	7:33:20	Savage 7 Marathon #3 (Ocala, FL)
439	12-29-2014	8:19:26	Savage 7 Marathon #4 (Ocala, FL)
440	12-30-2014	7:24:54	Savage 7 Marathon #5 (Ocala, FL)
441	12-31-2014	7:51:46	Savage 7 Marathon #6 (Ocala, FL)
442	01-01-2015	7:16:57	Savage 7 Marathon #7 (Ocala, FL)
443	01-11-2015	6:46:27	Walt Disney World Marathon (Lake Buena Vista, FL)
444	03-21-2015	7:03:23	Savin Rock Marathon (West Haven, CT)
445	04-29-2015	8:09:20	Independence Marathon #1 (Elkton, MD)
446	04-30-2015	8:14:03	Independence Marathon #2 (Bear, DE)
447	05-01-2015	7:30:11	Independence Marathon #3 (Birdsboro, PA)
448	05-02-2015	7:44:58	Independence Marathon #4 (Clinton, NJ)
449	05-03-2015	7:40:25	Independence Marathon #5 (New Platz, NY)
450	05-10-2015	6:26:48	Maine Coast Marathon (Biddeford, ME)
451	05-15-2015	9:52:10*	Three Days at the Fair 50k #1 (Augusta, NJ)
452	05-16-2015	43 miles*	Three Days at the Fair Augusta 24 Hour #2 (Augusta, NJ)
453	05-17-2015	41 miles*	Three Days at the Fair Augusta #3 (Augusta, NJ)
454	05-24-2015	9:36:16*	Pineland Farms 50k (New Gloucester, ME)
455	06-01-2015	7:17:55	Heartland Marathon #1 (Bryan, OH)
456	06-02-2015	7:28:50	Heartland Marathon #2 (Niles, MI)
457	06-03-2015	7:56:42	Heartland Marathon #3 (Anderson, IN)
458	06-04-2015	8:14:21	Heartland Marathon #4 (Bloomington, IL)
459	06-05-2015	7:55:25	Heartland Marathon #5 (Clinton, IA)
460	06-06-2015	7:32:30	Heartland Marathon #6 (Monroe, WI)
461	06-07-2015	8:26:28	Heartland Marathon #7 (Winona, MN)
462	06-28-2015	6:38:22	Bay of Fundy Marathon (Lubec, ME)
463	07-14-2015	7:38:32	Center of the Nation Marathon #1 (Baker, MT)
464	07-15-2015	8:39:59	Center of the Nation Marathon #2 (Bowman, MT)
465	07-16-2015	7:46:20	Center of the Nation Marathon #3 (Belle Fourche, SD)

466	07-17-2015	7:37:58	Center of the Nation Marathon #4 (Sundance, ND)
467	07-18-2015	8:14:25	Center of the Nation Marathon #5 (Chadron, NE)
468	07-19-2015	8:02:22	Center of the Nation Marathon #6 (Sterling, CO)
469	10-04-2015	6:54:26	Maine Marathon (Portland, ME)
470	10-18-2015	6:22:47	Mt. Desert Island Marathon (Bar Harbor, ME)
471	10-25-2015	7:23:52	Cape Cod Marathon (Falmouth, MA)
472	11-01-2015	6:15:31	Manchester City Marathon (Manchester, NH)
473	11-15-2015	6:26:28	Myles Standish Marathon (Plymouth, MA)
474	12-13-2015	7:19:38	Honolulu Marathon (Honolulu, HI)
475	12-26-2015	7:37:57	Savage 7 Marathon #1 (Ocala, FL)
476	12-27-2015	7:55:01	Savage 7 Marathon #2 (Ocala, FL)
477	12-28-2015	7:43:38	Savage 7 Marathon #3 (Ocala, FL)
478	12-29-2015	8:18:25	Savage 7 Marathon #4 (Ocala, FL)
479	12-30-2015	8:12:54	Savage 7 Marathon #5 (Ocala, FL)
480	12-31-2015	8:08:04	Savage 7 Marathon #6 (Ocala, FL)
481	01-01-2016	8:16:21	Savage 7 Marathon #7 (Ocala, FL)
482	01-10-2016	7:25:51	Walt Disney World Marathon (Orlando, FL)
483	03-26-2016	6:36:07	Two Rivers Marathon #1 (Two Rivers, PA)
484	03-27-2016	6:38:49	Two Rivers Marathon #2 (Two Rivers, PA)
485	04-17-2016	8:17:58	Riverboat Marathon series #1 (Winnsboro, LA)
486	04-16-2016	7:43:23	Riverboat Marathon series #2 (Lake Village, AR)
487	04-17-2016	7:45:47	Riverboat Marathon series #3 (Hollandale, MS)
488	04-18-2016	7:43:37	Riverboat Marathon series #4 (Millington, TN)
489	04-19-2016	7:44:07	Riverboat Marathon series #5 (Columbus, KY)
490	04-20-2016	7:42:42	Riverboat Marathon series #6 (Girardeau, MO)
491	04-21-2016	8:43:33	Riverboat Marathon series #7 (Vienna, IL)
492	05-12-2016	9:46:29	Three Days at the Fair 50k (Augusta, NJ)
493	05-13-2016	9:48:57	Three Days at the Fair 50k (Augusta, NJ)
494	05-14-2016	7:07:18	Three Days at the Fair Marathon (Augusta, NJ)
495	05-14-2016	8:09:49	Three Days at the Fair Marathon (Augusta, NJ)
496	05-17-2016	7:52:24	New England Marathon series #1 (Springfield, VT)
497	05-18-2016	9:25:05	New England Marathon series #2 (Northfield, MA)
498	05-19-2016	8:32:17	New England Marathon series #3 (Coventry, RI)
499	05-30-2016	7:50:53	Oh Boy Marathon (Waterbury, CT)
500	10-02-2016	8:29:39	Maine Marathon (Portland, ME)
501	10-13-2016	8:40:19	Mainly Marathon Appalachian Series (Seneca, NC)
502	10-14-2016	9:07:00	Mainly Marathon Appalachian Series (Unicoi State Park, SC)
503	10-15-2016	9:24:54	Mainly Marathon Appalachian Series (Guntersville, GA)
504	12-26-2016	8:32:02	Savage 7 Marathon #1 (Ocala, FL)
505	12-27-2016	7:58:30	Savage 7 Marathon #2 (Ocala, FL)
506	12-28-2016	8:46:30	Savage 7 Marathon #3 (Ocala, FL)